The EU Timescape

The manner in which time is institutionalized is critical to how a political system works. Terms, time budgets and time horizons of collective and individual political actors; rights over timing, sequencing and speed in decision-making; and the temporal properties of policy matter to the distribution of power; efficiency and effectiveness of policy-making; and democratic legitimacy. This book makes a case for the systematic study of political time in the European Union (EU) - both as an independent and a dependent variable - and highlights the analytical value-added of a time-centred analysis. The book discusses previous scholarship on the institutionalization of political time and its consequences along the dimensions of polity, politics and policy; reviews dominant perspectives on political time, which centre on power, system performance and legitimacy; and presents case studies that illustrate the importance of time in the governance of the EU.

This book was original published as a special issue of *Journal of European Public Policy*.

Klaus H. Goetz holds the Chair in German and European Politics and Government at the University of Potsdam, Germany.

Jan-Hinrik Meyer-Sahling is Associate Professor of European Politics at the University of Nottingham, UK.

Journal of European Public Policy Series

Series Editor: Jeremy Richardson is a Professor at Nuffield College, Oxford University

This series seeks to bring together some of the finest edited works on European Public Policy. Reprinting from Special Issues of the *Journal of European Public Policy*, the focus is on using a wide range of social sciences approaches, both qualitative and quantitative, to gain a comprehensive and definitive understanding of Public Policy in Europe.

Towards a Federal Europe
Edited by Alexander H. Trechsel

The Disparity of European Integration
Edited by Tanja A. Börzel

Cross-National Policy Convergence
Causes Concepts and Empirical Findings
Edited by Christoph Knill

Civilian or Military Power?
European Foreign Policy in Perspective
Edited by Helene Sjursen

The European Union and New Trade Politics
Edited by John Peterson and Alasdair R. Young

Comparative Studies of Policy Agendas
Edited by Frank R. Baumgartner, Christoffer Green-Pedersen and Bryan D. Jones

The Constitutionalization of the European Union
Edited by Berthold Rittberger and Frank Schimmelfenig

Empirical and Theoretical Studies in EU Lobbying
Edited by David Coen

Mutual Recognition as a New Mode of Governance
Edited by Susanne K. Schmidt

France and the European Union
Edited by Emiliano Grossman

Immigration and Integration Policy in Europe
Edited by Tim Bale

Reforming the European Commission
Edited by Michael W. Bauer

International Influence Beyond Conditionality
Postcommunist Europe after EU enlargement
Edited by Rachel A. Epstein and Ulrich Sedelmeier

The Role of Political Parties in the European Union
Edited by Björn Lindberg, Anne Rasmussen and Andreas Warntjen

EU External Governance
Projecting EU Rules beyond
 Membership
*Edited by Sandra Lavenex and
 Frank Schimmelfennig*

EMU and Political Science
What Have We Learned?
*Edited by Henrik Enderlein and
 Amy Verdun*

**Learning and Governance in the EU
 Policy Making Process**
Edited by Anthony R. Zito

**Political Representation and EU
 Governance**
*Edited by Peter Mair and
 Jacques Thomassen*

**Europe and the Management of
 Globalization**
*Edited by Wade Jacoby and
 Sophie Meunier*

Negotiation Theory and the EU
The State of the Art
*Edited by Andreas Dür,
 Gemma Mateo and
 Daniel C. Thomas*

**The Political Economy of Europe's
 Incomplete Single Market**
*Edited by David Howarth and
 Tal Sadeh*

**The European Union's Foreign
 Economic Policies**
A Principal-Agent Perspective
*Edited by Andreas Dür and
 Michael Elsig*

The Politics of the Lisbon Agenda
Governance Architectures and
 Domestic Usages of Europe
*Edited by Susana Borrás and
 Claudio M. Radaelli*

**Agency Governance in the European
 Union**
*Edited by Berthold Rittberger and
 Arndt Wonka*

The EU Timescape
*Edited by Klaus H. Goetz and Jan-
 Hinrik Meyer-Sahling*

The EU Timescape

Edited by
Klaus H. Goetz and
Jan-Hinrik Meyer-Sahling

LONDON AND NEW YORK

First published 2012
by Routledge
2 Park Square, Milton Park, Abingdon, Oxon, OX14 4RN

Simultaneously published in the USA and Canada
by Routledge
711 Third Avenue, New York, NY 10017

First issued in paperback 2017

Routledge is an imprint of the Taylor & Francis Group, an informa business

© 2012 Taylor & Francis

This book is a reproduction of *Journal of European Public Policy*, Volume 16, issue 2. The Publisher requests to those authors who may be citing this book to state, also, the bibliographical details of the special issue on which the book was based.

All rights reserved. No part of this book may be reprinted or reproduced or utilised in any form or by any electronic, mechanical, or other means, now known or hereafter invented, including photocopying and recording, or in any information storage or retrieval system, without permission in writing from the publishers.

Trademark notice: Product or corporate names may be trademarks or registered trademarks, and are used only for identification and explanation without intent to infringe.

British Library Cataloguing in Publication Data
A catalogue record for this book is available from the British Library

ISBN 13: 978-1-138-11729-7 (pbk)
ISBN 13: 978-0-415-69633-3 (hbk)

Typeset in Times New Roman
by Taylor & Francis Books

Publisher's Note
The publisher would like to make readers aware that the chapters in this book may be referred to as articles as they are identical to the articles published in the special issue. The publisher accepts responsibility for any inconsistencies that may have arisen in the course of preparing this volume for print.

Contents

Acknowledgements	ix
1. Political time in the EU: dimensions, perspectives, theories *Klaus H. Goetz and Jan-Hinrik Meyer-Sahling*	1
2. How does the EU tick? Five propositions on political time *Klaus H. Goetz*	23
3. The temporal constitution of the European Commission: a timely investigation *Luc Tholoniat*	42
4. Do elections set the pace? A quantitative assessment of the timing of European legislation *Laszlo Kovats*	60
5. Uses of time in the EU's enlargement process *Graham Avery*	77
6. Policies, institutions and time: how the European Commission managed the temporal challenge of eastern enlargement *Katja Lass-Lennecke and Annika Werner*	91
7. The evolving timescapes of European economic governance: contesting and using time *Kenneth Dyson*	107
8. *Politics in Time* meets the politics of time: historical institutionalism and the EU timescape *Simon Bulmer*	128
9. The EU timescape: from notion to research agenda *Jan-Hinrik Meyer-Sahling and Klaus H. Goetz*	146
Index	159

Acknowledgements

This special issue of the *Journal of European Public Policy* documents the work of Team 26 within the framework of EU-CONSENT. The funding provided by EU-CONSENT allowed the authors to meet on several occasions to present and discuss their ideas at academic workshops and panels at the University of Potsdam; the EUSA Biennial Conference in Montreal; the 4th ECPR General Conference in Pisa; the 4th Pan-European Conference on EU Politics in Riga; and at several EU-CONSENT Plenary Conferences. We wish to thank Attila Ágh, Esra LaGro, Philippe Schmitter and Ulf Sverdrup for their help in getting us off to an excellent start in Potsdam; and Frank Schimmelfennig and Radoslaw Zubek for their most constructive comments as discussants at the Montreal and Pisa events respectively. Goetz would also like to thank Morten Egeberg, Johan Olsen and Ulf Sverdrup for the opportunity to take part in CONNEX-sponsored workshops in Barcelona and London and for the invitation to talk to staff and students at ARENA in Oslo.

We owe a special debt of gratitude to Wolfgang Wessels, the Co-ordinator of EU-CONSENT, who placed great trust in our ability to produce an acceptable 'deliverable' out of what must have looked like a rather fanciful idea about temporality and the EU. We were both fortunate to be able to spend several months at the European University Institute in Florence in 2008, Goetz as Fernand Braudel Senior Fellow and Meyer-Sahling as Max Weber Postdoctoral Fellow. We would like to thank Yves Mény, the President of the EUI; Ramon Marimon, the Director of the Max Weber Programme; and Peter Mair, Chairman of the Department of Political and Social Sciences, for enabling us to work together intensively on the articles collected here. Finally, we are indebted to Jeremy Richardson, Editor of this journal, who threw caution to the wind by entrusting a special issue to two EU novices.

KHG
JHMS

Political time in the EU: dimensions, perspectives, theories

Klaus H. Goetz and Jan-Hinrik Meyer-Sahling

ABSTRACT The manner in which time is institutionalized is critical to how a political system works. Terms, time budgets and time horizons of collective and individual political actors; rights over timing, sequencing and speed in decision-making; and the temporal properties of policy matter to the distribution of power; efficiency and effectiveness of policy-making; and democratic legitimacy. This article makes a case for the systematic study of political time in the European Union (EU) – both as an independent and a dependent variable – and highlights the analytical value-added of a time-centred analysis. The article discusses previous scholarship on the institutionalization of political time and its consequences along the dimensions of polity, politics and policy; and then reviews dominant perspectives on political time, which centre on power, system performance and legitimacy. These perspectives tie in with diverse theoretical traditions in the study of the EU. Taken together, dimensions, perspectives and theories help to guide time-centred analyses of the EU political system.

WHY STUDY POLITICAL TIME?[1]

The Council of Ministers of the European Union (EU) is a permanent institution, but its presidency changes every six months. Members of the European Parliament (EP) are elected for a five-year term, but key posts in the EP – including those of the President, the Vice-President and committee chairs – are reallocated in mid-term. The President of the Commission and the Commissioners are appointed for five years, but most of the staff with whom they work are appointed on a permanent basis. The six members of the Executive Board of the European Central Bank (ECB) serve non-renewable eight-year terms, but their terms are staggered, i.e. scheduled to end in 2010, May and October 2011, and 2012, 2013 and 2014. The sequence as well as the respective rights and responsibilities of the Commission, the EP and the Council in the legislative process are subject to detailed provisions, but leave great scope for the acceleration of decisions, for instance, in the shape of so-called 'early agreements' under the co-decision procedure (see Corbett et al. 2007: 224ff.). Parliament, unlike the Council, is not a permanent institution, but legislation still pending at the end of a legislative term is routinely carried over into the newly elected legislature, so that the 'discontinuity principle' applied in most national legislatures is effectively suspended (Kovats 2009). Both the Commission and the Parliament have five-year mandates, but the parameters of the EU budget are determined through the multi-annual financial perspective in a seven-year cycle.

It is our central contention that these and many other temporal features of the EU political system deserve more sustained and systematic study than they have received so far. There is much to be gained from according political time a central place in EU scholarship: if we understand better 'how the EU ticks' (Goetz 2009), we will also gain insights into how it distributes opportunities for effective participation in decision-making; why it is good at doing some things – say, creating a single market – but bad at others – say, the promotion of growth and employment (Kok Report 2004); and why some of its procedures are seen as more legitimate than others. Put differently: research into the 'EU timescape' (see Meyer-Sahling and Goetz 2009) – both as a 'dependent' and an 'independent' variable – raises new questions about the EU and it opens up novel perspectives on long-standing debates.

Our main concern is *not* with historical analysis, in the sense of explaining developments *over time*, an interest that has featured prominently in EU studies, both in integration theory – most notably in neo-functionalist and historical institutionalist accounts of integration – and also in historical institutionalist policy analysis. As Bulmer's (2009) discussion in this volume makes clear, however, there are fruitful connections to be made between the study of 'politics in time' (Pierson 2004) and an agenda centred on political time and political timescapes. Nor do we focus on the impact of the past on the present – of 'governing with the past' – the importance of which Pollitt (2008) has recently emphasized in the context of administrative and policy analysis. Nor do we have much to say on how unforeseen and unforeseeable events, crises and 'bolts from the blue' may play havoc with well-laid plans and timetables. Rather, we are interested in the temporal features that are built into the political system of the EU and in how the specific manner in which they are institutionalized matter for power, performance and legitimacy.

By treating time as an institutional property we privilege an interest in temporal rules (broadly understood) and the temporal features of procedures. These can, of course, vary in precision, formality and authority (Stone Sweet *et al.* 2001: 6–7). We, therefore, share in the mainstream of institutionalist approaches to the study of Europe, which think of institutions as 'the structure in which social interaction – as opposed to random encounters – takes place; they tend to pattern behaviour in particular ways ... institutions make purposive action possible by providing individuals with a framework of shared expectations' (Stone Sweet *et al.* 2001 : 7). But we argue that the importance of time as an institution has been neglected in EU scholarship.

At the same time, we have to recognize that it is not always easy to determine unambiguously the analytical status of political time within the context of variable-oriented research designs that seek to distinguish clearly between independent, dependent and, possibly, intervening variables. For example, if we were to ask how the time horizon of a Commissioner affects the legislative initiatives that s/he is likely to undertake, we are bound to encounter feedback loops, in the sense that initiatives already undertaken influence future time horizons. Where aspects of time – be they terms, time budgets, time horizons, time rules in decision-making or temporal properties of policy – are used to explain something else, their effects can often only be detected through observation over longer periods of time during which 'effect may become cause' (Pierson 2004). Moreover, the effects of such temporal features of a political system can rarely be understood without reference to substance – what is substantively at stake – and also to space (especially important in a multi-level setting). This is why research into the institutionalization of political time and its effects needs to 'foreground' time (Adam 2008), but cannot necessarily treat it as a discreet variable.

Bearing in mind these analytical challenges, the success of previous efforts to put political time at the heart of comparative analysis has not been encouraging. As Schedler and Santiso (1998) noted in their 'invitation' from the late 1990s to concentrate research on 'political time', '[t]ime in its manifold manifestations represents a pervasive factor in political life', but 'as a rule, reflections on politics and time have remained unsystematic, implicit, and disperse, and our theoretical insights, conceptual tools, and empirical knowledge have remained severely limited' (Schedler and Santiso 1998: 5). A major German-language monograph on contemporary political time in national democratic settings published by Riescher (1994) has largely failed to inspire further empirical analysis. Similarly, the insightful work by Ekengren (1996, 1997, 2002) on the time of EU governance did not spark a wider discussion on the specific properties of political time in the EU and its consequences for the member states.

It is, perhaps, the ubiquity of political time that has tended to discourage its systematic analysis. For example, Schedler and Santiso's (1998) attempt to outline a future research agenda encompassed a very wide range of issues related to political time, including politicians' time horizons, the role of time constraints, the importance of institutional time rules, time strategies and also time discourses. The temporal categories that can be analysed are, in themselves, numerous. Empirical work has addressed issues of temporal location (when does something happen?); sequence (in what order do things happen?); speed (how quickly do things happen?) (Schmitter and Santiso 1998), and also duration (how long do things take?). But there are a host of other temporal features that matter in political life, including, for example, deadlining and punctuality, rates of recurrence, and, in particular, cycles and rhythms (Meyer-Sahling 2007).

Yet much of what we know so far about political time relates to differences between national political regimes (Schedler and Santiso 1998; Riescher 1994). Linz (1998) has reminded us that government *pro tempore* is a – or perhaps *the* – defining feature of democracies. Governments in non-democratic regimes do not face a similar constraint. 'The pro-tempore character of democratic government makes it essential that elections take place with reasonable frequency' (Linz 1998: 21). The limited time budget resulting from regular elections makes time a 'scarce resource' (Linz 1998: 22) in democratic politics and democratic politicians, in particular, a 'harried elite' (Linz 1998: 29). Following Linz, this inbuilt restriction of democratic time has a profound impact on the temporal ordering of the activities of governments and parliaments. Their term of office provides political decision-makers with an overall time budget, which they need to allocate wisely if they wish to be re-elected. It also marks their most important time horizon. What to do when, in what sequence, how speedily and for how long are, accordingly, enduring political preoccupations. In short, the electoral term is the most fundamental time unit of democracy and the electoral cycle to which the democratic limitation of time gives rise is its defining temporal feature.

Democracy's time constraint not only works at the polity level, notably the institutional terms of governments and legislatures. Time also matters at the levels of politics and policy. As regards the former, temporal rules governing political decision-making are of special significance. A good deal of work has, for example, examined how time rules in parliaments – notably as they affect the timing of legislative initiatives – influence the distribution of power both between the executive and parliament and within the legislature (for example Döring 1995, 2003, 2004). As regards the policy dimension, policy timing has been an enduring theme. Here, one thinks immediately of work on political business cycles, which has noted the link between electoral rules and resultant time budgets and time horizons of political decision-makers, on the one hand, and the 'opportunistic' timing of economic policy tools, on the other (for a review of much of this work, see Drazen 2001).

The case for analysing political time is supported by the fact that political time is intimately connected to power, system performance and legitimacy. The link between time rules and the allocation of power is probably too apparent to require much comment; but time rules also matter for the efficiency and effectiveness of political decision-making and political legitimacy. To recognize this point it may suffice to remind ourselves briefly of Hamilton's comments on 'The Duration in Office of the Executive' in the Federalist Papers No. 71. The argument in favour of a four-year term for an elected 'magistrate' (i.e. chief executive) rests on the likelihood that it will ensure the 'firmness and independence of the magistrate':

> It cannot be affirmed, that a duration of four years, or any other limited duration, would completely answer the end proposed; but it would contribute towards it in a degree which would have a material influence upon the spirit and character of the government. Between the commencement and termination of such a period, there would always be a considerable interval, in which the prospect of annihilation would be sufficiently remote, not to have an improper effect upon the conduct of a man indued with a tolerable portion of fortitude; and in which he might reasonably promise himself, that there would be time enough before it arrived, to make the community

sensible of the propriety of the measures he might incline to pursue . . . on the one hand, a duration of four years will contribute to the firmness of the Executive in a sufficient degree to render it a very valuable ingredient in the composition; so, on the other, it is not enough to justify any alarm for the public liberty.

In today's EU setting, very similar considerations are brought to bear when it comes to assessing its temporal features, though the way in which they are expressed is, of course, quite different. Thus, to give just two examples, the increasing duration of law-making is often seen as a sign of inefficient decision-making (König 2007; Kovats 2009), whilst the introduction of an elaborate multi-annual planning cycle in the Commission has been justified on grounds of better governance (Tholoniat 2009). As regards legitimacy, time rules relating to, for example, the rights of Members of the European Parliament (MEPs) and parliamentary groups in the legislative process are of critical relevance when it comes to assessing claims about the EU's democratization through parliamentarization. In short, the analysis of political time leads us to the core of contemporary scholarly and political debates about power, performance and legitimacy in the EU (Hix 2008; Menon 2008).

Against this background, this special issue of the *Journal of European Public Policy* makes the case for a more systematic study of time in the EU. In this introductory article, we first review previous scholarship on the institutionalization of political time and its consequences along the dimensions of polity, politics and policy. For each of the three dimensions, we identify the main properties and provide examples from debates in comparative politics and debates surrounding the EU political system. Second, we discuss dominant perspectives on political time, which centre on power, system performance and legitimacy. These perspectives tie in with different theoretical traditions in the study of the EU, which we discuss in our last section. Taken together, dimensions, perspectives and theories help to identify key questions in time-centred analyses of the EU political system, an issue that is taken up again in the conclusion (Meyer-Sahling and Goetz 2009) to this special issue.

INSTITUTIONALIZING POLITICAL TIME: POLITY, POLITICS AND POLICY

In its substantive emphases, previous scholarship on political time has tended to coincide fairly closely with the widely accepted distinction between polity, politics and policy dimensions in the analysis of political systems. This distinction has also been applied in the study of the EU (e.g., Hix 2005) and in much recent work on the Europeanization of domestic political systems (see, e.g., Goetz and Meyer-Sahling 2008; Graziano and Vink 2007). The three dimensions are concerned, respectively, with term lengths and configurations of political and senior administrative officeholders, their time budgets and time horizons; rights to influence the timing, sequencing, speed and duration of political decision-making processes; and the temporal properties of public policy, such as transposition deadlines or the duration of temporary derogations.

Polity: terms, time budgets, and time horizons

In a democracy, the most fundamental temporal unit is the electoral term, the maximum length of which tends to be fixed at the level of the constitution. The electoral term on which their temporal mandate is based determines the time budgets available to elected politicians; and, although they may, of course, plan beyond the next election date, it also exerts a major influence on their time horizons in office. The limitation on the length of terms of elected politicians (and often also other senior officeholders in non-majoritarian institutions such as courts or central banks) has a profound effect on how the key political institutions – government and parliament – organize their work over the electoral term, i.e. decisional cycles; and on the timing, sequencing, speed and duration of public policies, i.e. policy cycles. The electoral cycle, which combines decisional and policy aspects, thus constitutes the basic rhythm of a democratic political system, as it reflects recurring patterns of political processes, marked by a clear beginning and an end.

Given the far-reaching consequences of how terms are arranged, it is surprising that cross-country differences in terms, time budgets and associated time horizons do not feature prominently in comparative typologies of political systems. To be sure, it has been noted that the distinction between presidential and parliamentary systems has a temporal dimension (Riescher 1994). Whilst in parliamentary systems, parliament and government operate on the basis of the same time budget (a fact which helps to synchronize their respective timetables), this is not the case in presidential systems (the US is the paradigmatic case here). In the former, terms and cycles of parliament and government are aligned or, more precisely, synchronized. In presidential systems, by contrast, the terms of legislators and chief executives do not coincide. The lack of synchronization of electoral cycles has, accordingly, been identified as a major source of divided government in presidential systems (Shugart 1995). But the typological distinction between presidentialism and parliamentarism itself is oblivious to this basic difference in the institutionalization of political time. Similarly, the distinction between majoritarian and consensus democracies (Lijphart 1999) does not explicitly engage with the temporal constitution of these two ideal-types.

This is not to suggest, of course, that political scientists have ignored the importance of terms, time budgets and time horizons. For example, studies of constitution-making in countries that have undergone transitions from authoritarianism to democracy have analysed the importance of the choice of term lengths and term limits of parliamentarians, governments and, especially, presidents (Frye 1997; Shugart and Carey 1992). Students of executive–legislative relations have inquired into the impact of electorally restricted time budgets on how politicians time legislative initiatives over the parliamentary term (Martin 2004); similar work is now done on legislative planning within central executives (Zubek *et al.* 2007).

Of equal relevance is work that has inquired into how 'non-majoritarian' political institutions work (Thatcher and Sweet Stone 2002). The defining characteristic of such institutions is that they do operate at some remove from direct control by elected officials and, by implication, at a greater distance from a direct, time-limited electoral mandate. The most oft-discussed institution of this kind includes agencies, central banks and courts. Non-majoritarian institutions do not fit easily within the democratic chain of delegation (Strøm et al. 2003), nor, and this is crucial, are they subject to the same time budgets and time horizons as majoritarian, i.e. electorally based institutions. It is their capacity to take the 'longer view' and to operate at least partly outside the constraints of electoral terms that provides their key functional justification.

Within the context of the EU, non-majoritarian institutions – notably the Court, the ECB and a host of EU agencies – have received a great deal of attention, as part of the discussion of the EU as a 'regulatory state' (Majone 1997) and the emergence of a 'new executive politics in Europe' (Egeberg 2006; Curtin and Egeberg 2008). Analyses of the EU as a regulatory state draw attention to two of its features: what it does substantively; and how it is institutionalized. Similarly, analysts of the new European executive order highlight the importance of a wide variety of agencies and international and transnational policy networks in the EU, which, again, are much less sensitive to the constraints on electorally limited terms than analyses of democratic chains of delegation might suggest.

Yet, if we examine terms, time budgets and time horizons of key actors in the EU system we find a complex and partly contradictory picture (Goetz 2009), not least because, compared to basic term rules at national level, temporal rules in the EU have been fairly dynamic. On the one hand, electoral terms seem to matter progressively more. The key points here are the introduction of direct quinquennial elections to the EP in 1979 and the synchronization of the term lengths of the EP and the College of Commissioners under the Maastricht Treaty, so that both now operate within the same basic time budget. At the level of policy planning, the five-year planning cycle instituted in the Commission has further helped to synchronize activities between the Commission and Parliament. On the other, continuity, ongoingness and extended time horizons also have very powerful institutional bases, notably in the Commission – think, for example, of the powerful Commission bureaucracy or comitology – and in the Council, for instance, in the form of the Committee of *Permanent* Representatives (COREPER) and the Secretariat-General. Moreover, the ECB makes much of the long, secure tenure of the members of its Executive Board – eight years – and governors of national central banks, who belong to its Governing Council, must have a minimum term of office of five years.

But the picture is more complicated than a simple opposition between institutions and actors that are more or less directly subject to electorally limited terms and those operating to varying degrees outside such constraints would suggest. Central to analysis of the mobilization of actors in the EU is the operation of the six-monthly presidencies of the Council, which rotate amongst the member states (Hayes-Renshaw and Wallace 2006). It is the short term of the Council presidency, in particular, that introduces urgency into Council proceedings and often turns the Council into an 'impatient legislator' (Rittberger 2000) when compared to other participants in the EU legislative process that possess a larger time budget and longer time horizons. From this perspective, we might expect that the introduction of the two-and-a-half-year President of the European Council as envisaged by the Lisbon Treaty, rather than making the work of the Council more efficient and effective, might, in fact, serve to slow it down, as the sense of urgency created by a tightly limited six-month term evaporates. The central concern in the analysis of terms (their length and configuration), time budgets and time horizons then relates to the temporal outlook which they impose on collective and individual actors, how they influence their (scope of) actions, and what consequences they have for political outcomes.

Politics: time for decision-making

Much work on political time has focused on its property as a resource and a constraint in decision-making, notably in legislative procedures. What matters critically in this respect is the malleability and manipulability of time. As Schmitter and Santiso (1998: 71) have noted in relation to democratization, decision-makers 'learn how to manipulate time, that is, to turn it from an inexorably limited, linear and perishable constraint into something that could be scheduled, anticipated, delayed, accelerated, deadlined, circumvented, prolonged, deferred, compressed, parcelled out, standardized, diversified, staged, staggered, and even wasted – but never ignored'.

Decision-making analyses that pay attention to temporal rules direct attention to how political actors may seek to influence the temporal structure of decision-making both within and between institutions. These time rights include the power to initiate and thus to influence the timing for the start of the policy-making process; they refer to sequences in decision-making – a prominent concern in both rationalist and historical institutionalist analyses – and they are interested in possibilities to accelerate or delay. Time rules provide opportunities for some and create constraints for others. Along the politics dimensions, time is fundamentally about the discretion to make time-related choices in order to gain an advantage in political processes.

For example, with regard to inter-institutional relations, government control of parliamentary timetables has been analysed as a key resource for government to impose its will on parliament (Cox 2005; Döring 1995). Recent research has also identified different patterns of allocating time to the processing of bills in parliament. In Hungary and the UK, for instance, the government controls not only the timetable of parliament, but it is also unusual for the opposition parties to be given committee and plenary time for the consideration of their initiatives.

By contrast, in countries such as Germany and Poland, it is common practice that legislative time is allocated proportionally between government and opposition (Zubek 2008).

The power to use time in the political process has also been an important component of the political dynamics within institutions. Studies of committee–floor relations in the US Congress, for instance, have drawn attention to questions of sequencing and timing in parliamentary decision-making (Shepsle and Weingast 1987). Within government, recent research has examined legislative planning procedures that allocate time rights to central actors such as Prime Minister's Offices to determine the timing of legislative proposals, the sequence and generally the overall amount of time that will be devoted to individual bill proposals before they can be passed on to parliament (Zubek *et al.* 2007).

The importance of time for decisional politics – perhaps most notably legislative politics – has also, not surprisingly, been recognized in the study of the legislative process of the EU. The right of the Commission to initiate proposals gives the Commission the power to choose the timing for initiating new policies. This time right remains recognized in the Treaties, although it has also been partly undermined in practice (Rasmussen 2007a). The right of the EP to give an opinion under the consultation procedure has often been labelled as a 'power to delay' (Kardasheva 2008), which has historically been an important resource for Parliament in the legislative process (Corbett *et al.* 2007). As already noted, the 'lack of time' has, on the other hand, often been an important constraint for the Council in the negotiations with Parliament, because the shorter terms of Council presidencies have turned the Council into an 'impatient legislator' relative to the EP (Rittberger 2000). At the same time, the Council has, of course, the right to conclude the legislative process and failure to do so means that a bill cannot pass. In short, at the EU level, time rights are shared among the three core institutions, in that each of them has an important right to influence the temporal structure of the legislative process.

Time-related issues have also gained a great deal of attention with regard to the politics within EU institutions. For instance, *rapporteurs* are in a central position within the EP to accelerate the co-decision procedure in order to broker an early agreement with the Council (Héritier and Farrell 2004). Within the Commission, officials can take advantage of their permanence *vis-à-vis* EU Commissioners who are appointed for five-year terms. Commission officials can use this temporal advantage strategically, in that they can delay the policy-making process and wait for a Directorate-General (DG) leadership that is more favourable to their views. Commission officials are also known to become more reluctant to introduce new ideas and proposals at the end of a Commissioner's term, as there is too much uncertainty over the preferences of the succeeding Commissioner (Tholoniat 2009).

In contrast to the sustained interest in the instrumental use of time rules in decision-making – powers to move first or last, to change sequences, to accelerate or delay, to conclude or to keep processes open, etc. – political scientists have paid less attention to the dense grid of regular meetings in which politicians and officials spend much of their time. A first glance shows that the sheer frequency of meetings differs from one institution to another. The College of Commissioners, for instance, meets once a week; COREPER I and II meet once a week, but may meet for more than a day; the Council in its various configurations meets somewhat less regularly, but several times a month, and there are also regular informal ministerial meetings organized by the EU Presidency; the European Council meets two times during a six-monthly presidency, with one or two additional informal meetings of the heads of state and government; the EP meets for 12 four-day sessions in Strasbourg and six additional two-day sessions in Brussels; the Governing Council of the ECB meets twice a month.

The importance of dense schedules of regular meetings can hardly be overstated. They provide a temporal grid into which much decision-making has to be fitted. They set the basic rhythm for the work of the key EU institutions and also constrain the discretionary use of time in the member states, notably of executives and parliaments (Ekengren 2002; Jerneck 2000). They mobilize actors and are a routinized means of addressing intra-institutional and inter-institutional problems of synchronization.

Understanding time along the politics dimension thus requires attention both to opportunities for the instrumental use of time rules and to temporal grids. The latter create regularity, predictability, mobilize and synchronize actors; the former allow for flexibility and can be used both to lessen constraints or in an attempt to reduce temporal discretion. In the present context, the challenge for students of the EU is to gain greater insights into how decisional time rules and temporal grids work and, in line with our institutional outlook on time, how they 'pattern behaviour' within the EU system.

Policy: allocation in time

Along the policy dimension, political time is centrally concerned with the temporal allocation of values in society. EU policy, like national policy, provides an almost infinite number of examples for the intricate temporal structuring of policy. To give just one example, the reform of the Common Market Organization for wine, which came into force on 1 August 2008, foresees, amongst many other measures, that planning rights schemes 'are to be abolished by the end of 2015, with the possibility to continue them at a national level until 2018'; distillation schemes are to be phased out, with 'crisis distillation ... limited to four years at Member States' discretion until the end of 2011/2012, with maximum expenditure limited to 20 percent of the national financial envelope in year one, 15 percent in year two, 10 percent in year three and 5 percent in year four'; and a 'three-year voluntary grubbing-up scheme for a total area of 175,000 hectares with a decreasing level of premium over the three years' (http://ec.europa.eu/agriculture/capreform/wine/index_en.htm; accessed 24 August 2008).

The key issue along the policy dimension is then: when, in what sequence, how quickly and for how long are benefits to be provided and costs to be imposed? When should a new directive come into force? In what sequence should EU measures for combatting climate change be implemented and what is the appropriate time scale for action? How quickly should transitional arrangements be phased out? How long should a temporary derogation last?

Time rules are thus applied as tools of governance. They determine basic parameters such as the timing, start and end dates of policies. However, time rules are also used to address temporal dilemmas inherent to public policies. For instance, we have already noted how the debate on non-majoritarian institutions stresses their superiority in ensuring temporal consistency when compared to institutional solutions that are more closely related to the electoral cycle and, thus, more likely to be subject to behaviour that follows political business cycles. Thus, economists stress the benefits of politically independent central banks, because they take monetary policy instruments out of the hands of elected politicians with short-term interests (Kydland and Prescott 1977, McNamara 2002). Dyson (2009) shows how this discourse has influenced the institutionalization of European economic and monetary governance, but also how such time rules remain contested.

More generally, it is often argued that the last two decades have seen a marked shift towards the establishment of non-majoritarian agencies (Thatcher and Stone-Sweet 2002) at both national level and within the EU as a 'regulatory state' (Majone 1997). The desire to overcome problems of credible commitment, which are closely connected to relatively short, electorally determined time horizons, is often seen as a major force behind this institutional shift (Gilardi 2002). Delegation to independent regulatory agencies is then used as a tool to enhance temporal consistency.

If such temporal features of policy are to be treated as part of the institutional make-up of the EU, the question arises as to whether it is possible to detect regularities of EU policy time. At this stage, we may formulate three general expectations relating to the temporality of EU policy. A first expectation is that, on the whole, EU policy is more likely to be time consistent than policy at the national level, which is more closely controlled by majoritarian institutions. There has arguably been a trend towards establishing policy continuity and towards the reduction of time tools in the hands of politicians at the EU level. EU policies, as Goetz (2009) argues in more detail, tend to favour continuity through delegation and through the establishment of programmes that commit Commissioners, MEPs and Council members to think and act beyond their term in office. We would expect that policy in the EU is less likely to be subject to electorally sensitive, 'opportunistic' timing than in national contexts, where electoral politics matters much more. But so far, with the exception of monetary and economic policy (Dyson 2009), we know very little about how 'time consistent' EU policies are.

A second expectation concerns 'the politics of when' (Jacobs 2008), i.e. the intertemporality of policy in terms of distributing costs and benefits over time. Here, we would expect that EU policy, to the extent that it is made by non-majoritarian institutions, is more likely to time costs upfront than majoritarian institutions, which have an incentive to defer costs well into the future. EU policy might, therefore, not just be more time consistent; it might also be better at confronting the task of distributing costs and benefits equitably over time.

Finally, a third expectation relates to the temporality of policy reforms at EU level. Impressionistic evidence suggests a strong propensity for gradualism, elaboratedly scheduled reform in stages, with transitional clauses, and much phasing in and phasing out. This gradualism is underpinned by the fact that planning periods in key policies – such as agricultural policy and the structural funds programme - typically exceed the five-year mandates of Commissioners and MEPs. Instead they are aligned with the budgetary cycle, which has traditionally been seven years long (Lindner 2006), so that any substantive reform requires consent across two successive Commissions, two successive parliaments and several Council presidencies.

HOW DOES TIME MATTER? PERSPECTIVES ON THE STUDY OF POLITICAL TIME

The most critical question in the study of EU time is how the manner in which it is institutionalized shapes political action and outcomes. Scholarship that concentrates on time-related issues in political life tends to engage with one or more of three major themes, which are also amongst the central concerns of political science as a discipline: power, system performance and legitimacy.

Power

The first theme is, not surprisingly, how political time affects the distribution of power within a political system. Studies of democratization and constitution-making, for example, have pointed to the strategic importance of the terms of chief executives (Frye 1997). Longer terms are typically associated with enhanced power and with an increased time budget seen as resource that can be employed in the political process. In the case of parliaments, a great deal has been made of timetable control as a means of governments to impose their will on the legislature (Tsebelis 2002).

The relation between time and power is also at the centre of debates surrounding EU politics and policy-making. The short term of Council presidencies is not only considered to have a negative impact on the performance of the Council, but is also often seen to create a strategic disadvantage for the Council *vis-à-vis* the EP and the Commission. Thus, the EP, with its five-year mandate and the continuity option in legislation, may use its power of delay in order to strengthen its position in inter-institutional relationships (Hix 2002). Playing with and for time has, accordingly, been identified as one of the main resources of the EP to gain influence in the legislative process (Corbett *et al.* 2007). Finally, where policy is in flux and timetables are not yet as fixed as in long-standing policy areas, political and administrative entrepreneurs may seek to structure institutional and policy timetables in such a way as to maximize their own influence. The Commission's successful effort to become the time manager in enlargement policy provides a case in point (Avery 2009; Lass-Lennecke and Werner 2009).

Performance

Much debate in comparative politics and comparative political economy has concerned the performance of political systems and its determinants. To give just two examples: Lijphart (1999) has argued that consensual-type democracies perform better at both the input level of representation and the output level of economic and social performance than majoritarian systems. Similarly, Persson and Tabellini (2003) have addressed the consequences of constitutional design with regard to economic outcomes, such as welfare spending and the size of budget deficits. This concern with performance, efficiency and effectiveness is echoed in time-centred research. For example, the shortening of the presidential term together with the alignment of presidential and parliamentary elections in France have largely been justified with regard to the superior performance of the new institutional set-up (Cole 2002), as it reduces the risk of *cohabitation* and the risk of gridlock in a divided executive.

In the EU setting, temporal considerations are likewise often linked to considerations of performance. For example, the troika presidency has been justified on grounds of enhanced policy-making capacity of the Council (Ágh 2007). König's (2007) work has related the length of legislative processes to the efficiency of political decision-making. Time, it is assumed here, is costly and the growing amount of time that is needed to pass bills indicates a decline in system performance. To give another example, the 'early agreements' between Council and EP under the co-decision procedures are frequently regarded as an efficiency-enhancing device. The original understanding was that technical policy proposals and minor amendments would not require three readings. Yet, research by Héritier and Farrell (2004; Farrell and Héritier 2007) shows that political constellations between Parliament and Council are more important in explaining the use of the early agreement provision (see also Rasmussen 2007b).

Legitimacy

Finally, time-centred analysis shows an affinity to questions of legitimacy. To give two examples, in the context of her study of time rules in parliament, Riescher (1994, 1997) stresses the link between time rules, notably the rights of the opposition to demand time in committees and the plenary, and the legitimacy of the outcomes of parliamentary deliberation and decision-taking. Discussing the comparative experience of administrative reforms, Painter and Peters (forthcoming) note that one of the key reasons why radical, fast-track administrative reforms are rarely successful is the lack of time given to deliberation and the search for acceptance.

Legitimacy also has its place in trying to understand the institutionalization of political time in the EU and its consequences. One example may suffice: the establishment of longer programming cycles and the better regulation agenda more broadly have been linked to the desire to increase both the efficiency and the legitimacy of EU policy-making. Tholoniat (2009) explains how the use of regulatory impact assessments and consultation mechanisms with stakeholders increases the amount of time needed for the development of Commission proposals. But the additional time invested in policy-making should be compensated by the higher acceptance of EU policy.

THEORIZING EU TIME

So far, we have concentrated on how and why political time matters for political analysis. We hope to have shown that analysing the institutionalization of political time in the EU more intensively and systematically than has hitherto been the case can shed new light on the overarching questions of what kind of political system the EU is, what sort of problems it might be particularly good or bad at dealing with, and how political time affects political actors and outcomes.

But how best to approach the study of political time in the EU from a theoretical point of view? There are two broad issues at stake here. First, what are the main theoretical perspectives to draw on in trying to understand the effects of political time? Second, how can we account for the manner in which political time has evolved in the EU? In line with our understanding of political time as part of the changeable institutional make-up of the EU, we think that in answering these questions our efforts should concentrate – at least in the first instance – on drawing out the implications of the dominant approaches to the study of EU institutions and their effects and to integration, institutionalization and institutional change.

EU politics has arguably been a battlefield for different theoretical approaches to the study of institutions and their effects. They have been reviewed on numerous occasions and have been extensively criticized (Schneider and Aspinwall 2001; Jupille *et al.* 2003) and we do not make any claim to originality here. In a first step, it is sufficient to distinguish rational choice (Pollack 2006) and constructivist approaches (Checkel 2006) when asking how theory might help us to formulate hypotheses about the 'patterning' effects of political time. Seeing political time through the lenses of these two approaches serves to highlight its different properties and possible effects.

A rationalist perspective emphasizes actors' preferences over temporal qualities of mandates, decisional rules and policy, which are informed by the desire to maximize some material outcome, and highlights contestation and choice surrounding political time. Political time is a resource that can be used; it is instrumental and consequential. Rationalist approaches emphasize that temporal institutions act as opportunities and constraints on actors' strategies, affecting both when and how to act.

Constructivist perspectives, on the other hand, would emphasize the social embeddedness of temporal structures. Temporal features provide meaning and sense for individuals and collectivities, they have important symbolic values, and they provide orientation about the temporal appropriateness of action. Constructivist perspectives, therefore, resonate well with the notion of 'social time' and the social construction and interpretation of time (Nowotny 1994). Constructivism suggests that actors' views of temporal orders, choices, perceptions and discourses are not necessarily guided by instrumentality, but by ideas, principles, deeply embedded values and norms.

Accordingly, rationalist approaches seem well placed to ask questions about temporal opportunity structures, time rules and strategic advantages, calculations over policy timing, time-efficient decisions, and time consistency. Constructivist approaches direct our attention to themes such as clocks and rhythms as norms and values, temporal appropriateness, 'ripe time' (Goodin 1998), the value of temporal routines, and procedural-temporal legitimacy, for instance, the allocation of time to parliamentary minorities in legislative decision-making.

Rationalist arguments resonate with perspectives of political time that concentrate on its relationship to power and performance. The timing, sequencing, and conclusion of decision-making processes are geared towards maximizing benefits and minimizing costs. For instance, König's (2007) work on the length of legislative processes reflects a concern with the costs of decision-making. The debate surrounding the 'early agreements' under the EU co-decision procedure looks at the implications for the distribution of power between EU actors. Héritier and Farrell (2004), for instance, have shown that the early agreements have shifted power towards *rapporteurs* in the EP. Time-centred analysis from a constructivist perspective, by contrast, would seem to be particularly apt to explore the linkages between political time and legitimacy. For example, Ekengren (2002) emphasizes the 'social construction' of temporality when he points to the changing perception of time at the national level in response to progressive EU integration.

The second key question about theorizing political time in the EU concerns its historical evolution as part of the overall process of European integration. There is, of course, a very rich scholarship that has sought to explain this overall trajectory, including both the different strands of 'integration theory' and more recent work that focuses on the institutionalization of, and institutional change in, the EU (Stone Sweet *et al.* 2001; Héritier 2007). These studies have not, so far, dealt more comprehensively with explaining the development of the temporal properties of the EU system *over time*. But there is no reason why they should not be able to do so. For example, Héritier's (2007) recent analysis of institutional rules and change in the EU repeatedly also touches on temporal rules of decision-making (as, for example, in legislative procedures) and it is also explicitly concerned with explaining long-term institutional change. A similar analysis that focuses head-on on temporal institutional properties and their explanation promises much in terms of a greater understanding of both the trajectory and the interconnectedness of temporal properties. In short, we do not see the need for a 'theory of EU time', but rather encourage existing theory-oriented accounts of integration, institutionalization and institutional change to 'foreground' time as a key 'dependent' variable to be explained.

Finally, as Bulmer's (2009) contribution to this volume underlines, there is potentially also much to be learned from paying attention to how time helps to account for aspects of European integration that would otherwise be difficult to explain; in other words, it has a role to play as an 'independent' variable in explaining European integration. Historical institutionalist analyses – as exemplified by Pierson's (2004) work, in particular – with their stress on feedbacks, path dependencies, timing, sequences, and long-term processes are the most obvious point of departure. But it is interesting to note that neo-functionalism and 'neo-neofunctionalism' (Schmitter 2004) also accord initiation, priming, and transformative 'cycles' and the notion of 'asynchronic change' central explanatory status (Goetz, forthcoming).

A BRIEF OVERVIEW

The present article has sought to make a case for studying the manner in which political time is institutionalized in the EU. Studying time in the EU involves, in particular, an analysis of terms, time budgets, time horizons and their impact on the temporal ordering of activities; of the temporal features of decision-making; and of the time choices embedded in public policies. The article has sought to show that temporal features have important consequences for questions surrounding the distribution of power, the performance and the legitimacy of the EU political system. Different theoretical approaches are relevant for the study of time in the EU and shed light on different aspects of the institutionalization of political time in the EU. The articles assembled in this volume engage with different dimensions, perspectives and approaches in the study of political time in the EU and provide selective insights into the way political time matters for the EU.

The paper by *Goetz* (2009) discusses the manner in which political time has been institutionalized in the EU. The paper advances five propositions that focus on distinctive features of the EU timescape. The propositions stress the absence of a dominant political cycle comparable to the electoral cycle at the national level and resultant problems of mobilization and synchronization; an emphasis on linear political time, associated with continuity and open-endedness, as opposed to cyclical political time, which lends itself to discontinuity in political processes; intensive inter-institutional and intra-institutional bargaining over time-setting and a propensity for governing by timetable; the fragility of EU *Eigenzeit* and its sensitivity to external interference; and the impact of EU time on political time in the member states. Goetz argues that the balances struck in the temporal constitution of the EU are critical to its long-term future.

This is followed by an article by *Tholoniat* (2009) that focuses on temporal aspects in the work of the Commission; it highlights growing differentiation in the temporal organization of the Commission. Tholoniat notes how attempts at promoting good governance within the Commission have affected both institutional and policy time. Drawing on first-hand experience gained in the Commission, he stresses the changing clocks and time horizons within the Commission's work. In particular, he analyses the consequences of the introduction of a complex system of multi-annual planning and impact assessment and points out how they have contributed to power shifts both within the Commission and in inter-institutional relations.

Questions of timing are at the centre of the article by *Kovats* (2009). Kovats examines whether EU legislative activity is subject to distinct cycles comparable to national democracies. He finds that the Commission initiates more legislation at the end of the term of the EP, which contrasts with the prevalent patterns at the national level where legislative initiatives tend to peak at the beginning of the parliamentary term. Moreover, his analysis shows that the timing of the adoption of EU legislation is closely associated with the reallocation of agenda powers within the EP at mid-term rather than the timing of European elections and thus the end of MEPs' terms in office.

The three articles that follow link in different ways to polity, politics and policy concerns. The article by *Avery* (2009), a former long-time Commission official, underlines how the Commission sought to steer the enlargement process through governing by timetable. He discusses several examples of imaginative time-setting by the Commission, which helped to buttress its position *vis-à-vis* the Council, the EP and, above all, the candidate states.

Lass-Lennecke and Werner's article (2009) follows on from this analysis. They ask how the temporal and substantial policy challenges posed by Eastern enlargement led to institutional change inside the Commission, in particular, the creation of DG Enlargement and the establishment of new rules and procedures for time management. They thus grapple with the general question of how policy time affects institutional time. They note how policy time – aimed primarily at the accession states – fed back into the organization of the Commission's work, with DG Enlargement acting as a time-setter for much of the rest of the Commission and, to some extent, the Council.

The link between institutional and policy time is also explored in the contribution by *Dyson* (2009). He stresses how European economic governance has progressively become characterized by an *Eigenzeit*, with distinctive time rules and time horizons. This particular set of temporal features is typically justified with reference to the functional requirements of economic governance. But whilst performance arguments dominate, Dyson makes clear that the temporality of economic governance has also had a deep impact on political time in the member states.

The article by *Bulmer* (2009) focuses on the links between the study of political time, as advocated in this volume, and the concerns of historical institutionalism. Bulmer identifies overlaps and differences between the politics of time and the 'politics in time' (Pierson 2004) and examines how attention to the EU timescape can help to inform broader debates on the EU integration process since the very beginning, the specifics and dynamics of EU policy, and the impact of EU integration on institutional change in the member states that is discussed under the heading of Europeanization.

The final article by *Meyer-Sahling and Goetz* (2009) moves the debate from broad attention to political time in the EU to the systematic study of the EU timescape. Building on the papers collected in this special issue, the paper clarifies the concept of the EU timescape and outlines its value-added for debates surrounding EU enlargement, differentiated integration and the democratization of the EU. Taking forward the insights gained from the study of the EU political system, the article concludes that political systems can be generally characterized by the systematic patterning of temporal features. The authors thus make the case for the comparative study of democratic timescapes.

Biographical note: Klaus H. Goetz is Professor of German and European Politics and Government at the University of Potsdam, Germany, and Visiting Fellow at the European Institute, London School of Economics, UK. Jan-Hinrik Meyer-Sahling is Lecturer in European Politics at the University of Nottingham, UK.

ACKNOWLEDGEMENTS

We would like to thank the following for their most helpful comments on an earlier draft of this paper: Umut Aydin, Simon Bulmer, Simon Hix, Laszlo Kovats, Katja Lass-Lennecke, Anand Menon, Stephanie Lee Mudge, Johan P. Olsen, Anne Rasmussen, Richard Rose, and Annika Werner. The usual disclaimer applies.

NOTE

1 This article is informed by work carried out within the context of a working group on 'The Temporality of Europeanization and Enlargement', which was convened by the authors under the auspices of EU-CONSENT. The paper also draws on an ongoing study of political time in the EU, which is funded by the German Research Foundation (DFG) and led by the first author at the University of Potsdam.

REFERENCES

Adam, B. (2008) *Of Timescapes, Futurescapes and Timeprints*. Paper presented at Lüneburg University, 17 June.

Ágh, A. (2007) *The New Life Cycles of the Council: The Incoming Presidencies of the New Member States*. Paper presented at the CONSENT workshop 'The Temporality of Europeanization and Enlargement', University of Potsdam, 15–16 February 2007.

Avery, G. (2009) 'Uses of time in the EU's enlargement process', *Journal of European Public Policy* 16(2): 256–269.

Bulmer, S. (2009) '*Politics in time* meets the politics of time: historical institutionalism and the EU timescape', *Journal of European Public Policy* 16(2): 270–285.

Checkel, J. (2006) 'Constructivism and EU politics', in K.E. Jørgensen *et al.* (eds), *Handbook of European Union Politics*, London: Sage, pp. 57–76.

Cole, A. (2002) 'A strange affair: The 2002 presidential and parliamentary elections in France', *Government and Opposition* 37(3): 317–42.

Corbett, R., Jacobs, F. and Shackleton, M. (2007) *The European Parliament*, 7th edn, London: John Harper Publishing.

Cox, G. (2005) 'The organisation of democratic legislatures', in B. Weingast and D. Wittman (eds), *The Oxford Handbook of Political Economy*, Oxford: Oxford University Press, pp. 141–61.

Curtin, D. and Egeberg, M. (2008) 'Tradition and innovation: Europe's accumulated executive order', *West European Politics* 31(4).

Döring, H. (1995) 'Time as a scarce resource: government control of the agenda', in H. Döring (ed.), *Parliaments and Majority Rule in Western Europe*, Campus Verlag, pp. 223–246.

Döring, H. (2003) 'Party discipline and government imposition of restrictive rules', *Journal of Legislative Studies* 9(4): 147–63.

Döring, H. (2004) 'Controversy, time constraint, and restrictive rules', in H. Döring and M. Hallerberg (eds), *Patterns of Parliamentary Behaviour: Passage of Legislation across Western Europe*, Aldershot: Ashgate Publishing Ltd, pp. 141–68.

Drazen, A. (2001) 'The political business cycle after 25 years', *NBER Macroeconomics Annual 2000*.

Dyson, K. (2009) 'The evolving timescapes of european economic governance: contesting and using time', *Journal of European Public Policy* 16(2): 286–306.

Egeberg, M. (ed.) (2006) *Multilevel Union Administration: The Transformation of Executive Politics in Europe*, Basingstoke: Palgrave.

Ekengren, M. (1996) 'The Europeanization of state administration: adding the time dimension', *Cooperation and Conflict* 31: 387–415.

Ekengren, M. (1997) 'The temporality of European governance', in K.E. Jørgensen (ed.), *Reflective Approaches to European Governance*, Basingstoke: Macmillan, pp. 68–86.

Ekengren, M. (2002) *The Time of European Governance*, Manchester: Manchester University of Press.

Farrell, H. and Héritier, A. (2007) 'Co-decision and institutional change', *West European Politics* 30(2): 285–300.

Frye, T. (1997) 'A politics of institutional choice: post-communist presidencies', *Comparative Political Studies* 30: 523–52.

Gilardi, F. (2002) 'Policy credibility and delegation to independent regulatory agencies: a comparative empirical analysis', *Journal of European Public Policy* 9(6): 873–93.

Goetz, K.H. (forthcoming) 'Time and differentiated integration', in K. Dyson and A. Sepos (eds), *Whose Europe? The Politics of Differentiated Integration*, Basingstoke: Palgrave.

Goetz, K.H. (2009) 'How does the EU tick? Five propositions on political time', *Journal of European Public Policy* 16(2): 202–20.

Goetz, K.H. and Meyer-Sahling, J. (2008) 'The Europeanisation of domestic political systems', *Living Reviews in European Governance*, June.

Goodin, C. (1998) 'Keeping political time: the rhythms of democracy', *International Political Science Review* 19(1): 39–54.

Graziano, P. and Vink, M.P. (eds) (2007) *Europeanization: New Research Agendas*, Basingstoke: Palgrave.
Hayes-Renshaw, F. and Wallace, H. (2006) *The Council of Ministers*, 2nd edn, Basingstoke: Macmillan.
Héritier, A. (2007) *Explaining Institutional Change in Europe*, Oxford: Oxford University Press.
Héritier, A. and Farrell, H. (2004) 'Interorganizational negotiation and intraorganizational power in shared decision making: early agreements under codecision and their impact on the European Parliament and Council', *Comparative Political Studies* 37(10): 1184–212.
Hix, S. (2002) 'Constitutional agenda-setting through discretion in rule interpretation: why the European Parliament won at Amsterdam', *British Journal of Political Science* 32(2): 259–80.
Hix, S. (2005) *The Political System of the European Union*, 2nd edn, London: Palgrave.
Hix, S. (2008) *What's Wrong with the European Union and How to Fix It*, Cambridge: Polity Press.
Jacobs, A.M. (2008) 'The politics of when: redistribution, investment and policy making for the long term', *British Journal of Political Science* 38: 193–220.
Jerneck, M. (2000) 'Europeanization, territoriality and political time', *Yearbook of European Studies* 14: 27–49.
Jupille, J., Caporaso, J. and Checkel, J. (2003) 'Integrating institutions: rationalism, constructivism, and the study of the European Union', *Comparative Political Studies* 36: 7–40.
Kardasheva, R. (2008). *The Power to Delay: Explaining the European Parliament's Influence in the Consultation Procedure*. Paper presented at the ECPR Joint Sessions, Rennes, April 2008.
Kok Report (2004) *Facing the Challenge: The Lisbon Strategy for Growth and Employment*. Report from the High Level Group, chaired by Wim Kok, Brussels: European Communities. Available at: http://europa.eu.int/comm/lisbon_strategy/index_en.html
König, T. (2007) 'Divergence or convergence? From ever-growing to ever-slowing European legislative decision making', *European Journal of Political Research* 46: 417–44.
Kovats, L. (2009) 'Do elections set the pace? A quantitative assessment of the timing of European legislation', *Journal of European Public Policy* 16(2): 239–55.
Kydland, F.E. and Prescott, E.C. (1977) 'Rules rather than discretion: the inconsistency of optimal plans', *Journal of Political Economy* 85(3): 473–92.
Lass-Lennecke, K. and Werner, A. (2009) 'Policies, institutions and time: how the European Commission managed the temporal challenge of eastern enlargement', *Journal of European Public Policy* 16(2): 270–85.
Lijphart, A. (1999) *Patterns of Democracy: Government Forms and Performance in Thirty-Six Countries*, New Haven, CT: Yale University Press.
Lindner, J. (2006) *Conflict and Change in EU Budgetary Politics*, London: Routledge.
Linz, J. (1998) 'Democracy's time constraints', *International Political Science Review* 19(1): 19–37.
Majone, G. (1997) 'From the positive to the regulatory state: causes and consequences of changes in the mode of governance', *Journal of Public Policy* 17(2): 139–68.
Martin, L.W. (2004) 'The government agenda in parliamentary democracies', *American Journal of Political Science* 48(3): 445–61.
McNamara, K. (2002) 'Rational fictions: central bank independence and the social logic of delegation', *West European Politics* 25(1): 47–76.
Menon, A. (2008) *Europe: The State of the Union*, London: Atlantic Books.

Meyer-Sahling, J.-H. (2007) *Time and European Governance: An Inventory*. Paper presented at the Biennial Conference of the European Union Studies Association, Montreal, May 2007.
Meyer-Sahling, J.-H. and Goetz, K.H. (2009) 'The EU timescape: from notion to research agenda', *Journal of European Public Policy* 16(2): 325–36.
Nowotny, H. (1994) *Time: The Modern and Postmodern Experience*, Cambridge: Polity Press.
Painter, M. and Peters, B.G. (eds) (2009, forthcoming) *Administrative Traditions: Inheritances and Transplants in Comparative Perspective*, Basingstoke: Palgrave.
Persson, T. and Tabellini, G. (2003) *The Economic Effects of Constitutions*, Cambridge, MA: MIT Press.
Pierson, P. (2004) *Politics in Time: History, Institutions and Social Analysis*, Princeton, NJ: Princeton University Press.
Pollack, M. (2006) 'Rational choice and EU politics', in K.E. Jørgensen *et al.* (eds), *Handbook of European Union Politics*, London: Sage, pp. 31–56.
Pollitt, C. (2008) *Time, Policy, Management: Governing with the Past*, Oxford: Oxford University Press.
Rasmussen, A. (2007a) 'Challenging the Commission's right of initiative? Conditions for institutional change and stability', *West European Politics* 30(2): 244–64.
Rasmussen, A. (2007b) *Early Conclusion in the Co-decision Legislative Procedure*, European University Institute, Max Weber Paper 2007/3.
Riescher, G. (1994) *Zeit und Politik. Zur institutionellen Bedeutung von Zeitstrukturen in parlamentarischen und präsidentiellen Regierungssystemen*, Baden-Baden: Nomos Verlagsgesellschaft.
Riescher, G. (1997) 'Parlamentarische Zeitstrukturen zwischen geschichtlichen Traditionslinien und moderner Funktionalität', *Zeitschrift für Parlamentsfragen* 44: 101–15.
Rittberger, B. (2000) 'Impatient legislators and new issue-dimensions: a critique of the Garrett–Tsebelis "standard version" of legislative politics', *Journal of European Public Policy* 7(4): 554–75.
Schedler, A. and Santiso, J. (1998) 'Democracy and time: an invitation', *International Political Science Review* 19(1): 5–18.
Schmitter, P.C. (2004) 'Neo-neofunctionalism', in A. Wiener and T. Diez (eds), *European Integration Theory*, Oxford: Oxford University Press, pp. 45–73.
Schmitter, P. and Santiso, J. (1998) 'Three temporal dimensions of the consolidation of democracy', *International Political Science Review* 19(1): 69–92.
Schneider, G. and Aspinwall, M. (2001) *The Rules of Integration: Institutionalist Approaches to the Study of Europe*, Manchester: Manchester University Press.
Shepsle, K. and Weingast, B. (1987) 'The Institutional Foundations of Committee Power', *American Political Science Review* 81(1): 85–104.
Shugart, M.S. (1995) 'The electoral cycle and institutional sources of divided presidential government', *American Political Science Review* 89(2): 327–43.
Shugart, M.S. and Carey, J. (1992) *Presidents and Assemblies. Constitutional Design and Electoral Dynamics*, Cambridge: Cambridge University Press.
Stone Sweet, A., Fligstein, N. and Sandholtz, W. (2001) 'The institutionalization of European Space', in A. Stone Sweet *et al.* (eds), *The Institutionalization of Europe*, Oxford: Oxford University Press, pp. 1–28.
Strøm, K., Müller, W.C. and Bergman, T. (eds) (2003) *Delegation and Accountability in Parliamentary Democracies*, Oxford: Oxford University Press.
Thatcher, M. and Stone-Sweet, A. (2002) 'Delegation to independent regulatory agencies: pressures, functions and contextual mediation', *West European Politics* 25(1): 1–22.
Tholoniat, L. (2009) 'The temporal constitution of the European Commission: a timely investigation', *Journal of European Public Policy* 16(2): 221–38.

Tsebelis, G. (2002) *Veto Players: How Political Institutions Work*, Princeton, NJ: Princeton University Press.
Zubek, R. (2008) *Parliamentary Executives and Legislative Time.* Paper presented at PSA Annual Conference, Swansea, UK, 1–3 April 2008.
Zubek, R., Goetz, K.H. and Lodge, M. (2007) *Legislative Planning in Central Europe: Towards Strategic Management of Government Legislation*, London: LSE, Central European Observatory.

How does the EU tick? Five propositions on political time

Klaus H. Goetz

ABSTRACT In what manner is political time institutionalized in the political system of the EU? This article advances five propositions on political time in the EU and highlights their implications for the workings of the EU. The propositions stress: (i) the absence of a dominant EU political cycle, which creates problems of mobilization and synchronization, but also allows for temporal plurality; (ii) an emphasis on linear political time, associated with ongoingness and open-endedness, as opposed to cyclical political time, which favours discontinuity in institutional practices and policies; (iii) intensive bargaining over time-setting, which encourages governing by timetable; (iv) the sensitivity of EU political time to member state influence, on the one hand, and (v) the Europeanization of political time in the member states, on the other. The balances struck in the temporal constitution of the EU are critical to its future.

INTRODUCTION

In what manner is political time institutionalized in the European Union (EU)? What are the time rules, time budgets and time horizons in EU policy-making? Is EU time cyclical or linear? In short, how does the EU tick? The reason why we raise such questions is that 'time matters' and that research into, and reflection on, political time can advance our understanding of the nature of power, performance and legitimacy in the EU (Goetz and Meyer-Sahling 2009).

Many of the current debates in political science on the nature of the EU, the challenges its faces and its future prospects are linked to political time, although this connection is rarely made explicit. For example, the proposed introduction of the position of a President of the Council elected for a two-and-a-half-year term under the Lisbon Treaty and the new arrangements for troika presidencies constitute important changes in the timescape of the Council and the EU as a whole (Ágh 2007). These changes have tended to be justified politically on grounds of improved efficiency and effectiveness of Council decision-making. Such an emphasis mirrors academic comment, which amongst the weaknesses of the six-monthly rotating presidency has noted volatility – 'change at the helm results in new priorities'; discontinuity – 'frequent changes in personnel unsettling for external partners'; and its 'time-consuming' nature, because consultation and negotiation with all the member states 'requires considerable input of time' (Hayes-Renshaw and Wallace 2006: 155). But they are also likely to affect the inter-institutional balance of power, as they suggest a lengthening of the time horizons of the political tier of the Council, counterbalancing the five-year mandate of the College of Commissioners.

With these considerations in mind, the main aim of the present article is to stimulate debate on the nature of political time in the EU and its consequences through five broad propositions. There are good reasons why one would *not* want to generalize about political time in the EU: the EU has a complex institutional make-up; its political core institutions – the Council of Ministers and the European Council, the Commission and the European Parliament (EP) – are marked by high degrees of functional and organizational differentiation and specialization; it encompasses many different decision-making modes, including the traditional Community method, the EU regulatory mode, a distributional mode, policy co-ordination and 'intensive transgovernmentalism' (Wallace and Wallace 2006); and it touches on a very wide range of policy areas with big differences in the legal powers and competences for these institutions. Moreover, as Dyson's (2009) work on economic and monetary policy underlines, different policy fields are characterized by *Eigenzeiten*, i.e. their own distinct temporal frameworks. These include distinct time budgets that actors have at their disposal, time horizons that tend to be adopted, time rules that have to be observed and flexibility in the discretionary use of time. For example, where the Commission acts as a quasi-judicial authority – as in the antitrust area, mergers, cartels or state aid (Türk 2006) – the rules that it has to follow on the timing, sequencing, speed and duration of its actions as part of due process are likely to be more detailed, more strictly enforced and less discretionary than where it acts in a co-ordinating or advisory capacity.

Yet, it is in the nature of generalizations that they permit exceptions and invite qualifications. My purpose here is not to try to encapsulate the EU timescape (Meyer-Sahling and Goetz 2009) in its entirety, but to highlight some prominent features and to encourage debate on their consequences. Prominent features is *not* to be read as unique features, for any such claim could only be based on a systematic comparison with other international organizations or national political systems which is beyond this article.

FIVE PROPOSITIONS ON POLITICAL TIME IN THE EU

Proposition I: *There is no dominant political cycle in the EU. As a consequence, mobilization and synchronization of actors are difficult to achieve, but time is less of a constraint on policy-making than in systems with an overarching cycle.*

Our understanding of democratic political time is intimately tied to the notion of cycles. 'Much political time is caught up in *cycles*, both regular and irregular and of different lengths' (Loomis 1994: 10; emphasis in the original) and cycles 'are central to the structure of political life and its interpretation' (Loomis 1994: 12). Chief amongst these cycles at national level is the electoral cycle. It provides elected politicians with a finite time budget, which they need to allocate wisely if they wish to be re-elected; it acts as a major restriction on the time horizons that they are likely to adopt; and it also has a profound influence on the timing, sequencing, speed and duration of their political actions, such as, for example, the timing of bills over the course of a parliament (Martin 2004).

Under conditions of parliamentary government, the electoral cycle helps to synchronize government and parliament, because both draw on the same time budget and both are similarly constrained in the time horizons that they typically adopt. In short, the electoral cycle in democratic politics is central to understanding the mobilization of the electorate and politicians; and it provides for a considerable degree of synchronization amongst the key political institutions, although evidently more so in unitary parliamentary systems than in presidential, semi-presidential or federal systems, in which mandates and elections are less closely aligned. This is not to suggest, of course, that all cycles in national politics are tied to the electoral cycle. But it has traditionally constituted the basic rhythm of democratic life in national polities.

If we turn to the EU, we find no similarly dominant cycle – whether electoral or 'selectoral' (i.e. tied to regular selection or appointment processes, as in the case of the Commission)[1] and whether at the institutional or policy levels – which would provide the basic rhythm to the system as a whole. At the institutional level, cycles are most evident in the electoral cycle constituted by the regular quinquennial elections to the EP, and by the fixed periods of office of the Commission President and the Commissioners. Since, under the Maastricht Treaty, the lengths of the mandates of the EP and the Commission have been made to coincide and the appointment and approval of the Commission have become progressively tied to the EP (Moury 2007), the electoral term has certainly increased in importance as a time-setter in EU politics.

The length of the mandate of the Commission has a deep impact on how it arranges its work over time, as does the fact that the mandate is linked to the parliamentary term (Tholoniat 2009). The timing of initiatives and the planning of workflows owe much to the five-year mandate, the more so since the Commission has started to adopt five-year strategic objectives at the start of its term of office. The Commission bureaucracy needs to ensure that a sufficient number of major legislative initiatives have been developed up to a point where the new incoming President of the Commission and his fellow Commissioners can quickly establish their own distinct policy agenda. In this, the President of the Commission is at a temporal advantage. He is appointed and approved prior to the Commissioners and can use this period of time as a 'window of opportunity' to try to fashion the new Commission's priorities.

This need to come up with new initiatives early on in the life of a new Commission also suggests that, towards the end of the mandate, Commission officials will have less incentive to try to push proposals at the political level and may, instead, prefer to wait for the new incoming Commission. Similarly, outgoing Commissioners with little or no prospect of reappointment may not be much interested in launching new initiatives and prefer to concentrate on 'unfinished business' (or on securing their next job).

Yet, although the electoral term of the EP affects how the Commission and also the Council arrange their business, the electoral cycle does not provide the basic rhythm of EU politics. This is partly because EP elections do not hold the prospect of a fundamental alternation of power, and partly because much EU business is not directly tied to the electoral term. In the EP, there is no divide between government and opposition parties, so that cyclical elections do not hold the prospect of major change. Members of the European Parliament (MEPs) from the two major party groups – the European People's Party–European Democrats and the Socialist Group – have a high chance of securing re-election, and EP elections tend to be fought as second-order national contests. Both factors mitigate against electoral cycles assuming the same prominence in the temporal ordering of the EP's business that one can observe, although, of course, to varying degrees, in the member states. The fact that pending legislation is regularly carried over from one legislature to the next – the discontinuity principle in parliamentary legislation is effectively suspended – further militates against strong cyclical effects (Kovats 2009). In the Commission, as will be discussed below, there are still strong institutional forces that operate against marked cycles in how it organizes its work. Finally, the terms of office in the Council are, of course, dissociated from the electoral term, a fact that also minimizes electoral cyclicity.

There are policy cycles that arguably matter more than the electoral cycle. Chief amongst these is the budgetary cycle. It is constituted by a multi-annual financial framework that establishes upper spending limits per heading and is based on a binding agreement between the Commission, the EP and the Council. Importantly, it extends beyond the five-year mandate of the former two institutions, as the current agreement, adopted in 2006, covers seven years (2007–2013). The financing of the European Agricultural Guarantee Fund and the European Agricultural Fund for Rural Development is also determined for the same period. Finally, although it stretches the understanding of 'cycles', the rounds of treaty revisions since the mid-1980s – the Single European Act, the Treaty on European Union, the Amsterdam and Nice Treaties, the failed Constitution and the Treaty of Lisbon – have introduced an important additional rhythm to the operation of the EU.

What are the consequences of this absence of a dominant cycle? Two deserve highlighting. First, it makes mobilization and synchronization of political actors difficult. In national politics, the electoral cycle mobilizes actors and it synchronizes them at the same time – the minds of most political actors, whether in the legislature, government or the upper echelons of the bureaucracy, are focused by the next election. The absence of a similarly dominant cycle at EU level makes mobilization and synchronization – as key regulatory and steering functions of political time – very demanding. Mobilization, which is about the preferential allocation of time to tasks, is made difficult in the absence of a dominant cycle that could help to settle conflicts over the allocation of actors' time to clear temporal priorities. Where terms, time budgets and time horizons of different groups of actors differ as markedly as in the EU, agreeing on priorities in allocating time is not easy. Similarly, synchronization, i.e. making sure that a range of different activities is performed in a temporally co-ordinated fashion, is made more demanding in the absence of a dominant time-setter.

But this lack of a dominant rhythm also allows for temporal plurality. Within the Commission and the Council, in particular, powerful permanent bureaucracies both provide memory – knowledge about what has happened in the past – and a future time horizon that extends beyond the Commission mandate, a minister's tenure or a Council presidency. Different policies can run on different clocks, especially if they are of a regulatory nature and require little or no co-ordination with the EU budgetary cycle. Thus, policy-making in the EU may be less constrained by time than in systems with an overarching cycle.

Proposition II: *There is a strong emphasis on ongoingness in EU political time: it has a decidedly linear character. This encourages continuity in action over time, but it also lends a temporal subtext to the 'democratic deficit'.*

In one of the few systematic treatments of political time in contemporary politics, Gisela Riescher has suggested that political time remains fundamentally determined by the 'archaic' conception of cyclical, as opposed to the modern understanding of linear time.

> The 'cyclical element' characterizes the temporal structures of political systems much more than linearity. True: political planning and innovation, economic and technical progress and the establishment of strategies for future developmental opportunities ... are future-oriented linear 'time arrows' ... But political time is to a much larger extent characterized by recurring cycles. The reasons for this ... lie above all in the temporal limitation of democratic government.
> (Riescher 1994: 230; KHG's translation)

Although the distinction between cyclical and linear time is very common in writings on time, the two are not as easily distinguished as one might expect; more crucially, it would be misleading to see them as mutually exclusive. Rather, what matters for a political timescape is how they are combined.

Cyclical time is characterized by periodically repeated sequences of events with a clear beginning and end. The electoral cycle and the budgetary cycle, which is annualized in most democracies, are prime examples (Pollitt 2008: 51). Linear time, by contrast, is typically associated with 'time arrows', a succession or sequence of events that may occur with a high degree of regularity, but are not bounded by clear start and end points that would give rise to a new sequence. Political cycles are, therefore, strongly linked to the idea of discontinuity, institutionalized opportunities for renewal, even ruptures, in institutional practices, personnel and policy. Linear time, by contrast, tends to be identified with ongoingness, continuity of action and open-endedness. Fixed mandates, which are subject to regular renewal, accord with cyclical political time; open or extended mandates suggest linearity.

Yet, cyclical and linear time are complementary. As Adam points (2008: 2) out, 'whether we see cycles of repetition or change and linear succession is relative. It depends on our temporal framework of observation.' For example, if one follows the Commission's activities day by day, then the impression of linearity prevails; a longer period of observation – five years – shows signs of a cycle; a still longer period – say, two decades – shows cycles within a trajectory – an 'arrow' – of institutional and policy development.

This said, it is evident that there are many institutional arrangements in place in the EU that favour ongoingness, continuity of action and open-endedness.[2] As has already been noted, in the EP, electoral cycles are weakened by the absence of a government–opposition dynamic. The discontinuity principle in law-making is not invoked (Kovats 2009). Within the Commission, we find a powerful permanent bureaucracy charged with thinking ahead. The incentives for officials to look beyond the mandate are reinforced by the fact that Commissioners have little chance of returning to their portfolios in a new Commission. Of the 26 Commissioners in the Barroso Commission (2004–2009), only one, Joaquin Almunia, the Commissioner for Economic and Monetary Affairs, has held the same portfolio in the Prodi Commission, and another, Viviane Reding, Commissioner for Information Society and Media, retained part of her previous portfolio. This implies that, on the one hand, a Commissioner's own time horizons in relation to his or her portfolio are clearly limited, but also that officials – certainly towards the end of a mandate – need not be overly concerned about a Commissioner's preferences in forward planning.

It is not surprising, therefore, that major EU policy initiatives regularly extend beyond individual Commission mandates and parliamentary terms. One may mention, for example, the single market programme launched in 1986; the introduction of European monetary union (EMU) in three stages from 1990; the Lisbon Strategy launched in 2000; or enlargement policy (Avery 2009; Lass-Lennecke and Werner 2009). The proliferation of Community agencies also tends to reinforce linearity in the temporal constitution of the EU's institutions (Pollak and Puntscher Riekmann 2008; Trondal and Jeppesen 2008), since their activities are less closely tied to the five-year mandates of either the EP or the Commissioners than the Commission bureaucracy. It is perhaps not surprising, therefore, that the European Court of Auditors (2008) in its Special Report on the EU's regulatory agencies of July 2008 noted that the agencies had failed to set medium-term result and impact objectives.

Other institutional developments further underpin the ongoingness of EU business. If we look at the Council, the work of, and interaction between, the Council of Ministers, the rotating Presidency of the Council and the European Council is governed by a set of formal and informal temporal rules that combine rotation and permanence. The work programme of the rotating half-year Presidency, co-ordinated with the Commission's annual strategic work programme, acts as an important mobilizing device, since the success of Presidencies is in part measured by their ability to deliver on the deadlines set in the work programme. It is precisely this dynamic which, at first sight paradoxically, allows the 'discontinuous' institution of the EP to exert concessions from the 'permanent' institution of the Council of Ministers (see, e.g., Bergström *et al.* 2007). The formal and informal meetings of the European Council also act as a further major mobilizing force.

The central elements of continuity in the Council of Ministers include the Committee of the Permanent Representatives (COREPER I and II), with its weekly meetings; similar top-level committees staffed with national civil servants in different policy domains; working groups; and also the Council's General Secretariat. COREPER, in particular, is the institution that 'keeps the clock ticking'. Thus, weekly meetings and other forms of exchange (such as weekly luncheons or informal trips) create a strong 'dynamic of ongoingness in COREPER's work' (Lewis 2003: 289). Dense scheduling allows business to be driven forward. Highlighting 'insulation' as one of the secrets of COREPER success, Lewis (2003: 291) quotes an unnamed permanent representative: 'We are better placed than the capitals to know what are the real interests of our countries. We are less exposed to the pressures, the short-term problems of the time. This affects us much less.' Ongoingness is further buttressed through the Council's General Secretariat, which has been greatly expanded over the years, appears to have increasingly assumed a brokerage role, and is charged with providing continuity in Council proceedings (Christiansen and Vanhoonacker 2008).

What follows from this strong orientation towards ongoingness and open-endedness? On the one hand, to the extent that the temporal operating principles of the key EU institutions resemble those of non-majoritarian institutions, they encourage continuity in action, 'temporal consistency' and, by implication, longer-term policy credibility (Majone 1996). Equally importantly, the powerful institutional foundations of linear political time in the EU, coupled with long time horizons, imply that the EU may not just be adept at dealing with 'transboundary policy problems' (Menon and Weatherill 2008), but also at tackling what one might call analogously 'transtemporal policy problems', i.e. those where there is a long time gap between action and likely effects. Its timescape is well suited to taking substantive actions that the electoral calendars of domestic politics make unlikely (at least in systems where electoral contests are closely fought and alterations in power likely).

By the same token, however, linear political time reduces the likelihood that political decisions are revisited and reversed; note the sacrosanctity of the *acquis*. The EU policy profile is, of course, anything but static; but dynamism stems as much from the accretion of new tasks, responsibilities and instruments than from major reviews, reforms and reversals. In this sense, linearity also comes at a considerable democratic cost.

Proposition III: *There is intensive bargaining over timetables. Governing by timetable is a prominent feature of EU governance.*

Students of national parliaments have shown how timetable control may rival agenda control as an effective power resource both in executive–legislative relations and within parliament (notably between the governing parties and the opposition and between committees and the plenary) (Döring 1995). But timetabling – how and by whom timetables are set and the substantive time rules that they establish – is about more than the distribution of power. It is also intimately linked to ideas about performance (notably the efficiency and effectiveness of decision-making) and the legitimacy of decision-making processes and their outcomes.

Timetabling, in addition to supporting mobilization and synchronization, is, to employ Riescher's (1994) categories, concerned with 'stabilization', which implies 'to give time, to let things mature, to institutionalize a protected time as duration, to give a decision the opportunity to prove itself in time and to mature' (Riescher 1994: 201; KHG's translation), and 'rationalization', which means 'to keep decision situations open and to use the present not as a moment, but as duration, so as to let the moment in time pass and to be able to take decisions without time pressure, with greater calm' (Riescher 1994: 201; KHG's translation). Crucially, timetabling, under democratic conditions (Riescher 1994: 213ff.), serves to maintain the separation and limitation of power; helps to enforce the majority principle and to protect (parliamentary) minority rights; and ensures procedural legitimation by stipulating authoritative time rules to be adhered to.

It is not surprising, therefore, that we find intensive intra-institutional and inter-institutional bargaining over timetables. This relates to both decisional timetables, which establish the timing, sequence, speed and duration of decision-making processes, and policy timetables, which determine the temporal properties of policies (say, for example, how speedily a directive is to be implemented, in what sequence policy measures are to be phased in, or how long a transitional measure is to stay in place). Basic decisional timetables tend to be regulated at high levels, including in constitutions or treaties, and in great detail, for example, in laws and, in particular, standing procedures. Thus, the Treaty on European Union and the Treaty establishing the European Community (in future to be known as the Treaty on the Functioning of the European Union) as amended by the Lisbon Treaty are replete with temporal rules, notably in the institutional provisions and the financial provisions. So are, not surprisingly, the rules of procedure of the EP, the Commission and the Council. Amongst policy timetables, budgetary policy, at the national level, is regularly amongst the most intensively regulated in its temporal features, and this is replicated in the EU.

Decisional timetables can never be sufficiently encompassing or detailed to prevent exploitation in the pursuit of substantive objectives – setting timetables for decision-making, in particular when it comes to strongly contested issues, is often a key political battleground. For several interconnected reasons, this general observation applies with special force in the context of the EU.

First, the emphasis on openness and ongoingness in EU business noted above means that there is greater scope for the discretionary fixing of timetables even in routine policy-making than where cycles with clear cut-off points are the norm. In particular, ongoingness offers greater scope for 'giving time', but also for claiming that time is not yet 'ripe'. Goodin (1998: 41), in the context of his discussion of reasons behind political claims of 'unripe time', goes as far as suggesting that 'while allusions to political time might be more or less successful in their manipulative intent, the attempt seems ... nonetheless manipulatory across the whole range of the phenomenon.'

Second, the fact that the key EU institutions do not run to the same clock and that, internally, their time rules, time budgets and time horizons also differ provides both additional incentives and additional scope for playing timetable politics. Third, even in EU legislative politics, an area which in national contexts is often governed by very dense temporal rules, one finds considerable discretion in timetabling. Thus, for example, deadlines are missing regarding the first readings of Council and the EP in the co-decision procedure. This indeterminacy of temporal legislative rules – and, thus, the potential scope of political bargaining over timetabling – has been stressed by Farrell and Héritier (2007) in their discussion of the institutionalization of the 'early agreements' provisions (the current practice of early agreements under the co-decision procedure is set out in Corbett *et al.* 2007: 224ff.). Their analysis also provides a very telling illustration of how (initial) indeterminancy of temporal rules may be exploited in the pursuit of enhanced institutional power (in this case by the EP).

Fourth, whilst timetables may be more or less predetermined for routine policy-making, both the politics of continuous Treaty revisions and successive enlargements and an orientation towards 'grand projects' in the EU raise a host of time-setting issues that cannot be resolved by recourse to established routines. To give just one recent example: following the Dutch and French referendums on the European Constitution in May/June 2005, Europe's leaders decided to 'buy time' or, in the language introduced above, they sought to use time for 'stabilization'. The Heads of State and Government called for a 'period of reflection' to allow for debate and rethinking. Initially expected to last one year, the period was extended in mid-2006 and was only officially brought to an end at the Brussels European Council of June 2007, when it was decided to launch an Intergovernmental Conference to adopt a new Treaty.

When it comes to policy schedules, i.e. the temporal ordering of public policies, it scarcely requires much comment as to why these are the subject of intensive contestation. The dynamism of the *acquis* through continuous deepening and widening has meant that in many cases there have been no templates in place to guide the temporal grid of policy, either because the policy had previously fallen outside the EU's remit or because the procedures involved were, in themselves, new. In many instances, discussions over decisional and policy timetables are inextricably intertwined. An example has been enlargement policy (Avery 2009; Lass-Lenneke and Werner 2009), in which the key objective, accession, was agreed by all parties to the negotiations, so that discussions revolved to a considerable extent around decisional timetabling – for example, when and in which sequence should the individual negotiation chapters be opened and preliminarily closed – and policy timetabling – for example, how long should transitional periods and temporary derogations last. As Avery (2009) and Lass-Lennecke and Werner (2009) discuss at some length, the Commission consistently used time management as a means of both mobilizing other actors and shoring up its own position in enlargement governance.

Enlargement policy provides a telling illustration of 'governing by timetable', which constitutes a prominent feature of EU governance. Governing by timetable through authoritative scheduling over often long time horizons that go beyond the political mandates of the political decision-makers is encouraged by the fragility of EU *Eigenzeit* (see below), as it helps to protect EU institutional and policy time against external disturbance. Whilst leaving more or less scope for future substantive decision-making, governing by timetable seeks to structure the clock of future decision-making processes sometimes far in advance. Temporal governing devices such as roadmaps are means to establish a time budget; serve as a mechanism for allocating time; and, at the same time, act as monitoring and, if necessary, enforcement devices for time rules. Sequencing and deadlining tend to play a key role in this context, as in the single market programme launched in 1986, with its 1992 deadline; the introduction of EMU in three stages from 1990; or the Lisbon Strategy launched in 2000 with its 2010 deadline.

Governing by timetabling is not just a response to challenges of synchronization and mobilization; it may also be interpreted as a functional response to the problem of ensuring commitment over time. All democratic political systems face this problem, and the EU is no exception. It does, however, confront a special challenge, which relates, in particular, to the Council. It is, of course, a continuous institution, but it is marked by constant changes in its membership; the same applies to the European Council. The commitment challenge is reinforced by the six-monthly rotation in the Presidency.

Given frequent turnover in national governments, those supposed to commit and comply have often not had any part in the original decision. The temptation to reorder priorities, to reopen negotiations, to set aside decisions and to delay or avoid compliance is, therefore, high. Where Euroscepticism is rife and there is little common ground amongst domestic parties on EU policy, the likelihood of attempted defection increases further. Of course, the threat of defection is quite effectively contained by the 'shadow of the future' (Axelrod 1984), which, because decision-makers can assume that they will 'meet again', encourages co-operative behaviour in EU negotiations. But the history of the EU provides many examples where this shadow has not been long enough to prevent member states from trying to 'go back to the drawing board'.

Moreover, compared to the national level, commitment and compliance tools – beyond enshrining policy in law – are weak. For example, if we draw an, admittedly not unproblematic, analogy between the Council and national cabinets, key devices regularly employed to stop ministers from 'defecting' from collectively taken decisions and to ensure ministerial 'reliability' (Blondel and Manning 2002) do not operate at European level. This applies, for example, to party programmes, coalition agreements or, as an ultimate sanction, the power of prime ministers to sack unreliable cabinet members. In contrast to what tends to be the case in national governments, members of the Council do not 'hang together', as they are not collectively answerable for their decisions either to an elected legislature or a common electorate. Constant turnover in Council membership, owing to changes of government in the 27 member states, only exacerbates problems of 'reliability'. Under these conditions, timetables, especially with long time horizons and fixed dates and sequences, assume a crucial role as commitment and compliance tools. By structuring the future, they seek to bind future entrants in decision-making.

Proposition IV: *The EU's political time is highly sensitive to influences from the member states.*

It is not difficult to see why European policy-makers, notably the Commission and the administrative layers in the Council, favour a time framework that stresses ongoingness and dense advance scheduling. For while the time of EU decision-making may not be strongly cyclical and time horizons extended, the European institutions are hardly in full control of their timetables. On the contrary: the EU's *Eigenzeit* is fragile and sensitive to interference, notably from the member states.

Theories of institutionalization generally regard autonomy as a prime yardstick for assessing degrees of institutionalization. In the case of political time, what matters, in particular, is the extent to which an organization – or cluster of organizations – is able to establish its *Eigenzeit* (own time) (Nowotny 1994), which it is able to protect from, and, ideally, impose upon, its environment. Evidently, this autonomy can never be absolute. In the case of the EU, owing to its multi-level character, political time is especially sensitive to external influences, the most important of which are the political and, in particular, electoral calendars of the major member states. To give just one recent example: the temporal planning of the initiative by the German EU presidency in the first half of 2007 to agree on the mandate of an Intergovernmental Conference was heavily influenced by the timing of the French presidential elections, on the one hand, and the likely date of the resignation of Tony Blair, the British Prime Minister, on the other. No major substantive decisions could be taken before the French elections had taken place; at the same time, there was a widely held view that Blair would wish to stay on until a deal on an Intergovernmental Conference had been reached. With the German presidency ending on 30 June 2007, the 'window of opportunity' was, therefore, narrow.

Temporal autonomy becomes more difficult to establish and maintain, the greater the number of member states and, more importantly, the more EU-level decisions become subject to partisan and electoral competition within the member states. Growing contestation of European matters in national party competition (Marks and Steenbergen 2004), thus, bears heavily on the scope of the EU institutions for working to 'their own clocks'.

But the fragility of the EU's *Eigenzeit* is not just connected to potential clashes with the political calendars of member states or other states and international organizations. *Eigenzeit* is also fragile because of problems of mobilization of temporal resources, which again arise, in particular, in the relations between the EU institutions and the political and administrative institutions of the member states. The latter have to 'make time' so as to allow the timely preparation of EU-level decisions; enable EU-level decisions to be taken 'on time', i.e. avoid unnecessary delays due to a lack of inputs from national policy-makers; and also, and in particular, ensure the timely implementation of such decisions. In all of this, there is a permanent danger that national policy-makers give temporal priority to national issues and concerns. The issue here is not one of timetable 'clashes' and political convenience, but of limitations in the time budgets of national policy-makers and the restrictions in time allocation that they imply. The oft-noted problems of member states in meeting transposition deadlines are a case in point.

The temptation to allocate time to domestic matters at the expense of EU business is present both at the level of elected national politicians (most of whom operate within incentive systems that encourage them to give time to their national voters, constituencies, parties and interests rather than devote their time to 'Europe'), and that of those national officials who work outside the EU core executive, i.e. those institutions that deal more or less exclusively with EU-related matters. Perhaps paradoxically, the more EU policy-making involves ministerial administrations across the board (rather than a select few ministries), the more conflicts over 'making time' are likely to increase. Such problems of mobilization can be expected to be especially severe where, as in the case of the German Federal ministerial administration since the early 1990s, progressive Europeanization has been accompanied by large cuts in the size of departmental staff. Mobilization is, therefore, especially problematic under conditions of a multi-level decision-making system in which incentives governing the allocation of time resources are ill-aligned.

In sum, there is a close connection between a preference for ongoingness and sensitivity to the political calendars and time constraints of the member states: the responsiveness of EU decisional time to the political calendars of the member states – which is most pronounced in the case of the intergovernmental Council of Ministers and the European Council – is to some extent compensated for by the extended time horizons of administrative decision-makers in the Council and the Commission and also of elected politicians in the EP. They can afford to 'take the long view'; but they also need to do so, not only for reasons of institutional complexity, which makes for lengthy decision-making (König 2007; Kovats 2009), but also because of the specific temporal challenges of synchronization and mobilization.

Proposition V: *EU integration Europeanizes national political time, with ambiguous consequences for the discretionary use of time in national politics.*

How does EU integration in general, and EU political time in particular, affect the democratic timescapes of the member states? Put differently, in what ways has political time in the member states been Europeanized? In reflecting on this question, we should avoid two common pitfalls that have been highlighted in the literature on the Europeanization of national political systems (Goetz and Meyer-Sahling 2008; Graziano and Vink 2007). First, as should have become clear from the above discussion, the member states are not just 'time-takers', in the sense of adapting to EU time, but also time-setters, notably through the Council, but also, for example, through their participation in comitology. The member states both shape EU time and are influenced by it. Second, it is difficult to isolate integration from other forces that impact on the member states' timescapes. In many instances, Europeanization is part of a broader story of change and transformation in the temporal framework of national politics.

Not much work has been done that focuses directly on the Europeanization of democratic timescapes of the member states; hence there is a good deal of speculation in the trends highlighted in the following. Yet, existing work has almost uniformly noted a decline in the domestic discretion over political time. In the *polity* domain, Ekengren (1996, 1997, 2002), in particular, has argued that EU time leads to a 'squeezed national present' in national administrations: 'the national present is, if not altogether disappearing, seriously squeezed between demands for quick action by overlapping European timetables' (2002: 84). EU time, by changing the time budgets and time horizons of national actors, is, therefore, an important driver of 'shifts of balance and concentration of powers ... within the central governmental structure' (Ekengren 2002: 153). In the *politics* domain, integration would appear to make it more difficult for national politicians to respond to the temporal priorities and time horizons of their national electorates. Discretion in the temporal ordering of decision-making processes is seen to decline:

> national time strategies can be applied less independently in a system of European governance. The national political process has to adjust firmly to different decision-making rhythms and detailed calendars of supranational processes of decision-making and negotiation ... [T]he necessities of the external synchronization of politics may decrease rather than increase national decision-makers' latitude as regards the free choice of the domestic allocation of time.
>
> (Jerneck 2000: 39)

Finally, in the policy domain, opportunities for fashioning political business cycles are said to decrease (Donohue and Warin 2007). Each of these arguments deserves some further comment.

It is noteworthy that many of the substantive arguments about the Europeanization of core state institutions are informed by considerations of time. This is most clearly the case in the work by Ekengren, who focuses explicitly on the institutional implications of European time. He argues:

> The fact that EU deadlines are diffused deeply down into the European and national bureaucracy has both centralising and decentralising effects. On the one hand, all European policymakers have to follow centrally decided time disciplinary norms and rules. On the other hand, there is less time for the individual department, group or official to be instructed from higher-level authorities which leads to decentralised autonomous policy-making.
> (Ekengren 2002: 153)

The effect of EU time at the level of national administrations is, thus, both centralizing and decentralizing. Centralization in response to time pressures has also been highlighted in recent research on the role of executive organization in explaining transposition records in the Central and Eastern European accession states (Zubek 2008).

Similarly, appeals to time pressures and differential mobilization feature in discussions about the impact of integration on the relationship between national politicians and officials or national parliaments. For example, Lægreid et al. (2004) point to domestic time pressures on politicians as a key reason for their comparative under-involvement in European policy-making when compared to officials. Goetz (2003), with reference to the German ministerial bureaucracy, has suggested that the incentives for executive politicians to devote part of their time budget to European affairs are, on the whole, much less strong than in the case of senior officials. Finally, it is worth noting that references to the speed of decision-making in the Council of Ministers; weak incentives for allocating time to EU business in national legislatures; and problems of synchronization between national parliamentary timetables and EU timetables feature prominently in writing on the Europeanization of member state legislatures and the oft-stated claim of a strengthening of national executives at the expense of legislatures (for a review, see Goetz and Meyer-Sahling 2008).

Overall, what has been written on the topic so far suggests that it is national politicians, in particular, in parliament, but also in government, who are progressively 'timed out' by integration. This effect would seem to be reinforced when it comes to the temporal framework for national politics. Much recent debate on the implications of integration for democracy in the member states (Schmidt 2006; Mair 2007) notes how integration limits substantive policy choices and, by default or by design, serves to reduce 'substantially the stakes of competition between political parties, to dampen down the potential differences wrought by successive governments, and to reduce the scope for classical opposition' (Mair 2007: 14). The discussion here suggests that the restrictive effects of integration may concern as much the timing, sequencing, speed and duration of decision-making processes as the substantive choices to be made.

Of course, the EU is by no means the sole force behind such a shift. There has been quite a pronounced trend in many EU states to dissociate growing parts of political decision-making from electorally determined time altogether – agencification, the rise of non-majoritarian institutions and progressive judicialization all point in this direction (Stone Sweet and Thatcher 2002). Such reforms are welcomed by those who identify short time horizons and the alleged short-sightedness of politicians who are incapable of looking beyond the next election as a central drawback of democratic politics and call for long-term action and greater time consistency. Agencies, courts and policy networks are not immune to opportunistic timetabling; but in their calculations, the electoral calendar will weigh less heavily than in the case of politicians facing re-election.

Research on the Europeanization of policy appears to bear this out. Whilst there has been a great deal of work on substantive change in national policies, less is known about how their temporal characteristics have changed in response to progressive integration. One key finding, with potentially profound implications, is that the opportunities for fashioning domestic political business cycles have declined markedly over the years. Thus, Donahue and Warin (2007: 436), examining national fiscal policy before and after the introduction of a deficit and debt ceiling under the Stability and Growth Pact, show that 'there is a PCB [political business cycle] across countries in Europe for the period 1979–1993, but after 1993, internal political pressures are overwhelmed by the constraints imposed on fiscal policies by the Treaty of Maastricht and the subsequent rule: the SGB [Stability and Growth Pact].' They also note, however, that this is not the same as arguing that countries may not adopt 'moral hazard behaviour', i.e. breach the SGP, as, of course, France and Germany, amongst others, have done. Further, Dyson (2009) demonstrates how, with monetary policy at its core, European economic governance has developed its distinct *Eigenzeit*, which reduces the scope for control of policy time by domestic political élites.

Whether this tendency towards a restriction of the discretionary temporal structuring of policy at the national level can be generalized beyond economic governance will need to be answered on the basis of further empirical research. Recent work on transposition, for example, underlines that European deadlines are by no means sacrosanct and compliance can be difficult to enforce (Sverdrup 2007).

More generally, Europeanization research cautions against over-emphasizing domestic restrictions resulting from integration to the neglect of domestic opportunities, as many examples of the domestic 'usage of Europe' underline (Jacquot and Woll 2004). One potential group of beneficiaries of the Europeanization of national political time has already been noted: national officials, who may gain in relative power and influence *vis-à-vis* politicians, as the latter's discretion over political timing appears to decrease and as they are increasingly drawn into a multi-level Union administration (Egeberg 2008). But there may well also be advantages for politicians *vis-à-vis* their national electorates. The central point here is not the opportunity for blame-shifting from the national to the EU level in cases where 'untimely' decisions have to be taken, though that can certainly be a convenient option. Rather, to the extent that the decisional timetables and the temporal features of major public policies – economic, monetary, or security-related – are increasingly determined at EU level (though, of course, with participation by the member states), national politicians may well be encouraged to engage in the opportunistic timing of substantively less momentous but electorally appealing initiatives. In this way, the ongoingness and openness of EU business may, paradoxically, foster short-termism and opportunistic timing in those fields where member states retain substantive temporal discretion.

CONCLUDING REMARKS

The emergence of a temporal order is part and parcel of the overall institutionalization of the EU's political system. To the extent that the distribution of power in the EU, its performance – notably, but by no means solely, its efficiency and effectiveness – and its legitimacy remain contested, so will be the contours of political time. This article has drawn attention to some of the key tensions in the institutionalization of the emergent EU timescape: between cyclical time, which allows for discontinuity, renewal and innovation, and linear time, which provides for continuity, stability and predictability; between the emergence of *Eigenzeiten* specific to particular organizations, decision-making modes and policy domains and effective co-ordination within and across organizations, procedures and domains; between authoritative time rules, which provide for effective mobilization and synchronization, and ambiguity and indeterminacy, which allow scope for bargaining and compromise; and between necessary time-setting authority *vis-à-vis* the member states and problematic restrictions on national political time. No amount of 'temporal engineering' will be able to resolve these tensions – but the balances struck in the temporal constitution of the EU are critical to its long-term future.

Biographical note: Klaus H. Goetz is Professor of German and European Politics and Government at the University of Potsdam, Germany, and Visiting Fellow at the European Institute, London School of Economics, UK.

ACKNOWLEDGEMENTS

I would like to thank the following for their most helpful comments on an earlier draft of this paper: Graham Avery, Simon Bulmer, Simon Hix, Laszlo Kovats, Anand Menon, Johan P. Olsen, Jan-Hinrik Meyer-Sahling, Christopher Pollitt, Richard Rose and Annika Werner. The usual disclaimer applies.

NOTES

1 I owe this term to Philippe Schmitter.
2 In contrast to what is suggested here, Ekengren (2002), in his analysis of EU time, stresses the cyclic character of EU time. He associates this quality, in particular, with recurringness: 'the meeting rhythms and decision-making procedures shaping time practices recur on a very regular basis over time' (Ekengren 2002: 143). In my view, this dense, regular, open-ended scheduling is, by contrast, an expression of the linearity of EU time; for it to be cyclical, it would need to be marked by clear beginnings and ends to established sequences of actions or events. Instead, the timetables that Ekengren has analysed so insightfully are mostly open-ended and not linked to specific points in time – the start of one cycle, the beginning of another – at which basic change (in participants, preferences and priorities) is likely to occur.

REFERENCES

Adam, B. (2008) *Of Timescapes, Futurescapes and Timeprints*. Paper presented at Lüneburg University, 17 June 2008.
Ágh, A. (2007) *The New Life Cycles of the Council: The Incoming Presidencies of the New Member States*, Paper presented at the CONSENT workshop 'The Temporality of Europeanization and Enlargement', University of Potsdam, 15–16 February 2007.
Avery, G. (2009) 'Uses of time in the EU's enlargement process', *Journal of European Public Policy* 16(2): 256–69.
Axelrod, R. (1984) *The Evolution of Cooperation*, New York: Basic Books.
Bergström, C.-F., Farrell, H. and Héritier, A. (2007) 'Legislate or delegate? Bargaining over implementation and legislative authority in the EU', *West European Politics* 30(2): 338–66.
Blondel, J. and Manning, N. (2002) 'Do ministers do what they say? Ministerial unreliability, collegial and hierarchical governments', *Political Studies* 50(3): 455–76.
Christiansen, T. and Vanhoonacker, S. (2008) 'At a critical juncture? Change and continuity in the institutional development of the Council Secretariat', *West European Politics* 31(4): 751–70.
Corbett, R., Jacobs, F. and Shackleton, M. (2007) *The European Parliament*, 7th edn, London: John Harper Publishing.
Donahue, K. and Warin, T. (2007) 'The Stability and Growth Pact: a European answer to the political budget cycle', *Comparative Political Studies* 5(5): 423–40.
Döring, H. (1995) 'Time as a scarce resource: government control of the agenda', in H. Döring (ed.), *Parliaments and Majority Rule in Western Europe*, Frankfurt: Campus Verlag, pp. 223–46.
Dyson, K. (2009) 'The evolving timescapes of European economic governance: contesting and using time', *Journal of European Public Policy* 16(2): 286–306.
Egeberg, M. (2008) 'European government(s): executive politics in Europe', *West European Politics* 31(1/2): 236–57.
Ekengren, M. (1996) 'The Europeanization of state administration: adding the time dimension', *Cooperation and Conflict* 31: 387–415.
Ekengren, M. (1997) 'The temporality of European governance', in K.E. Jørgensen (ed.), *Reflective Approaches to European Governance*, Basingstoke: Macmillan, pp. 68–86.

Ekengren, M. (2002) *The Time of European Governance*, Manchester: Manchester University Press.
European Court of Auditors (2008) *The European Union's Agencies: Getting Results*, Special Report No 05/2008; http://eca.europa.eu/portal/pls/portal/docs/1/1227518.PDF.
Farrell, H. and Héritier, A. (2007) 'Co-decision and institutional change', *West European Politics* 30(2): 285–300.
Goetz, K.H. (2003) 'The federal executive: bureaucratic fusion versus governmental bifurcation', in K. Dyson and K.H. Goetz (eds), *Germany, Europe and the Politics of Constraint*, Oxford: Oxford University Press, pp. 55–72.
Goetz, K.H. and Meyer-Sahling, J.-H. (2008) 'The Europeanisation of domestic political systems', *Living Reviews in European Governance*, June.
Goetz, K.H. and Meyer-Sahling, J.-H. (2009) 'Political time in the EU: dimensions, perspectives, theories', *Journal of European Public Policy* 16(2): 180–201.
Goodin, C. (1998) 'Keeping political time: the rhythms of democracy', *International Political Science Review* 19(1): 39–54.
Graziano, P. and Vink, M.P. (eds) (2007) *Europeanization: New Research Agendas*, Basingstoke: Palgrave.
Hayes-Renshaw, F. and Wallace, H. (2006) *The Council of Ministers*, 2nd edn, Basingstoke: Macmillan.
Jacquot, S. and Woll, S. (eds) (2004) *Les Usages de l'Europe*, Paris: L'Harmattan.
Jerneck, M. (2000) 'Europeanization, territoriality and political time', *Yearbook of European Studies* 14: 27–49.
König, T. (2007) 'Divergence or convergence? From ever-growing to ever-slowing European legislative decision making', *European Journal of Political Research* 46: 417–44.
Kovats, L. (2009) 'Do elections set the pace? A quantitative assessment of the timing of European legislation', *Journal of European Public Policy* 16(2): 239–55.
Lægreid, P, Steinthorsson, R. and Thorhallsson, B. (2004) 'Europeanization of central government administration in the Nordic states', *Journal of Common Market Studies* 42(2): 347–69.
Lass-Lennecke, K. and Werner, A. (2009) 'Policies, institutions and time: how the European Commission managed the temporal challenge of eastern enlargement', *Journal of European Public Policy* 16(2): 270–85.
Lewis, J. (2003) 'National interests: COREPER', in J. Peterson and M. Shackleton (eds), *The Institutions of the European Union*, Oxford: Oxford University Press, pp. 277–98.
Loomis, B. (1994) *Time, Politics and Policies: A legislative Year*, Lawrence, KS: University of Kansas Press.
Mair, P. (2007) 'Political opposition and the European Union', *Government & Opposition* 41(1): 1–17.
Majone, G. (1996) *Temporal Considering and Policy Credibility: Why Democracies Need Non-Majoritarian Institutions*, European University Institute, Working Paper, RSC No. 96/57.
Marks, G. and Steenbergen, M.R. (eds) (2004) *European Integration and Political Conflict*, Cambridge: Cambridge University Press.
Martin, L.W. (2004) 'The government agenda in parliamentary democracies', *American Journal of Political Science* 46(3): 445–61.
Menon, A. and Weatherill, S. (2008) 'Transnational legitimacy in a globalising world: how the European Union rescues its states', *West European Politics* 31(3): 397–416.
Meyer-Sahling, J.-H. and Goetz, K.H. (2009) 'The EU timescape: from notion to research agenda', *Journal of European Public Policy* 16(2): 325–36.
Moury, C. (2007) 'Explaining the European Parliament's right to appoint and invest the Commission', *West European Politics* 30(2): 367–91.

Nowotny, H. (1994) *Time: The Modern and Postmodern Experience*, Cambridge: Polity Press.
Pollak, J. and Puntscher Riekmann, S. (2008) 'European administration: centralisation and fragmentation as means of polity-building', *West European Politics* 31(4): 771–88.
Pollitt, C. (2008) *Time, Policy, Management: Governing with the Past*, Oxford: Oxford University Press.
Riescher, G. (1994) *Zeit und Politik. Zur institutionellen Bedeutung von Zeitstrukturen in parlamentarischen und präsidentiellen Regierungssystemen*, Baden-Baden: Nomos Verlagsgesellschaft.
Schmidt, V.A. (2006) *Democracy in Europe: The EU and National Polities*, Oxford: Oxford University Press.
Sverdrup, U. (2007) 'Implementation', in P. Graziano and M.P. Vink (eds), *Europeanization: New Research Agendas*, Basingstoke: Palgrave, pp. 197–211.
Thatcher, M. and Stone Sweet, A. (2002) *The Politics of Delegation: Non-Majoritarian Institutions in Europe* special issue of *West European Politics* 25(1).
Tholoniat, L. (2009) 'The temporal constitution of the European Commission: a timely investigation', *Journal of European Public Policy* 16(2): 221–38.
Trondal, J. and Jeppesen, L. (2008) 'Images of agency governance in the European Union', *West European Politics* 31(3): 417–41.
Türk, A.H. (2006) 'Modernisation of EC antitrust enforcement', in H.C.H. Hofmann and A.H. Türk (eds), *EU Administrative Governance*, Cheltenham: Elgar, pp. 215–43.
Wallace, H. and Wallace, W. (2006) 'Overview: The European Union, politics and policy-making', in K.E. Jørgensen *et al.* (eds), *Handbook of European Union Politics*, London: Sage, pp. 339–58.
Zubek, R. (2008) *Core Executive and Europeanization in Central Europe*, Basingstoke: Palgrave.

The temporal constitution of the European Commission: a timely investigation

Luc Tholoniat

ABSTRACT This paper examines the main temporal factors impacting on the European Commission and sheds light on its particular relationship to time. By way of illustration, it discusses two relatively recent, but increasingly significant, features of the Commission's work: its planning and programming cycle and its use of impact assessments. These two techniques are at the core of the Commission's quest for exemplary management and of its endeavour to promote 'better regulation' principles. Taken together, they can transform EU policy-making and bring about a greater predictability and transparency of EU action. They cannot, however, fully capture the more political and discretionary role of the Commission, which must adapt to a diverse and changing EU agenda.

1. INTRODUCTION

As well as being the guardian of the Treaties of the European Union (EU), the European Commission is the guardian of the 'European clock', in charge of steering the EU decision-making process, monitoring the timely implementation of EU policies and ensuring respect of EU deadlines. It is itself a strictly regulated administration, with tight internal and inter-institutional rules of procedures.

Much is known about the functioning of the Commission and its ability to influence decision-making at EU level (Egeberg 2007; Fischer *et al.* 2007; Spence and Edwards 2006; Christiansen 2006; Dimitrakopoulos 2004). Recent research highlights the extent of organizational changes experienced by the Commission since the 1990s and draws attention to the broader implications that these developments may have on the wider EU policy-making process (Bauer 2008; Curtin and Egeberg 2008). In this discussion, time is a dimension which is often neglected or addressed in a patchy way (Goetz and Meyer-Sahling 2009), with a less than systematic account of the nature of the temporal rules applied within the institution and scarce discussion of their impact on the wider EU timescape (Meyer-Sahling and Goetz 2009).

The purpose of this paper is to shed light on the temporal constitution of the Commission, defined in a broad sense as the set of – internal and external, formal and informal – temporal rules impacting on the Commission's actions. The paper proposes a first typology of the main time variables of interest to the study of the Commission (section 2) and reflects on the importance of temporal rules for the development of the EU agenda (section 3). By way of illustration, it discusses two relatively recent, but increasingly significant, features of the Commission's work: its planning and programming cycle and, as part of this cycle, its use of impact assessments (section 4). These two techniques are at the core of the wider endeavour of the EU to adopt and promote 'better regulation' principles, in which the Commission is increasingly invited, and willing, to lead by example. Although their impact must be qualified, these instruments can potentially transform the wider EU inter-institutional policy-making (section 5).

2. THE EUROPEAN COMMISSION'S RELATIONSHIP TO TIME: A FIRST OVERVIEW

In order to study the temporal constitution of the Commission, it is important to bear in mind some of its distinctive features both as an institution and as an administration. Table 1 proposes a first overview of temporal parameters of interest for the study of the Commission.

The proposed distinction between 'time as a resource' and 'time as a constraint', between 'temporal variables', 'rules' and 'devices' and between 'internal' and 'external' factors would deserve a more elaborate discussion, which goes beyond the scope of this article (see Goetz and Meyer-Sahling 2009). In particular, it would be interesting to reflect further on the Commission's characteristics in comparison to other EU and (inter)national institutions, on the relative significance of each of the associated temporal variables and on the extent to which the rules which the Commission sets for itself contribute to the Europeanization of institutional and administrative timescapes. With this important caveat in mind, the proposed categorization may nevertheless help us to highlight some key parameters of the Commission's relationship to time.

Time is a resource that, given its role among the EU institutions, the Commission is well placed to use strategically in order to shape EU policy-making. The following three functions are particularly illustrative of its role.

An agenda-setter: the Commission enjoys a quasi monopoly of the right of initiative at EU level. Although this can be contested by a proactive Council (e.g. the role of successive Presidencies and of EU summit conclusions) and a more assertive Parliament (e.g. the use of 'sunset clauses' setting compulsory deadlines for the adoption of new proposals), the Commission can effectively influence the timing of a large range of EU initiatives.

A building-block: while the Commission's day-to-day activities are largely determined by the priorities of its five-year College, the time horizon of its administrative action is almost unlimited and its knowledge of EU affairs is

Table 1 Key temporal parameters for the study of the European Commission

Key temporal variables	Corresponding temporal rules and devices
Time as a potential resource	
The Commission as an agenda-setter	Political and institutional rules and devices leading the Commission to decide on the timing and time horizons of EU initiatives
The Commission as a building-block	Political and institutional rules and devices leading the Commission to use its accumulated experience and serve as a reference for the pursuit of EU policies over time
The Commission as a broker	Political and institutional rules and devices giving the Commission a pivotal, time-saving and efficiency-enhancing role in policy-making at EU level
Time as a constraint: external factors	
The political, institutional and socio-economic context	Temporal provisions of the EU Treaties
	Temporal requirements of the EU legislative and comitology decision-making process
	Deadlines set by EU legislation, Council conclusions and Parliament's resolutions
	Timetable of EU Council preparations
	Multi-annual work programme of EU Presidencies
	Organization of Parliament's plenary and committee work
The EU electoral cycle	The Commission's five-year mandate
	Synchronization with national electoral cycles
The EU budgetary process	The EU multi-annual budgetary programme
	The EU annual budgetary cycle
	Spill-over effects at national and regional level
The multi- and supranational regime	Co-ordination requirements for EU-level and national actors
	Implications of subsidiarity and proportionality 'checks'
	Effects of the EU language regime
Time as a constraint: internal factors	
The 'collegiality' principle and internal organizational set-up	Internal rules of procedures
	Rules governing inter-service consultations
	Preparation of 'weekly' College meetings
The choice of policy horizons and timeliness of data	Choice of policy targets and monitoring mechanisms
	Choice of indicators, availability and timeliness of data

(*Continued*)

Table 1 Continued

Key temporal variables	Corresponding temporal rules and devices
'Better regulation' and administrative rules	The planning and programming cycle
	Impact assessment guidelines
	Minimum standards for public consultations
	Temporal effects of 'simplification'
	Effects of the Commission's civil service career system
The communication imperative	Sequence and recurrence of policy themes at EU level
	'Midday express' press conferences and releases
	Temporal considerations in the development of EU-level communication strategies

Source: Luc Tholoniat (author).

without equivalent. Moreover, its role as guardian of the EU Treaties leads it to play a central role in the timely enforcement of EU law. The experience of the Commission is therefore a unique resource to develop EU policies and it is a warrant of the consistency of EU action over time.

A broker: with 27 member states and pressures for co-ordinated action at global level, for instance for trade or climate negotiations the Commission is ideally placed to identify interests and create synergies among EU actors. It is also naturally led to liaise between the Council and the Parliament, as well as with EU lobbies and expert groups (Gornitzka and Sverdrup 2008; Borrás 2007). Taking contact with the Commission is often the best shortcut to identify key EU players and access information. Giving the Commission a mediation role can also reduce transaction costs and facilitate deals at EU level. In other words, using the Commission can save time.

In practice, the capacity of the Commission to perform these three functions depends on a series of temporal variables constraining its action. Many such factors are set independently of the Commission's day-to-day action ('external factors'); others can be considered self-imposed ('internal factors'). Among the former, the following four would seem of particular importance.

The wider political, institutional and socio-economic context. Except for times of high-level politics where the Commission can influence its environment, for instance a Treaty negotiation, the temporal context in which it operates appears largely set: the procedural provisions of the EU Treaties, the inter-institutional rules governing EU decision-making, the conclusions of EU summits, the work programmes of EU Presidencies – all these provide a prescriptive framework for the daily work of Commission services. The nature and pressure of the EU institutional and policy context vary over time, and the Commission must constantly reassess the ranking and time horizon of its priorities. In the recent period, for example, the debate over the draft EU

Constitution was both time-consuming and a source of uncertainty for many EU actors, and for the Commission in particular (Kassim and Dimitrakopoulos 2007). Moreover, unforeseen events – frequent and perceived crises, such as an environmental disaster or a major economic setback – will require urgent attention and swift reaction from the Commission.

The EU electoral cycle. The five-year mandate of the College provides an important time reference for the work of the Commission. As for national electoral cycles, new Commissioners are commonly expected to shape the agenda of their portfolios by presenting major initiatives early in their mandate, while the end of their term is dedicated to policy consolidation and implementation. The electoral cycles of the member states may also be of importance for the development of initiatives at EU level, with the risk of 'backlash' or 'freeze' in periods of electoral campaigns. However, both the legal obligations to act at EU level and the difficulty of accounting for the political situation of 27 member states may limit room for manoeuvring the timing of EU action in practice.

The EU budgetary process. The EU multi-annual budgetary programme and the choice of a reference period (currently 2007–2013) provide an overarching framework for the activities of the Commission as EU executive. This is particularly significant for services in charge of the negotiation, management, evaluation and auditing of the EU funding programmes. Annually, the requirement to commit and spend EU money, as well as to report on financial execution, also has direct consequences on the planning of activities of most departments. Beyond the Commission, the multi-annual budgetary cycle is also of importance for stakeholders in charge of implementing the EU budget and it often serves as a reference for national and regional public investment cycles.

The multi- and supranational regime. The very nature of the EU creates temporal constraints for the various actors involved, such as the need for EU representations and lobbies to co-ordinate their positions with their national or corporate headquarters, or the requirement for the Commission to consult national parliaments in application of the subsidiarity and proportionality principles. One of the most emblematic, and possibly overlooked, attributes of the EU relates to its linguistic regime. With now 23 official languages, translation requirements may radically impact on the way in which Commission services conceive the timing and content of their policy initiatives. For instance, as a result of the 2004 enlargement, the Commission was led to reduce the average size of its 'Communications' – its main non-regulatory policy instrument – and to limit the translation of documents of lesser importance. The capacity of the Commission to deliver translations in time is also important for the decision-making process at large, as discussion in Council and Parliament may be postponed pending the availability of the required linguistic versions.

In contrast to the above factors, the following four 'internal' factors would seem more directly subject to the Commission's own will.

The 'collegiality' principle and the Commission's organizational set-up. The Commission's internal rules for procedures reflect one of its essential characteristics: the Commission must 'speak with one voice' and the efficiency of internal decision-making should not go against the need to build consensus and ensure cohesion within the institution (European Commission 2005a). With 27 Commissioners and about 40 Directorates-General, effective internal consultation and co-ordination, although they prove time-consuming, are more than ever necessary to avoid overlaps, gaps or cacophony. Hence, compulsory temporal rules are in place to organize inter-service consultations and prepare the weekly 'Wednesday meetings' of the College, with the Secretariat General playing both a 'secretariat' and a 'general' role in the respect of deadlines and processing of proposals via the registry (the 'greffe').

The choice of policy horizons and timeliness of data. In developing new policy initiatives, the Commission is often led to suggest policy objectives and proposals for the coming years. This is typically the case for 'EU action plans' listing forthcoming initiatives in specific policy domains. An important consideration for such planning is the amount of preparatory work already 'in the pipeline' and the possibility of relying on sound and mature evidence at the time of the proposal. The availability, robustness and timeliness of data, which may vary significantly across policy fields, are particularly necessary for the choice of policy targets and indicators. For policy processes and funding programmes with a medium-term horizon, it is common to foresee dedicated follow-up and monitoring mechanisms, such as annual reporting and mid-term reviews. The management of past EU enlargement provides an instructive example of such planning devices (Avery 2009).

'Better regulation' and administrative rules. 'Better regulation' has many facets (Radaelli and De Francesco 2007). The remainder of this article focuses on planning and impact assessment techniques. Other aspects could be worth considering, such as the use of public consultations (European Commission 2002a) and the temporal cost-effectiveness of efforts at simplifying EU law and reducing 'administrative burdens' (European Commission 2008b).

The communication imperative. In the light of the above constraints, adjusting the timing of EU initiatives to maximize their media impact may seem a daunting task. On a daily basis, the tempo of the Commission's communication activities is set by its 'midday express' press conferences and press releases. Throughout the year, the Commission also pays attention to the sequencing of its activities, which may imply devoting specific days for 'big-bang' packages focusing on a single theme. This, incidentally, may entail pushing forward or postponing individual proposals, while respecting their associated legal requirements and meeting the political expectations of their corresponding audiences. Further research into the Commission's communication strategy may also help to reflect on the Europeanization of the communication space (Trenz 2008).

3. OVERCOMING THE 'SOFT LAW PARADOX'

The capacity of the Commission to combine an institutional role of policy steer and a more administrative role of EU executive makes it very well placed to shape EU policies. Yet, this double role also often confronts it with a paradox. On the one hand, the Commission is prone to policy activism, i.e. the need to fuel the policy process with new initiatives and to build and maintain an 'attractive' EU policy agenda. On the other hand, this agenda must be 'effective', and the Commission must rely on institutional predictability, i.e. a fixed machinery, set timetables and agreed administrative arrangements, to develop policies and ensure successful implementation over time.

Policy activism at EU level does not just originate from the Commission. It is also largely the result of the tendency of each Presidency or member state to export its views to the EU level, as well as of the natural bias of EU political forces for new policy initiatives. Such activism is necessary and useful to allow for a diversity of views to emerge and to update EU action in the light of changing political and socio-economic realities. Yet, it also bears the risk of an unstable policy agenda, with frequent shifts in policy priorities, an overstretch of resources and weak delivery.

Against this background, a certain degree of stability in policy priorities and institutional set-up may seem desirable in order to make EU initiatives operational and to secure implementation. This is also of importance for stakeholders at national and local levels, who often have difficulty in keeping track of EU developments. Yet, too much stability also has a risk, that of an administrative routine that would appear too dull or too cumbersome for member states and EU stakeholders to adhere to. This would reduce interest in the related EU instruments and possibly call their legitimacy and existence into question. This would also fuel the negative perception of the EU as a 'gas factory' lacking political relevance and policy responsiveness.

This double-bind between the need for policy momentum, on the one hand, and the need for institutional predictability, on the other, is particularly apparent in 'soft law' areas operated through the open method of co-ordination (OMC), such as the Lisbon Strategy for Growth and Jobs and the EU Sustainable Development Strategy, as well as employment, social inclusion, education and migration policies. Such processes are particularly exposed to calls for revision: their policy objectives combine various and sometimes divergent ideological and national views into a single framework; their co-ordination mechanisms often lack a legal anchor in the EU Treaties; and their credibility largely relies on the good will of member states in terms of political support and reporting. At the same time, these mechanisms are also particularly exposed to accusations of administrative overload. Most competences in these domains lie at national or local levels and these authorities may be ill-equipped or reluctant to engage in reporting at EU level; comparison between countries is complex and requires the construction of new and possibly constraining EU benchmarks and indicators; and the requirement to report at frequent intervals may be deemed excessive given the pace of socio-economic change and the time necessary to carry out and evaluate policy reforms.

In practice, the EU must therefore often navigate between the Charybdis of an 'all-out political agenda' and the Scylla of the 'bureaucratization trap', with time as its best compass. In the case of the OMC, this has led the Commission to propose, and the EU to adopt, specific temporal rules, including quantified targets and systems of annual or biennial reporting at national and EU levels, with the conclusions of the European Council providing regular guidance. For instance, in just a few years, the timetables of Lisbon-related EU processes have been redefined to ensure greater synchronization in the preparation of the Spring European Council, thereby giving it a pivotal role in the discussion of EU socio-economic priorities every year (Tholoniat and Fischer 2006).

4. NEW TEMPORAL RULES AS PART OF THE 'BETTER REGULATION' AGENDA

Since the late 1990s, the Commission has gradually developed its so-called strategic planning and programming (SPP) cycle and defined its own methodology for the use of impact assessments. These two techniques are central elements of the Commission's endeavour to adopt exemplary management as a way of justifying its action. They are also an essential aspect of the EU commitment to improve the quality of the EU regulatory environment as part of the wider 'better regulation' agenda.

These developments can be read as the combined result of a dynamics of internal reform and a more general move towards better governance of EU affairs. Both techniques were introduced against the background of the Commission's White Paper on European Governance of July 2001 (European Commission 2001) and the 'better law-making' action plan of June 2002 (European Commission 2002c). These new instruments share similar roots as the 'Kinnock reforms', which entailed a significant overhaul of the Commission's internal management and the spread of new public management, methods such as activity-based budgeting and a more performance-based career structure (Kassim 2004, 2008; Schön-Quinlivan 2008). Overall, the reform can be read as a further move from the initial Continental model of administrative management towards Anglo-Saxon and Scandinavian models (Balint *et al.* 2008).

The Commission's planning and programming cycle: no room for discretion?

The essence of the new SPP system is to be found in the White Paper on Administrative Reform adopted by the Commission in 2000 (European Commission 2000). This document established the Annual Policy Strategy (APS) and the Commission's Legislative and Work Programme (CLWP) as the main vehicles for the Commission to define its priorities and optimize the use of its resources on an annual basis. It also led to the creation of a SPP function in the Secretariat General of the Commission. Figure 1 highlights the main milestones in this cycle.

The overall policy framework is set by the multi-annual strategic objectives adopted by the College at the beginning of its term (European Commission 2005d). On this basis, the Commission presents every year its APS (European

THE EU TIMESCAPE

YEAR 'N–2'

December: Letter from the President and/or College orientation debate and circular to the services to prepare the Annual Policy Strategy for the year 'n'.

YEAR 'N–1'

February: Commission adopts Annual Policy Strategy for the year 'n' including draft roadmaps listing planned initiatives + start of dialogue with Parliament and Council.

March: Commission adopts its preliminary draft budget for the year 'n' + start of dialogue with Parliament and Council.

October/November: Commission adopts its Legislative and Work Programme and catalogue of initiatives for the year 'n' including more detailed roadmaps.

November/December: Each Directorate-General adopts its Annual Management Plan for the year 'n' describing how its activities and resources will contribute to the overall priorities of the Commission.

December: Inter-institutional adoption of the budget for the year 'n'.

YEAR 'N'

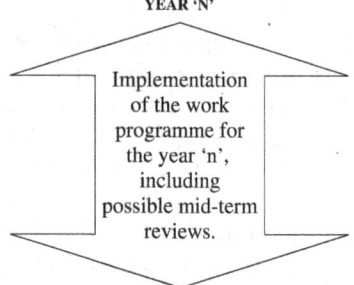

Implementation of the work programme for the year 'n', including possible mid-term reviews.

YEAR 'N+1'

January: Commission's President gives 'State of the Union' speech to the Parliament.

By March: Each Directorate-General presents an Annual Activity Report reviewing achievements for the year 'n'.

June: Commission adopts its Annual Synthesis Report summarizing how it has met its management and internal control standards for the year 'n'.

Figure 1 The strategic planning and programming cycle of the European Commission
Source: Luc Tholoniat (author), on the basis of information available from the website 'The European Commission at work' (http://ec.europa.eu/atwork/index_en.htm).

Commission 2008a), setting out broad priorities and estimating associated human and financial resources for the following year. The APS is adopted early in the year to allow sufficient time for inter-institutional discussion and feedback into the adoption of the CLWP in the autumn (European Commission 2007a). Routine items and initiatives of a more technical nature are listed in a 'catalogue' annexed to the CLWP. Both the CLWP and the catalogue can be adapted and complemented during the year to which they relate.

The Commission is committed to reporting on implementation the following year, with its President giving a 'State of the Union' speech to the Parliment every January and an annual Synthesis Report detailing how the Commission has met its management and internal control standards in the previous year. Within the Commission, the Secretariat General plays a central role in defining SPP rules and mainstreaming the process throughout the institution, and is also pivotal in its co-ordination. At the same time, each Directorate-General is called upon to contribute to the cycle and build up its administrative capacity, with co-ordination units inheriting new tasks in monitoring and oversight.

The unrolling of the SPP cycle is now considered a structural feature of the Commission's work on an annual, if not daily, basis. It implies, for instance, that in the winter of every year each department is expected to prepare its Annual Management Plan for the coming year, to contribute to the definition of priorities for the subsequent year and to report on achievements of the previous year. Throughout the year, the process also requires constant administrative co-operation between services and cabinets, with 'bottom-up' and 'top-down' co-ordination mechanisms, so as to adjust the content and timing of the planned initiatives: co-ordination units in the various Directorates-General call upon operational units to review the state-of-play of past or new initiatives; these are checked with the respective cabinets and Commissioners and discussed with the Secretariat General; and the APS and CLWP go through a process of inter-consultation and adoption by the College.

The SPP cycle is also of importance for wider EU policy-making, as it reinforces the transparency and predictability of the Commission's activities. The cycle basically requires the Commission's services to announce planned initiatives on average 12–24 months before these could eventually be adopted. And it takes on average nine months between the time when a proposal is first made public in the form of a preliminary roadmap in the APS and the time when it is confirmed as part of the work programme, leaving room for stakeholders to lobby for additions or withdrawals. Once the work programme is adopted, the Commission will naturally be quite wary of its capacity to deliver according to the original timetable.

Recourse to impact assessments: no room for hazard?

The recourse to impact assessments (IAs) was introduced to the Commission in 2003 (European Commission 2002c) and the system has been refined several times since then (European Commission 2008b, 2007b, 2006, 2005b). The term IA refers to the *ex ante* analysis of the potential economic, social and environmental effects of a decision to take or not to take action in response to an identified policy problem. The current Commission's IA system is closely linked to the SPP cycle presented above: all major legislative and policy proposals scheduled in the Commission's work programme should be subject to an IA report which is made public alongside the proposal to which it refers. The number of IA has increased steadily: 284 IA, were carried out from 2003 to 2007, with 180 more expected in 2008, a 50 per cent increase compared to 2007 (European Commission 2008b).

A typical IA may take between 6 and 12 months to be developed and the depth of the analysis varies depending on the importance of the issue at stake ('proportionate' IA). The reports are prepared by inter-service groups composed of officials from relevant departments, under the responsibility of a lead service, with the Secretariat General playing the role of advocate of IA guidelines. Consultation is an integral part of the IA process: it may be restricted to key stakeholders (e.g. existing committees) or it can concern the public at large. In the latter case, standard Commission consultation procedures should apply, notably the minimum standard of eight weeks of consultation (European Commission 2002b). Recourse to external expertise is also frequent in the course of the IA.

Late in 2006, the Commission established an internal, yet functionally independent, IA board of senior officials to review the quality of the IA reports before publication (European Commission 2006). In practice, while IA reports and the corresponding proposals were generally developed in parallel, the lead service is now expected to submit the IA report to the IA board at least a month before it intends to launch the formal inter-service consultation, i.e. on average two months before the adoption of the proposal, thereby adding an extra month to the preparation phase. For the sake of transparency, some EU actors may have wished to go even further, by requesting the Commission to publish and hold an inter-institutional discussion on IA reports before it could register an initiative in its work programme. This, in practice, would significantly alter the Commission's right of initiative and slow down its capacity to act.

Throughout 2007, the Commission reviewed its IA system and published the results of an external evaluation (The Evaluation Partnership 2007). In January 2008, it presented proposals for improvements, including suggestions to reinforce the preventive and proactive role of the IA board in the assessment of the IA reports (European Commission 2008b).

5. THE QUEST FOR EXEMPLARY MANAGEMENT: ACHIEVEMENTS AND LIMITS

Albeit of relatively recent origin, the SPP cycle and IA system already seem to be yielding results. Arguably, the most significant impact at this stage is to be seen within the Commission itself, but these techniques also have the potential to transform the wider EU decision-making process, by altering the balance of power, the performance and the legitimacy of the Commission *vis-à-vis* other institutions (Goetz and Meyer-Sahling 2009).

Achievements and potential

The SPP cycle and IA system are now embedded in the working practices of the Commission, with visible effects at all levels of the institution (European Commission 2007c, 2008b, 2008c, 2008d; Kurpas *et al.* 2008; The Evaluation Partnership 2007). In particular:

- The new SPP cycle contributes to a greater transparency and predictability of the activities of the Commission's services, through the obligation to plan ahead, produce roadmaps, set objectives and keep track of achievements. The main novelty of the system is to establish a central and open process of priority-setting, while seeking to link the allocation of staff and financial resources with these priorities.
- The requirement to carry out IA reports is considered to have contributed positively to the quality of the proposals. In particular, it is said to have introduced a new culture of administrative action, forcing services to consider a wider range of options and leading them to engage more systematically in internal and external consultations before taking action. At the same time, early co-ordination between services may contribute to limiting dissensions during the last stages of finalization of the proposal.
- As proposals have to be announced well in advance, it is easier for the Commission to bundle initiatives together, thereby ensuring consistency and maximizing media impact, as was done, for instance, for the energy package in January 2007, the single market review of November 2007 or the climate change package of January 2008.
- The combination of SPP–IA tools may have contributed to the (re)centralization, consistency and collegiality of the internal decision-making process. The Secretariat General plays a key role in the operation of these instruments and it has contributed to spreading a culture of 'upstream co-ordination', inviting services to plan ahead and revisit the timetable of their initiatives in the light of the overall priorities of the College. It also plays an increasingly pivotal role in steering and screening new policy initiatives, with the possibility of being associated with, or to take over the leadership for, essential files. At the same time, the system creates incentives for other Directorates-General to become more transparent and co-operative. As part of the SPP cycle, each Directorate-General is incentivized to compete for staff and financial resources by presenting convincing Annual Management Plans. Moreover, greater co-operation is expected from them in the development of IA reports. Finally, in a context of intense organizational restructuring, with the creation of new departments and the arrival of new staff and Commissioners, the requirement to disclose intentions and associate other services

in developing new proposals can serve to reinforce mutual trust between internal actors and reduce risks of policy fragmentation.

Beyond the Commission itself, these techniques also have the potential to affect the wider EU decision-making process. In particular:

- By taking more time, providing more evidence and seeking to build a consensus in support of new proposals, the protracted preparation phase of the Commission may, in turn, help to speed up the inter-institutional decision-making process and facilitate implementation.
- The early announcement of initiatives and more frequent and longer consultation periods are valuable resources for other EU institutions, stakeholders and lobbies to take early action and mobilize in favour of or against a proposal.
- The greater focus on evidence-based initiatives, including recourse to external expertise, may increasingly shift the burden of proof back to the member states and the Parliament when amending a proposal from the Commission and lead them to step up their own IA standards.
- The standards set by the Commission may trickle down to the national level, with 'better regulation' seen as a central aspect of the Lisbon Strategy for Growth and Jobs (Radaelli 2007). One such example is the goal to reduce unnecessary administrative burdens, understood essentially in terms of information obligations imposed on business. While the concept was initially developed as part of the Commission's IA system, the target of a 25 per cent reduction at EU level by 2012 was endorsed by the 2007 Spring European Council and member states were invited to set national targets at a comparable level.

The limits of planning and transparency

Overall, the combined SPP–IA system is considered beneficial by the Commission (European Commission 2008b). It also has some intrinsic limitations which are worth bearing in mind. First, the system is demanding and resource-consuming to operate: it requires a machinery of officials at all levels of the administration, as well as time-consuming co-ordination, programming and reporting mechanisms. The system requires a greater involvement of units in charge of co-ordination and resources within each department to call on operational units to define priorities and report on results. It also involves a collective capacity to foresee policy issues over a time horizon of one to five years, which may prove particularly challenging in practice. For some scholars, this push towards 'modernization' has translated into new and irreversible 'bureaucratization' trends (Ellinas and Suleiman 2008).

Second, the system covers only parts of the Commission's activities: in particular, it does not apply to the decisions taken every day by the Commission as part of its regulatory and enforcement power, for instance to remedy cases of infringements of EU law. Although gross numbers can be estimated from one year to the other, such decisions cannot be planned and stem from legal obligations to act set directly in EU primary and secondary law. These decisions are also subject to a different adoption process often involving fast-track inter-service consultations.

Third, the system cannot fully capture the more political and discretionary nature of the Commission's work. In particular, the requirement to conduct an IA may prove cumbersome for political documents produced in response to new events or for a pressing political mandate. For instance, it is unlikely that the complete list of topics on the agenda of EU summits will be known far in advance, which often leads the Commission to present 'last-minute' contributions on topical subjects. Moreover, the system is ill-suited for more confidential, diplomatic or trade negotiation documents. In practice, the risk exists that only the most easily planned items will be registered in the work programme while key, but unforeseen, political initiatives will not, thereby reducing the credibility and use of the instrument. The Commission has, therefore, become used to updating its work programme half-way through its implementation.

Fourth, while the system contributes to improving transparency and planning within the institution, stakeholders outside the Commission may not yet be fully aware of the opportunities it creates. For instance, the roadmaps do not seem to be widely reacted to, and the use of the IA in the wider EU decision-making process may vary.

Fifth, and more generally, by seeking to cast in stone possible initiatives over the medium run, the system is partly a challenge to itself. There is indeed an intrinsic paradox in the way the system is constructed. While annual strategies and work programmes are meant to contribute to the predictability of the Commission's initiatives, they cannot, and should not, prejudge the exact content of the proposals, as this remains subject to the outcome of the IA exercise. The timetable of the IA is also difficult to foresee as additional consultation and expertise may prove necessary. The use of the IA therefore maintains a degree of uncertainty as to whether and when a proposal will be adopted, and what its exact nature will be. It also creates a tension between the political need to make early announcements, make public commitments and deliver swift results, and the more expert and administrative work of submitting new initiatives to a thorough and possibly lengthy programming and IA process.

Finally, the system is also a challenge for the EU institutions in general, as it requires greater co-operation between them in order to plan ahead and co-ordinate their legislative activity. Since the 'better law-making' inter-institutional agreement of December 2003, it was agreed that the EP, the Council and the Commission would each come forward with their respective annual legislative timetables and seek to agree a joint annual programme (European Parliament 2005; European Parliament, Council, Commission 2003). It has also now become practice that the Presidency troïka – three successive Presidencies - publishes a joint 18-month work programme, as was done in view of the German Presidency in early 2007. Improving inter-institutional co-operation further is a central element of the proposals put forward by the Commission in early 2008 (European Commission 2008b).

6. CONCLUSION

The European Commission plays a distinctive role in the European policy-making process and the temporal rules it sets for itself affect the wider European timescape. A more systematic reflection about the temporal constitution of the Commission should help to highlight the key parameters affecting the content, sequence and pace of its action, and the effect that this may have on the EU system. In so doing, such research should contribute to the literature on the effects of organizational changes on policy outputs (Bauer 2008), as well as to the wider reflection on the use of political time at EU level (Goetz 2009).

Such an investigation is particularly timely in the light of recent developments. Since the late 1990s, the Commission has gone a long way in reforming its internal decision-making processes and it has passed important milestones in its quest for exemplary management. This required the development of new temporal rules as a way of structuring its new planning and programming cycle and IA techniques. These instruments cannot fully capture the more political and discretionary essence of the work of the Commission, which must accommodate the diverse and changing nature of the EU agenda. In spite of all programming efforts, some room for manoeuvre remains necessary for the Commission to cope with unforeseen events and offer rapid political (re)actions, as well as to preserve some form of confidentiality.

Yet, the impact of these new instruments appears significant, as evidence suggests that they have radically altered the way in which the Commission's services conceive, plan and develop policy initiatives. By contributing to a greater predictability and transparency of the Commission's action, these techniques also set a precedent for other EU and national institutions. Further evaluation should show to what extent these techniques have resulted in improving the quality of the Commission's proposals, and whether this has contributed to their chances of success during the decision-making and implementation stages.

These developments are exemplary of the 'consolidation' phase in which the Commission has been engaged and which has resulted in a significant streamlining of its internal management in recent years (Kurpas *et al.* 2008; Tholoniat 2007). The accusations of mismanagement which led to the resignation of its College in 1999 and the calls for greater accountability prompted the Commission to engage in a far-reaching internal modernization and to embrace the 'better regulation' agenda.

This consolidation trend responded partly to internal considerations, but it can also be read as a strategic response to wider institutional and policy developments. In the late 1990s, the Commission had to digest the new competences given to it by the Amsterdam Treaty and adjust to the rapid growth of policy fields such as justice and home affairs, employment and social affairs, consumer and environmental policies, which led to the creation of several new departments. Over the last five years, it had to accommodate the arrival of about 4,000 new staff from 12 additional member states, as well as additional Commissioners. More generally, it had to cope with the general 'freezing' and questioning of the overall EU project, from the run-up to enlargement to the failure of the draft Constitution. In such a context, the dominant paradigm of the EU discourse has shifted from a 'missionary' reflection about the nature and values of the EU – very much present at the time of the European Convention – to a more pragmatic focus on achieving 'a Europe of results', with the 'better regulation' vocabulary gradually taking over the 'better governance' spirit of the late 1990s.

What was initially a constraint may have become a resource. By European standards, the Commission may be perceived today much more as a case of good management. But this achievement can prove to be two-edged. First, by engaging in a process of critical self-assessment and internal overhaul, there is always the danger of 'giving the stick to be beaten', confirming previous criticisms and laying the ground for additional requests to emerge. Second, the multiplication of administrative hurdles to overcome before a decision is taken may result in increasing bottlenecks at EU level and in a lack of responsiveness, if not a neutralization, of EU action. Finally, by communicating on its internal procedures and limiting its room for discretion, the Commission always runs the risk of reinforcing its bureaucratic image of an administrative machinery, at the expense of its more political role as an EU government.

Biographical note: Luc Tholoniat is a researcher on EU affairs and an administrator in the European Commission. At the time of writing this article, he was on leave from the Commission and employed at Econ Pöyry, an Oslo-based research and consulting company. This paper reflects his personal views and does not commit his employers.

ACKNOWLEDGEMENTS

While being solely responsible for any mistakes or inaccuracy, the author owes credit to the editors of this special issue and to colleagues in the European Commission with whom he had the pleasure to work. Their experience and knowledge have provided first-hand inputs to this article.

REFERENCES

Avery, G. (2009) 'Uses of time in the EU's enlargement process', *Journal of European Public Policy* 16(2): 256–69.

Balint, T., Bauer, M.W. and Knill, C. (2008) 'Bureaucratic change in the European administrative space: the case of the European Commission', *West European Politics* 31(4): 677–700.

Bauer, M.W. (ed.) (2008) 'Reforming the European Commission', *Journal of European Public Policy* 15(5), Special Issue.

Borrás, S. (2007) 'The European Commission as network broker,' *European Integration online Papers (EIoP)* 11(1).

Christiansen, T. (2006) 'The European Commission: the european executive between continuity and change', in J. Richardson (ed.), *European Union: Power and Policy-Making*, 3rd edn, London: Routledge, pp. 99–120.

Curtin, D. and Egeberg, M. (eds.) (2008) 'Towards a new executive order in Europe?' *West European Politics* 31(4), Special Issue.

Dimitrakopoulos, D.G. (ed.) (2004) *The Changing Role of the European Commission*, Manchester: Manchester University Press.

Egeberg, M. (2007) 'The European Commission', in M. Cini (ed.), *European Union Politics*, 2nd edn, Oxford: Oxford University Press, pp. 133–47.

Ellinas, A. and Suleiman, E. (2008) 'Reforming the Commission: between modernization and bureaucratization', *Journal of European Public Policy* 15(5): 708–25.

European Commission (2008a) *Annual Policy Strategy for 2009*, COM(2007)72 of 13.2.2007 (annual edition).

European Commission (2008b) *Second Strategic Review of Better Regulation in the European Union*, COM(2008)32 of 30.1.2008.

European Commission (2008c) *Impact Assessment Board: Report for the Year 2007*, SEC(2008)120 of 30.1.2008 (annual edition).

European Commission (2008d) *General Report on the Activities of the European Union – 2007*, SEC(2007)1000 of 25.1.2008 (annual edition).

European Commission (2007a) *Commission Legislative and Work Programme 2007*, COM(2007)640 of 23.10.2007 (annual edition).

European Commission (2007b) *Better Regulation and Enhanced Impact Assessment*, SEC(2007)926 of 28.6.2007.

European Commission (2007c) *Better Lawmaking 2006*, COM(2007)286 of 6.6.2007 (annual edition).

European Commission (2006) *A Strategic Review of Better Regulation in the European Union*, COM(2006)689 of 14.11.2006.

European Commission (2005a) *Rules giving Effect to the Rules of Procedure*, COM(2005)4416 of 15.11.2005.

European Commission (2005b) *Impact Assessment Guidelines*, SEC(2005)791 of 15.6.2005.

European Commission (2005c) *Better Regulation for Growth and Jobs in the European Union*, COM(2005)97 of 16.3.2005.

European Commission (2005d) *Strategic Objectives 2005–2009 – Europe 2010: A Partnership for European Renewal – Prosperity, Solidarity and Security*, COM(2005)12 of 26.1.2005.

European Commission (2002a) *Towards a Reinforced Culture of Consultation and Dialogue – General Principles and Minimum Standards for Consultation of Interested Parties by the Commission*, COM(2002)704 of 11.12.2002.

European Commission (2002b) *Action Plan on Simplifying and Improving the Regulatory Environment*, COM(2002)278 of 5.6.2002.

European Commission (2002c) *European Governance: Better Lawmaking*, COM(2002)275 of 5.6.2002.

European Commission (2001) *European Governance: A White Paper*, COM(2001)428 of 25.7.2001.

European Commission (2000) *Reforming the Commission: A White Paper*, COM(2000)200 of 5.4.2000.

European Parliament (2005) *Revised Framework Agreement on the Relations between the European Parliament and the Commission*, P6_TA(2005)0194 of 26 May 2005.

European Parliament, Council, Commission (2003) *Interinstitutional Agreement on Better Lawmaking*, Official Journal of the European Union, C321/1 of 31 December 2003.

Fischer, R., Karrass, A. and Kröger, S. (eds) (2007) *Die Europäische Kommission und die Zukunft der EU*, Berlin: Verlag Barbara Budrich.

Goetz, K.H. (2009) 'How does the EU tick? Five propositions on political time', *Journal of European Public Policy* 16(2): 202–20.

Goetz, K. and Meyer-Sahling, J.-H. (2009) 'Political time in the EU: dimensions, perspectives, theories', *Journal of European Public Policy* 16(2): 180–201.

Gornitzka, Å. and Sverdrup, U. (2008) 'Who consults? The configuration of expert groups in the European Union', *West European Politics* 31(4): 725–50.

Kassim, H. (2004) 'An historic achievement: administrative reform under the Prodi Commission', in D.G. Dimitrakopoulos (ed.), *The Changing European Commission*, Manchester: Manchester University Press, pp. 33–62.

Kassim, H. (2008) '"Mission Impossible", but mission accomplished: the Kinnock reforms and the European Commission', *Journal of European Public Policy* 15(5): 648–68.

Kassim, H. and Dimitrakopoulos, D.G. (2007) 'The European Commission and the future of Europe', *Journal of European Public Policy* 14(8): 1249–70.

Kurpas, S., Grøn, C. and Kaczynski, P.M. (2008) *The European Commission after Enlargement: Does More Add Up to Less?*, Special Report of the Center for European Policy Studies (CEPS), February 2008.

Meyer-Sahling, J.-H. and Goetz, K.H. (2009) 'The EU timescape: from notion to research agenda', *Journal of European Public Policy* 16(2): 325–36.

Radaelli, C.M. (2007) 'Whither better regulation for the Lisbon agenda?' *Journal of European Public Policy* 14(2): 190–207.

Radaelli, C.M. and De Francesco, F. (2007) *Regulatory Quality in Europe: Concepts, Measures and Policy Processes*, Manchester: Manchester University Press.

Schön-Quinlivan, E. (2008) 'Implementing organizational change – the case of the Kinnock reforms', *Journal of European Public Policy* 15(5): 726–42.

Spence, D. and Edwards, G. (2006) *The European Commission*, 3rd edn, . London: John Harper Publishing.

The Evaluation Partnership Limited (2007) *Evaluation of the Commission's Impact Assessment System*, Final Report, April 2007.

Tholoniat, L. (2007) 'The European Commission: an introduction', in R. Fischer, A. Karrass and S. Kröger (eds), *Die Europäische Kommission und die Zukunft der EU*, Berlin: Verlag Barbara Budrich, pp. 21–40.

Tholoniat, L. and Fischer, G. (2006) 'The European employment strategy in an enlarged EU', *Zeitschrift für ArbeitsmarktsForschung*, Institut für Arbeitsmarkt- und Berufsforschung 39(1): 123–42.

Trenz, H.J. (2008) 'Measuring the Europeanization of public communication: the question of standards', *ARENA Working Paper*, Oslo. No. 3, February 2008.

Do elections set the pace? A quantitative assessment of the timing of European legislation

Laszlo Kovats

ABSTRACT Many parliamentary systems are marked by regular periods of higher and lower legislative activity. This legislation cycle is characterized by an increase in the legislative output shortly ahead of elections and a decrease in legislative initiatives in the second half of the legislative term. This article shows that legislative cycles at the European level are different. First, it shows that the initiation of legislation peaks at the end of parliamentary terms rather than at the beginning. Second, the article shows that the adoption of legislation is only partially connected to the electoral cycle. Instead, the reallocation of agenda powers within the European Parliament twice during a legislature better explains the timing of the adoption of bills than the end of Parliament's term. This finding is especially relevant for legislation adopted under the co-decision procedure. The 'procedural cartel theory' of Cox and McCubbins (2005) combined with the 'economic theory of legislation' provide the theoretical basis that may explain this finding.

1. INTRODUCTION

The basic characteristic of democracies is that the ruling majority regularly faces the threat of losing its legislative and executive powers. The polling day therefore constitutes the most important landmark in the political life of every elected representative. The possibility of losing or winning office through the poll induces representatives to apply strategic manoeuvres in order to obtain enough votes to secure their (re-)election. Besides public opinion measures to boost the popularity of the government or a single candidate, policy measures are used for similar strategic purposes. The literature on political business cycles (PBC) has discussed and empirically shown that governments are responsive to an upcoming ballot and try to manipulate economic indicators to increase their chances of re-election (Drazen 2000). Similarly, the economic theory of legislation assumes that legislation has redistributive effects. Accordingly, it can also be used strategically to maximize the vote share.

This logic can be applied to explain the occurrence of distinct patterns of legislative activity. In parliamentary systems, the scores of initiatives should decrease in the second half of a legislative term whereas completed acts should be adopted more frequently in the run-up to elections. Martin (2004) finds this kind of empirical pattern for initiatives in four European parliamentary systems, while Lagona and Padovano (2007) demonstrate for the Italian case that legislative output increases shortly before scheduled parliamentary elections.

This article examines the extent to which these patterns apply to the European Union (EU) legislative system. Goetz (2009) argues that the EU system is characterized by the absence of a dominant political cycle. This article therefore asks to what extent EU legislation reacts to structural ruptures, in particular, the elections to the European Parliament (EP) in accordance with the expectations that were developed for member state democracies. Owing to the particularities of EU legislative procedures, the article develops two separate models to examine the initiation and the adoption of bills. First, it examines whether the timing of legislative initiatives is related to the Commission's term in office. Second, the article examines whether the output of European legislation increases at the end of the EP's term or whether the reallocation of agenda powers within the EP constitutes a more important structuring factor for the initiation and adoption of EU legislation.

The article is divided into four sections. Section 2 locates the research question in the debate on temporal features of European legislation. Section 3 presents four possible explanations that could produce patterns in the timing of European legislation. It first develops two competing hypotheses to explain the initiation of European legislation. They are followed by two hypotheses to explain the timing of the adoption of legislation. The hypotheses will be developed on the basis of the economic theory of legislation (Stigler 1971; Peltzman 1976; McCormick and Tollison 1981; Lagona and Padovano 2007) and the procedural cartel theory (Cox and McCubbins 2005). Section 4 delivers up-to-date summary statistics on European legislation from the PreLex database, and presents the empirical analysis and interpretation of the statistical calculations. Section 5 concludes.

2. POLITICAL TIME AND LEGISLATION

Political actors in democracies are not only constrained by a broad distribution of power but also by the limitation of legislative and executive office terms. This democratic setting determines the scope of action of those involved in the political business. Goetz and Meyer-Sahling (2009), in the introduction to this special issue, argue in this regard that the electoral cycle represents the basic rhythm of democratic systems of government. Therefore, all kinds of political action, and in particular the policy-making process, adapt to this cycle and one is able to observe recurring political phenomena that appear regularly depending on the current phase of the legislative term.

Legislation cycles

Power in democracies is limited in time. The outcome of future elections is uncertain and neither incumbents nor candidates for political posts can be sure of achieving their desired election outcome. The political horizon that they can reasonably oversee is their current legislative period (Riescher 1994). Van Schagen (1997) finds that in most (Western European) democracies this disruption of the political process comes with substantial discontinuity: legislative acts not completed at the end of a legislative period lapse automatically. If the new legislator wants those initiatives to become enacted it needs to start the whole legislative process again. Of course, such a legislative reset entails costs that an actor may not want to bear. However, if the ruling majority is unable to produce complete legislation the electorate may perceive it as incompetent and will probably vote for the opposition in the next elections (Heller 2001; Manow and Burkhart 2007a). So, if the chances of passing legislation successfully are small the ruling majority has to adapt its strategy. *Ceteris paribus*, this probability is highest if legislation is initiated at the beginning of a parliamentary term and decreases thereafter. At a certain point in the term it may be too late for a government and its supporting majority to initiate an act without risking their reputation.

Accordingly, the ruling majority may seek to adopt as many laws as possible at the end of a parliamentary term to prove its competence shortly before the elections. All in all, one may observe a legislation cycle with a decreasing number of initiatives towards the end of the legislative term as well as a peak in the number of adoptions.

The impact of the time elapsed during a parliamentary period on legislation has been examined for the national level. Becker and Saalfeld (2004) survey the legislative processes in 17 Western European parliaments and conclude that the 'choices of actors may be highly time-dependent, especially with regard to the electoral cycle' (Becker and Saalfeld 2004: 89). As regards the content of legislative text Manow and Burkhart (2007a; 2007b) find that the time left to the next elections does matter. They demonstrate that in times of differing majorities in the 'Bundestag' and 'Bundestag', initiatives for federal legislation are much more consensual if the election date is near. Martin (2004) studies the probabilities of legislative initiatives of coalition governments in Belgium, Germany, Luxembourg and the Netherlands over one legislative period. Overall, he finds that proposed activity in these countries remains stable between the sixth and the thirty-sixth week. In the year before the elections the frequency of legislative proposals drops significantly. Schindler (1998) confirms this finding for initiatives in the German second chamber, the Bundestag. His figures also show an increase in legislative output in the first two quarters of the last year of the German legislatures. Lagona and Padovano (2007) analyse the legislative activity of the Italian Parliament and find that legislative output is significantly higher at the end of legislative period. This mostly popular legislation is intended to secure the votes of the electorate ahead of upcoming elections – so they argue. The authors assume that those ruling majorities that are not able to produce legislation, for example owing to coalition deadlock, accordingly face a higher risk of losing the elections.

Time in the EU legislative system

In the literature on the political system of the EU time has mainly been captured as an indicator in order to draw conclusions on the power relations within the Council and between the institutions. Spatial analysis of legislative decision-making builds on the interplay of member state preferences, institutional preferences and decision-making rules to explain policy outcomes. If temporal aspects are considered they are applied as a proxy for decision-making efficiency. The duration of legislation is regarded as a good indicator to determine the decision-making capability of the EU system.

Schulz and Koenig (2000) measure the time lag between a Commission proposal and the decision by the Council to analyse the decision-making efficiency of the EU. Koenig (2007) identifies the duration of all EU legislation between 1984 and 1998. Both articles find that the broader application of qualified majority voting (QMV) in the Council has speeded up legislative procedures although further participation of the EP partly counters this effect. The authors see diverging positions of the member states in the Council as the main factor that slows down European legislation. They conclude that a further expansion of the EU increases the heterogeneity of Council positions which leads to ever slower decision-making. Golub (2007) reaches roughly the same results, but disagrees about the effect of EU enlargements. He argues that qualified majorities in the Council are always connected winning coalitions. Therefore, the probability of obtaining the necessary threshold is higher with a larger number of voters.

Farrell and Héritier (2004, 2007) explain how the time that a bill has spent in the co-decision procedure impacts on its outcome. In a nutshell, they argue that the EP has advantages in interstitial bargaining with the Council. So, if an agreement is reached in the early stages of the process, bargaining has probably taken place outside the formal legislative path. As the EP copes better with such negotiations this may translate into legislative output that reflects the position of the EP more closely.

However, temporal aspects of EU decision-making that exert their own influence on legislative outcomes have so far received little attention in the literature. In contrast to its dependent character when used as an indicator, time may also come as an independent variable in the causal explanation of EU legislation. Time is rarely conceptualized in this way. In particular, the direct effect of the time that has passed during a legislative term on the emergence of legislation cycles at the EU level has so far not been considered. This could be due to special characteristics of the political system of the EU. They create difficulties for the application of models that are taken from the analysis of traditional presidential or parliamentary systems. On the one hand, the supranational nature of the EU is marked by features that are more similar to international organizations; for instance, in the areas of foreign and security policy. On the other hand, it exercises real sovereignty when adopting legislation that is binding for its members and which can be enforced by an independent judicial system.

When applying public choice theories like the economic theory of legislation and the procedural cartel theory to the EU context, the lack of definitional clearness creates specific problems. These theories make assumptions about the relation between the electorate, political actors and legislation in a democratic system and demonstrate how and why they influence each other. In the case of the EU, one may have difficulties in identifying institutional set-ups that can be easily regarded as equivalents to those in national democratic systems. For instance, the EP is elected by national instead of European electorates, the quality of EU legislation depends on the policy area and real parliamentary oversight is restricted, and an executive that depends on a parliamentary majority and has to face regular elections is effectively non-existent. Accordingly, one could cast doubt on whether these public choice theories can help to explain the functioning of the political system of the EU.

Yet even if the structural setting of the EU differs from traditional states, there are some striking similarities. Elections follow fundamental democratic principles, an increasing number of legislative acts are negotiated between two co-equal legislative bodies, there is parliamentary involvement and oversight in core areas such as the budgetary process, and the office terms of the Commission and the EP have been synchronized. The gradual democratization of the EU system is strongly assumed to have a real impact on the appearance of phenomena known from the context of states. Latest research on the EP has found evidence that its cleavage structure resembles those of parliamentary systems across Western Europe. In a series of contributions, Simon Hix and his colleagues have analysed voting patterns in the EP since 1979 (Hix *et al.* 2005, 2006, 2007). The overall result was that the increase of the power endowment of the EP has led to greater competition among the party groups along the left–right dimension. Hix (2008) argues that this was a sign of the increasing competitiveness of the actors for influence within the EU system. As the powers of the EP are gradually being extended, it becomes attractive for political actors to gather a large vote share in elections to the EP. So, in this respect the exact composition of the institutions may be less decisive for the application of public choice theories.

To sum up, political actors of the EP compete for votes in elections to gain power and influence. This feature of the EU may lead to phenomena that are also observed at the national level, and can be explained by using the economic theory of legislation and the procedural cartel theory framework.

3. CYCLES IN EU LEGISLATION

The initiation and adoption of EU legislation is strictly divided between the institutions. Whereas initiatives and withdrawals are exclusively within the responsibility of the Commission, acts are adopted either by the Council alone or in co-operation with the EP. Owing to the structural separation of the Commission and the legislative bodies, the timing of initiatives and adoptions is assumed to follow different logics. Therefore, they are treated in separate models. Two rival explanations for fluctuations in the initiation and adoption rates will be tested for plausibility.

The basic underlying assumption that the following hypotheses have in common is that the legislative institutions of the EU establish an increasingly tight web of co-ordination and bargaining that exceeds the formal requirement for co-operation. Farrell and Héritier (2004) argue that individual agents of the Council and EP keep in touch throughout the entire legislative processes and communicate with each other about the ongoing negotiations in their institutions. This smooths inter-institutional bargaining and eventually allows for compromises at an early stage of the procedures. However, this co-operation implies that strategic measures in one legislative institution may be taken to influence the final legislative outcome. In other words, political actors with high stakes in a legislative procedure may be able to influence decision-making in areas that they formally do not control in terms of both content and timing.

Initiation of the legislative process

Martin (2004) sees a pattern in the rate of initiatives in four parliamentary democracies which is closely connected to the legislative period. This period structures the agenda of coalition governments in such a way that they have to initiate acts strategically to produce complete legislation and prove their competence in the eyes of the electorate. In what follows, Martin's reasoning will be applied to legislative initiatives by the Commission. At first sight, one might expect that the Commission would behave in a similar way to a national initiator of legislative acts and issue fewer initiatives in the last months of its office term.

However, considering the structure of the Commission and its position within the EU system, one could cast doubt on whether this holds true. The Commission does not face a direct vote by the electorate and in its daily business it is independent from majorities in the Council and the EP. Thus, it is well protected from any kind of electoral competition. Additionally, the Commission does not have to fear that its proposals will lapse without a formal decision because of the end of the parliamentary term. There is no effective discontinuity principle that restricts the duration of legislative procedures to the term during which they have been initiated. Consequently, decisions about initiatives do not need to entail a strategic component referring to elections or the end of the Commission's term in office. Hence, one does not need to expect significant fluctuations in the number of initiatives related to these dates. Hypothesis 1a can be formulated accordingly:

H1a: With respect to the end of the Commission's term in office, the number of legislative initiatives remains stable.

Hypothesis 1a suggests that the Commission is completely free in its decisions on legislative initiatives. However, an alternative scenario is also conceivable.

Institutionalist approaches to the EU (Tsebelis and Garrett 2000, 2001; Schneider and Aspinwall 2001) consider the institutional setting as a framework that impacts on the decision-making of the single parts of the system. In this respect, the Commission may account for majorities in the other institutions and adjust its legislative activity. Consequently, the Commission may issue initiatives when it believes it has the best chances for successful passage, or may wait for more favourable conditions.

This logic has been applied to the interplay between the Commission and the Council while the EP has been regarded as keeping a fixed position. What the institutionalist approach has paid less attention to is the possibility that the EP is not as homogenous as expected, and that the allocation of power within the EP may change. In some respects, this can happen even if no election has taken place. Halfway through the parliamentary term the Presidency of the EP changes between the two large European party groups. This alternation comes with the redistribution of committee chairs, a measure assumed to be influential. In the EP the actual legislative work is carried out within the 20 standing committees and a number of temporary and sub-committees. In particular, the committee chairs have considerable agenda powers. They organize the business of the committees (Hix 2005) and can use this power to determine when a topic is dealt with, or if it is dealt with at all. This characteristic of agenda has been outlined by Cox and McCubbins (2005) in their procedural cartel theory framework. So, if competitiveness between the European party groups in the EP has increased and their positions have become more distinct, the Commission may react to the rotation of committee chairs just as national initiators of legislation react to elections. Hence, if the EP plays a decisive role in the legislative process, the Commission may initiate fewer proposals at the end of the term of the two EP Presidencies because it knows that the actual committee chairs will not be able to promote initiatives late in their own term. The Commission may prefer to wait and see who follows in that important seat.

Hypothesis 1b can be formulated accordingly:

H1b: The number of initiatives in the co-decision procedure is significantly lower at the end of an EP Presidency term.

Finalization of the legislative process

Lagona and Padovano (2007) have found a pattern in the Italian legislative system which may be transposed to the European legislative system. They applied the economic theory of legislation to explain an increase in the legislative output shortly before parliamentary elections in Italy. In this respect, the authors shifted the focus away from the question 'who is supplied with legislation?' (Lagona and Padovano 2007: 2) to 'when it is politically most rewarding' (Lagona and Padovano 2007: 2) to do so. For a short explanation of the theory one has to go back to the theory of economic regulation by

Stigler (1971), who argues that the state regulates to redistribute economic wealth in favour of special interest groups. Peltzman (1976) formalized Stigler's model and 'integrated both consumers and producers in a rent-seeking struggle' (Mueller 2003: 344). On the one side, politicians, who seek to maximize their vote share, supply the consumer with regulative acts. On the other, consumers, in particular interest groups representing a certain section of the electorate, pay for the regulation with their votes. McCormick and Tollison (1981) extended the model to all types of legislation and so the theory developed into the economic theory of legislation.

The reasoning of Lagona and Padovano is intuitive: shortly before the parliamentary elections the ruling majority adopts batteries of legislation to secure the votes of certain electoral groups. This, they argue, explains the significant increase in adopted legislation near the election date as the governing majority campaigns for votes with its legislation.

Accordingly, it is assumed here that, on the one hand, the suppliers of legislation – namely the elected European politicians – try to finalize as many acts as possible at the end of a legislative term to stress their importance and competence in the light of upcoming elections. On the other hand, the consumers of legislation – namely the benefited electorate represented by European interest groups – vote for the candidate. Lengthy and complicated procedures reinforce the tendency to adopt legislation late in the parliamentary term. Although legislation does not lapse automatically at the end of a legislative period, elections constitute a rupture in the composition of the EP. The uncertainty concerning future majorities creates an incentive to accelerate the legislative process towards the end of the EP's term. In other words, if the electoral process works effectively, a *de facto* discontinuity principle may be observed even though it is not formally codified. As elections to the EP constitute the structural factor here, hypothesis 2a is restricted to the co-decision procedure where the EP has substantive legislative power:

H2a: The number of bills adopted in the co-decision procedure increases near the end of a legislative term.

The complicated legislative system of the EU and the lack of accountability of its institutions, parties or individuals, as well as the elections taking place in a national environment, are good reasons to question the connection between legislative action and voting decisions. In other words, facing the EU machinery the individual voter is not assumed to be able to evaluate the real impact of EU legislation. Therefore, the voter will cast his or her vote on the basis of factors other than legislative outcome. Knowing this, the EU legislator is geared rather to internal procedures that help to promote the actors' interests. Seen from this perspective, legislation is a tool for individual politicians who hold legislative posts to strengthen their personal position in the European party groups, in national parties and/or to implement personal beliefs or party ideology in EU legislation. The aim to win as many votes as possible in the elections remains, but elections are won by other potentially more effective means. In other words, the production of legislation and the voting of the electorate are detached from each other.

As argued above, the allocation of agenda powers may influence the outcome of legislation. Consequently, the reallocation of agenda powers during the parliamentary term of the EP may have similar effects to elections at the national level. Knowing that they will soon lose their agenda powers, the committee chairs may want to use their influence to finalize as much legislation as possible and thus secure the future support of their clientele. The later they present their success, the clearer the signal they send. Long and complex legislative procedures add to the tendency to finish business late, and so one may see an increase in legislative output shortly before halfway through and at the end of a parliamentary term. However, the EP can substantially control only a small number of legislative acts and there is no formal requirement that the argument should hold for legislation in which the Council decides alone. Hypothesis 2b can accordingly be formulated:

> *H2b: The number of bills adopted in the co-decision procedure increases in the periods before the EP Presidency and the committee chairmen alternate, i.e. in the middle and at the end of a parliamentary term.*

4. EMPIRICAL FINDINGS

The database used for the following calculations is a reproduction of the PreLex data on European legislation by the Commission. This database provides detailed information on every legislative process that takes place in the EU. It has been made accessible with special software developed at the Hasso Plattner Institute, the University of Potsdam. It automatically reads every piece of information available on the PreLex pages and enters it into one single file. Both software and file will be made available on the homepage of the author.

The hypotheses presented in section 2 establish a link between the number of acts, which is the dependent variable, and the point of time in the parliamentary period as the independent variable. Whether a systematic correlation exists between the two will be explored with a regression model for count data. These indicate how often an incident occurs in a given period of time. They follow a Poisson distribution, and therefore it may be adequate to fit an exponential Poisson regression curve. However, such data are likely to suffer from over-dispersion which may lead to inefficient and biased coefficient estimates. In such a case, Long and Freese (2003) recommend a negative binomial regression model (NBRM). The data at hand are indeed over-dispersed. Therefore, to avoid inefficient and biased estimates NBRMs are fitted to the data.

Initiatives

Two models will be calculated that are intended to assess which of the hypotheses from section 2 are supported by the data. Model 1 refers to hypothesis

H1a and tests for a significant increase in the number of initiatives at the end of the Commission's term of office. Therefore, the number of initiatives is counted on a monthly basis. A time dummy variable that marks a three-month period before the end of a Commission's term of office are included. The regression of the number of initiatives per month on the dummy variables is supposed to reveal whether the Commission changes its activity, knowing that its time in office will end soon. In other words, does the number of initiatives decrease in the periods defined by the dummy variables? The observation period reaches from one year before the first election to the EP (June 1978) until April 2008.

The negative binomial regression equation looks accordingly like this:

$$\mu = \exp(\beta 0 + \beta 1 x 1 + \beta 2 t 1 + \beta 3 t 2 + \beta 4 t 3 + \beta 5 t 4)$$

μ stands for the count of initiatives per month. It is not restricted to a particular procedure but refers to the whole legislative activity. x1 depicts the quarters preceding the end of a Commission's term of office, t1 to t4 represent fixed effects dummies for the legislative periods with the fifth parliamentary period representing the reference category. They are intended to stabilize the calculations by controlling for influential term-specific effects that may confound the results.

Model 2 refers to hypothesis H1b and tests if decisions of the Commission on initiatives are influenced by the allocation of agenda power in the EP. More specifically, Model 2 counts the number of initiatives per month and correlates these figures to time dummy variables that define three-month periods before agenda power in the EP is redistributed. The negative binomial regression equation has the following form:

$$\mu = \exp(\beta 0 + \beta 1 \times 1 + x\beta 2 x 2 + \beta 3 t 1 + \beta 4 t 2 + \beta 5 t 3 + \beta 6 t 4)$$

Again μ stands for the count of initiatives per month. However, in the second model only initiatives in the co-decision procedure are considered. x1 represents the dummy variable that marks the three-month period before half-time in a parliamentary term. x2 is the dummy variable that marks the quarter before the end of a parliamentary term. At these two dates the agenda power is reallocated in the EP. t1–t4 account for fixed effects of the legislative periods; the fifth parliamentary period is again the reference category. Table 1 summarizes the regression results of Models 1 and 2 for initiatives.

Technically, the results are to be interpreted as follows. Compared to quarters not marked by the time dummy variables, the number of bills initiated changes according to the coefficients. For a better understanding of their substantial meaning the changes are expressed in percentages.

Model 1 finds that in the quarter before the term of office of the Commission ends the number of initiatives increases by 29.5 per cent. The fact that the figure is highly significant tells us that there is probably a real correlation between the

Table 1 Dependent variable: counts of initiatives

	Model 1 (election)		Model 2 (agenda powers)	
	Coeff.	% change	Coeff.	% change
End of office	0.258*** (0.009)	29.5	–	–
Pre election	–	–	−0.253 (0.190)	−22.3
Pre mid-term	–	–	0.637*** (0.057)	89.1
EP1	−0.095*** (0.015)	−9.1	−2.12 (1.06)	−88.0
EP2	0.269*** (0.012)	30.9	−2.26*** (0.537)	−89.6
EP3	0.226*** (0.012)	25.4	−1.09*** (0.093)	−66.5
EP4	0.057*** (0.013)	5.8	−0.475*** (0.048)	−37.8

Notes: Model 1: N = 352 monthly counts; model 2: N = 178.
***0.01 significance level; **0.05 significance level; *0.1 significance level; standard deviations in parentheses.

dummy variable and the number of initiatives. This result clearly contradicts hypothesis H1a which predicts no significant change. It also shows that the Commission does not work as a national initiator of legislative acts. In national settings, one sees a decrease in the number of initiatives at the end of terms of office, i.e. when the election date approaches. Obviously, the Commission initiates more acts just before it is replaced by a new one.

Model 2 also produces unexpected results. In the last three months before the elections to the EP, the number of initiatives of bills in the co-decision procedure decreases by 22.3 per cent. This result is on the brink of the significance level of 1 per cent which makes it less trustworthy compared to the other figures in the model. In contrast, the mid-term effect is much more distinct: in the last quarter before the EP Presidency changes, the number of initiatives increases by 89.1 per cent. The figure is highly significant. Taken together, the results do not represent a coherent picture. On the one hand, Model 2 finds a decrease in initiatives just before the elections to the EP take place – as predicted by hypothesis H1b. On the other hand, more bills are initiated just before the EP Presidency changes – the opposite of what hypothesis H1b predicts.

On combining the results of both models, one could infer that the Commission increases the number of initiatives before agenda powers are reallocated in the EP halfway through the parliamentary term as well as shortly before its own term in office is up. The impact of the election date is minor. The correct explanation for this pattern is neither clearly provided by models derived from national contexts nor by the alternative agenda-setting model. However, it seems to be case that the Commission is indeed not affected by the electoral cycle.

Figure 1 illustrates the summary statistic of Model 2. The bars indicate how many bills in the co-decision procedure have been initiated in the three-month periods over the EP terms. The significant increase in the middle of

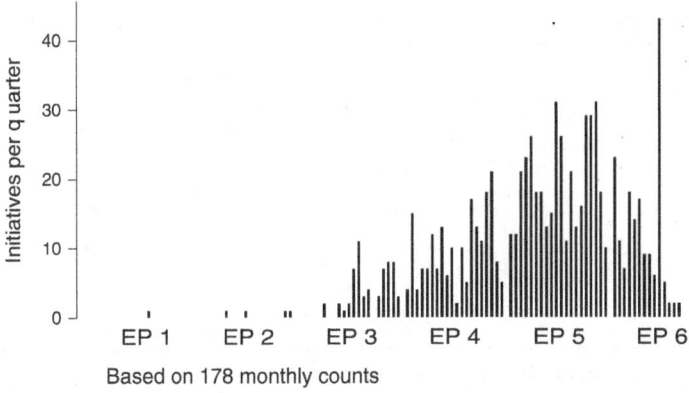

Figure 1 Initiatives in the co-decision procedure

the parliamentary terms is indeed observable – especially in EP6. But other fluctuations are also evident. This may cause interpretative problems that will be addressed later in the paper.

Adoptions

Two rival hypothesis were formulated to explain the timing of the adoption of EU legislation. Hypothesis H2a argues that the approaching election date provokes the legislators to finalize more acts whereas hypothesis H2b expects the reallocation of agenda powers in the EP to have this effect. Which of the two explanations finds more support in the data can be tested in one model that incorporates time dummy variables for both periods. Accordingly, the negative binomial regression equation has the following form:

$$\mu = \exp(\beta 0 + \beta 1 x1 + \beta 2 x2 + \beta 3 t1 + \beta 4 t2 + \beta 5 t3 + \beta 6 t4)$$

μ stands for the count of adoptions per month. Here, the acts under consideration are restricted to those agreed upon in the co-decision procedure. x1 is a time dummy variable that represents a three-month period before the elections to the EP take place. x2 is also a time dummy variable that accounts for a three-month period before the agenda powers in the EP are redistributed. This happens first halfway through the parliamentary period as laid down in the EP's Rule of Procedure 16 and, of course, in elections after a full parliamentary term. Therefore, if hypothesis H2a is correct, the regression should produce a peak in the number of acts adopted at the end of the legislative period only. If hypothesis H2b is correct, one should observe two peaks: one before halftime and one before the end of a parliamentary term. As both hypotheses are tested in one model it is termed Model 12. Table 2 summarizes the results of the negative binomial regression.

Table 2 Dependent variable: counts of adoptions

	Model 12	
	Coeff.	% change
Pre election	1.297*** (0.078)	265.9
Pre mid term	0.885*** (0.075)	142.3
EP1	no	no
EP2	no	no
EP3	−1.43*** (0.258)	−75.9
EP4	−0.859***(0.073)	−57.6

Notes: no = no observation; N (adoption) = 142.
***0.01 significance level; **0.05 significance level; *0.1 significance level; standard deviation in parenthesis.

The technical interpretation of the coefficients and the percentage changes is identical to the interpretation of Models 1 and 2 for initiatives. Substantially, they mean that in the quarter before of the elections to the EP the number of adoptions in the co-decision procedure is 265.9 per cent higher than in other periods. The quarter before the change in the EP Presidency is also marked by an increase in legislative output of 142.3 per cent. The fixed effects for the legislative terms account for possible term-specific interfering variables. Including them does not alter the results but makes them more distinct.

The main finding of Model 12 is that these are two clear peaks in the number of legislative adoptions in the co-decision procedure; first, in the middle of, and, second, at the end of the parliamentary term. This supports hypothesis H2b which argues that it is not the elections that influence legislative action but the distribution of agenda powers. The stronger effect in the quarter before the election date may be due to higher uncertainty about the future composition of the EP. This may induce the decisive political actors in the legislative bodies of the EU to push even harder for the finalization of ongoing procedures. Figure 2 illustrates the findings of Model 12. The bars indicate how many bills in the co-decision procedure have been initiated per three-month periods over the EP terms.

The distinct peaks as predicted by hypotheses 2a and 2b are obvious. However, the greatest pitfall in the interpretations of the regression result is also evident. The strong results are mainly due to two very influential quarters in EP5 and EP6. From today's perspective it is difficult to judge whether these two quarters are sufficient to confirm the hypotheses from section 2 or whether they are outliers. The co-decision procedure is a relatively new procedure and the period of observation is short. As the number of cases in a count data model depends on the period of observation, the analysis of the co-decision procedure leaves us with only a limited number of cases. In particular, the decisive observations marked by the dummy variables are infrequent. If the two strong

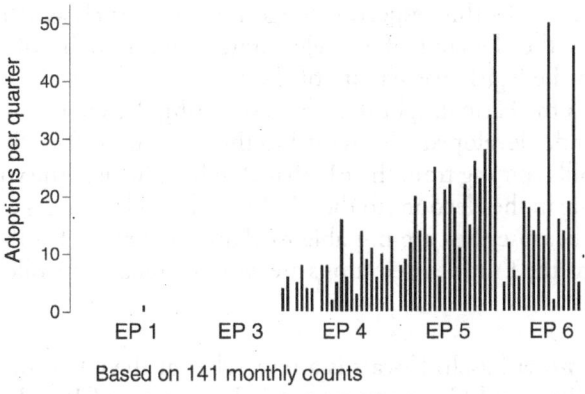

Figure 2 Adoptions in the co-decision procedure

effects in the fifth and sixth EP were indeed outliers or due to other factors, the results here could be biased. From today's point of view, however, we cannot, judge whether this is the case. The same critique applies to Models 1 and 2 for the analysis of initiatives.

Another cautionary point concerning the inferences of the statistical calculations needs to be made. Figures 1 and 2 indicate that adoptions and initiatives are subject to considerable fluctuations. The effects predicted by the hypotheses and found by the calculations indicate which of the rival hypotheses fits the data better. This implies that the results presented here do not mean that any of the hypotheses explain the timing of EU legislation best.

5. CONCLUSION

The basic aim of this article was to find evidence for legislation cycles in EU legislation similar to those at the national level. The central finding of the article is that, as far as the co-decision procedure is concerned, cycles in EU legislation are present. However, they look different compared to what we know about national democracies. First, a significantly higher number of bills is initiated shortly before the EP Presidency changes halfway of the parliamentary term. Moreover, considering proposals in all procedures, the results show that shortly before the Commission steps down it initiates a higher number of bills compared to other periods during its time in office.

Second, the article has shown that the number of acts adopted under the co-decision procedure peaks every time the agenda powers in the EP are reallocated. This happens twice during the parliamentary term and leads to the conclusion that internal factors, such as the allocation of agenda powers, may be more influential for the timing of adoptions than external factors, such as the date of European elections. In other words, an important structuring factor for legislation in the co-decision procedure can be traced back to measures and processes internal to the EP. In this respect, external influences such as elections, which should express the demand of the electorate, appear to be of second-order importance in the legislative activity of the EP.

This leads to the basic insight that the relationship between voters and representatives is underdeveloped with regard to the EU. Put differently, it is not the substance of bills coming from the EU that chiefly influences the voting decision of the electorate in the elections to the EP. Instead, EU legislators face a problem of legitimacy because they are not able to claim the reward for their legislative work as long as the European elections are won in arenas controlled by national political actors.

Biographical note: Laszlo Kovats is a researcher at the Chair of German and European Politics and Government at the University of Potsdam, Germany He is working on the project 'The Politics of Time: The Temporality of EU Enlargement and Europeanization' financed by the German Research Foundation – DFG (Project No. D76) and led by Professor Klaus H Goetz.

ACKNOWLEDGEMENTS

I would like to thank Professor Felix Naumann for his co-operation and in particular Tobias Vogel – both from the Hasso-Plattner Institute at the University of Potsdam – who developed the software necessary to build the database. Previous versions of this paper were presented at the ECPR Joint Sessions in Rennes and at the ECPR Pan-European Conference on EU Politics in Riga. I thank the workshop leaders and discussants at both conferences – namely Marianna Llanos, Natalia Ajenjo, Nicolas Jabko and Jonas Tallberg. I also thank colleagues from the working group on the 'Timescape of the EU' at the University of Potsdam, Katja Lass-Lennecke, and Annika Werner, and Klaus Goetz for their comments.

REFERENCES

Becker, R. and Saalfeld, T. (2004) 'The life and times of bills', in H. Doering and M. Hallerberg (eds), *Patterns of Parliamentary Behaviour: Passage of Legislation Across Western Europe*, Aldershot: Ashgate, pp. 57–90.

Cox, G.W. and McCubbins, M.D. (2005) *Setting the Agenda: Responsible Party Government in the U.S. House of Representatives*, Cambridge: Cambridge University Press.

Drazen, A. (2000) 'The political business cycle after 25 years', in B. Bernanke and K. Rogoff (eds), *NBER Macroeconomics Annual Number 15*, Cambridge, MA: The MIT Press.

Farrell, H. and Heritier, A. (2004) 'Interorganizational negotiation and intraorganizational power in shared decision making: early agreements under codecision and their impact on the European Parliament and Council', *Comparative Political Studies* 37(10): 1184–212.

Farrell, H. and Héritier, A. (2007) 'Codecision and institutional change', *West European Politics* 30(2): 285–300.

Goetz, K.H. (2009) 'How does the EU tick? Five propositions on political time', *Journal of European Public Policy* 16(2): 202–20.

Goetz, K.H. and Meyer-Sahling, J.-H. (2009) 'Political time in the EU: dimensions, perspectives, theories', *Journal of European Public Policy* 16(2): 176–97.

Golub, J. (2007) 'Survival analysis and European Union decision-making', *European Union Politics* 8(2): 155–79.

Heller, W.B. (2001) 'Making policy stick: why the government gets what it wants in multiparty parliaments', *American Journal of Political Science* 45: 780–98.

Hix, S. (2005) *The Political System of the European Union*, Basingstoke: Palgrave Macmillan.

Hix, S. (2008) *What's Wrong with the European Union and How to Fix It*, Cambridge: Polity Press.

Hix, S., Noury, A. and Roland, G. (2005) 'Power to the parties: cohesion and competition in the European Parliament, 1979–2001', *British Journal of Political Science* 35(2): 209–34.

Hix, S., Noury, A. and Roland, G. (2006) 'Dimensions of politics in the European Parliament', *American Journal of Political Science* 50(2): 494–511.

Hix, S., Noury, A. and Roland, G. (2007) *Democratic Politics in the European Parliament*, Cambridge: Cambridge University Press.

König, T. (2007) 'Divergence or convergence? From ever-growing to ever-slowing European legislative decision making', *European Journal of Political Research* 46: 417–44.

Lagona, F. and Padovano, F. (2007) 'The political legislation cycle', Public Choice online publication from 20 June

Long, S. and Freese, J. (2003) *Regression Models for Categorical Dependent Variables Using Stata*, College Station, Texas: Stata Press.

Manow, P. and Burkhart, S. (2007a) 'Legislative self-restraint under divided government in Germany, 1976–2002', *Legislative Studies Quarterly* 32(2): 167–91.

Manow, P. and Burkhart, S. (2007b). 'Delay as a technique under divided government? Evidence from Germany, 1976–2005'. Paper presented at the ECPR General Conference, Pisa, September 2007.

Martin, L.M. (2004) 'The government agenda in parliamentary democracies', *American Journal of Political Science* 48(3): 445–61.

Mueller, D.C. (2003) *Public Choice III*, Cambridge: Cambridge University Press.

McCormick, R.E. and Tollison, R. (1981) *Politicians, Legislation and the Economy: An Inquiry into the interest-group Theory of Government*, Leiden: Nijhoff.

Peltzman, S. (1976) 'Toward a more general theory of regulation', *Journal of Law and Economics* 19(2): 211–40.

Riescher, G. (1994) *Zeit und Politik. Zur institutionellen Bedeutung von Zeitstrukturen in parlamentarischen und präsidentiellen Regierungssysteme*, Baden-Baden: Nomos Verlag.

Schindler, P. (1998) *Datenhandbuch zur Geschichte des Deutschen Bundestages 1949–1999*, Baden-Baden: Nomos Verlagsgesellschaft.

Schneider, G. and Aspinwall, M. (2001) 'Institutional research on the European Union: mapping the field', in G. Schneider and M. Aspinwall (eds), *The Rules of Integration: Institutionalist Approaches to the Study of Europe*, Manchester: Manchester University Press.

Schulz, H. and König, T. (2000) 'Institutional reform and decision-making efficiency in the European Union', *American Journal of Political Science* 44(4): 653–66.
Stigler, G. (1971) 'The theory of economic regulation', *Bell Journal of Economic and Management Science* 2: 3–21.
Tsebelis, G. and Garrett, G. (2000) 'Legislative politics in the European Union', *European Union Politics* 1(1): 9–36.
Tsebelis, G. and Garrett, G. (2001) 'The Institutional Foundations of of Intergovernmentalism and Supranationalism in the European Union', *International Organisation* 55(2): 357–90.
Van Schagen, J. (1997) 'The principle of discontinuity and the efficiency of the legislative process', *The Journal of Legislative Studies* 3(4): 115–25.

Uses of time in the EU's enlargement process

Graham Avery

ABSTRACT The instruments of temporality played a key role in driving institutional action and political decision in the process of expansion of the European Union (EU) from 15 to 27 members. The Opinions made by the European Commission in 1997 on the countries of Central and Eastern Europe interpreted for the first time the 'Copenhagen criteria' for EU membership, and by using a 'medium-term' horizon introduced an important time-factor. The 'roadmap' developed by the Commission and approved by the Council of Ministers in 2000 effectively structured the decisive stages of the accession negotiations. In the 'battle of dates' with the applicant countries concerning the prospective timing of their accession, the EU refused to commit itself to a precise date until the last stages of the negotiations. Overall, it used time-factors in such a way that the existing members and the applicant countries were mobilized to reach a timely conclusion.

INTRODUCTION

This paper describes a number of cases of 'temporality' in which I was personally involved in the period 1996–2002 when I was working in the European Commission on the enlargement of the European Union (EU) to include the countries of Central and Eastern Europe.[1] It analyses the way in which time-rules and time-horizons structured and mobilized the process which led to the accession of ten countries to the EU in 2004 and two more in 2007, and it discusses some of the challenges that were encountered in using the time-factor as a device for managing the system.

Since the enlargement of the EU is an ongoing process (at present, seven countries are considered as prospective members, and at least ten others could potentially apply for membership), past experience can and should be instructive for policy-makers. Indeed, an important indicator of the dynamics of the EU's present enlargement policy is the way in which temporality figures in the political and institutional framework for the countries concerned.

The cases considered in this paper are:

1 *The medium term.* By this I refer to the 'medium-term' time-frame employed in the analyses made by the Commission in its Opinions in

1997 on the membership applications from ten Central and Eastern European countries.
2. *The roadmap*. This case concerns the so-called 'roadmap' developed by the Commission in 2000 which effectively structured the accession negotiations up to their conclusion in 2003.
3. *The demand for a date*. This section discusses the dialogue between the applicant countries and the EU concerning the prospective date for accession – the 'battle of dates' – which led finally to the choice of 1 May 2004 as the date for the enlargement from 15 to 25 members.

Having already published some general remarks (Avery and Cameron 1998; Avery 2004) on these cases, I comment on them here in more detail.

1. THE MEDIUM TERM

In 1996 when the Commission began the preparation of its Opinions on the applications for membership from ten countries of Central and Eastern Europe, I was asked to co-ordinate this exercise within the Commission. Together with my colleague Françoise Gaudenzi[2] I led a small team working in the Directorate-General for External Political Relations (DG IA), alongside the larger group in the same DG responsible for bilateral relations with the countries of Central and Eastern Europe and for the management of the EU's programme for financial aid and assistance (PHARE).[3]

Since I had already co-ordinated the Commission's Opinions on Sweden, Finland and Norway in 1992–93,[4] I was not a novice in this field. However, it soon became evident to me that the introduction of accession criteria by the European Council in Copenhagen in 1993 required a more sophisticated analysis than in the past. At Copenhagen the EU's leaders concluded that 'Membership requires:

1. that the candidate country has achieved stability of institutions guaranteeing *democracy*, the *rule of law, human rights* and respect for and protection of *minorities*;
2. the existence of a functioning *market economy* as well as the capacity to cope with competitive pressure and market forces within the Union;
3. and presupposes the candidate's ability to take on the obligations of membership including adherence to the aims of political, economic and *monetary* union.'

Our task was to put these 'Copenhagen criteria' into operational mode in the analyses which we made for the Opinions. None of our team had been involved in the formulation of the criteria,[5] so we approached their interpretation with an open mind. It surprised me to discover that no one in the EU institutions seemed to know what some of these phrases really meant. Although the Copenhagen criteria later assumed an almost biblical status, and created a veritable industry of monitoring reports, between 1993 and 1996 no one seemed to have confronted the question 'what do they mean, and how should we apply them?'.

I realized that for the Opinions on the Central and East European countries the temporal parameters required particular attention. Preceding Opinions had not posed the question 'When will this country meet the criteria for joining the EU?' for before Copenhagen there were no explicit criteria. They addressed rather the question 'What will be the consequences of this country's accession [implicitly, in the short term] and what problems will need to be discussed in accession negotiations?' It is interesting to recall that when the Commission in its 1976 Opinion on Greece took a longer-term view, and proposed a period of preparation before Greek membership, it was rejected by the Council of Ministers.

How therefore to deal with the Copenhagen criteria? I considered that if the Opinions on the Central and East European countries addressed the question 'Do these countries fulfil the conditions for membership at the present time?', the conclusion in every case would surely be 'no', and the exercise would be brief and of limited utility. On the other hand, if they addressed the question 'Will these countries fulfil the conditions at some (unspecified) date in the future?', the conclusion would surely have to be 'yes'. So we developed the idea of assessing the capacity of each country to assume the *acquis* at a specific time in the future. We introduced for this purpose a 'medium-term' horizon, which we defined in a conventional way as five years.[6] Consequently, when in the autumn of 1996 and the spring of 1997 we requested from the other services of the Commission their 'medium-term' evaluations of the applicant countries for each chapter of the *acquis*, we specified 2002 as the time-horizon.

The use of 2002, even as a technical working hypothesis, led to some objections from within the Commission, on the grounds that the year 2000 had recently been mentioned by both Bundeskanzler Kohl and President Chirac in speeches that were understood as signalling to Poland that it could be the year of its accession. Surely the Commission could not risk a disagreement on such a sensitive matter with these political leaders? But as time passed, the year 2002 began to be accepted as a realistic time-horizon: when the accession negotiations began in 1998 they were generally expected to last much longer than the negotiations with Austria, Sweden and Finland (one year) but, it was hoped, less long than those with Spain and Portugal (seven years). Later, 2002 was even considered optimistic, and it was finally abandoned in favour of 2004.

The evaluation of the applicants' capacity to take on the *acquis* within five years was a difficult exercise. But we reckoned that it was feasible, and colleagues in the other services of the Commission took up the challenge in a co-operative way. However, in the case of the 'political' criteria defined at Copenhagen – democracy, human rights, etc. – we decided that it would be an error to attempt an evaluation on a future basis, partly because for such elastic concepts (undefined in the EU's *acquis*) it is impossible to forecast how a country's situation will develop, and partly because by their nature they are in a different class from economic and administrative criteria. Although one could accept conducting accession negotiations with a country whose administrative, legislative and economic standards still require improvement, could one accept doing so with a country that is not yet democratic?

So we decided in the case of the political criteria to make the evaluation on a present basis, and thus we developed the principle that fulfilment of these criteria constitutes a precondition for the opening of accession negotiations. This approach of giving priority to the political criteria over the other Copenhagen criteria was corroborated by the decision at the Amsterdam European Council in June 1997 to modify the Treaty so that respect for democracy and human rights became an explicit condition for countries to apply for membership of the EU.

When the Opinions were finalized in 1997, it seemed to me important to include an explicit mention of the five-year horizon, in order to underpin the credibility of the evaluations. For some of the applicant countries, the Commission was not going to recommend the opening of negotiations, and I knew that 'disappointed' countries would be motivated to challenge our analysis. So I took care to insert in the final text in July 1997 the phrase 'without prejudging the actual date of accession, the Opinion is based on a medium-term time-horizon of approximately five years'. Although the date of 2002 was not cited, it was easy to calculate that it was implied.

This use of temporality had an important place in the development of the EU's approach to enlargement. It encouraged the applicant countries to develop a realistic time-horizon for their accession, and to construct a calendar of preparation. In the 'screening' exercise which followed the opening of negotiations, the countries were required to submit their plans for the implementation of the *acquis*, and naturally they based these plans to a large extent on the working hypothesis of 2002. This activity of planning in turn obliged their administrators and legislators to prepare for accession in a concrete way.

But in the absence of an endorsement of 2002 by the EU as an official objective, the date was soon subject to 'slippage'. Already when the accession negotiations commenced in 1998, Poland and others were basing their accession plans on 2003. Only Hungary, always wanting to be the best pupil in the class, retained 2002 as its target, and even Hungary finally converted its official target date from 1 January 2002 to 31 December 2002.

2. THE ROADMAP

In February 2000 the accession negotiations, which had been proceeding since 1998 with the six countries of the 'Luxembourg' group, were enlarged to include the remaining six applicant countries. This development was not welcome to the countries of the Luxembourg group, who feared that it would slow the process and delay their accession, and they began to demand more dynamism in the negotiations. Already in October 1999 and again in June and November

2000 their foreign ministers urged the EU to accelerate the process and conclude the negotiations in the course of 2001.

The European Council at Feira in June 2000 was a disappointment for them: they had hoped for a commitment to a 'qualitatively new phase', but the EU's leaders only promised to 'maintain the momentum' of negotiations. In fact, for many chapters of the negotiations the EU had not yet developed 'common positions' of substance; it had even fallen into the habit of responding to positions presented by the applicant countries with so-called 'common positions' that were no more than a series of additional questions.[7]

Faced by discontent on the part of the applicant countries, the French Presidency in the second half of 2000 began to talk of introducing a 'roadmap' (*feuille de route*) for the negotiations. They described this idea as 'a scenario without dates' without giving any clearer indication of what its contents might be. It thus fell to the European Commission, in the Strategy Paper which it presented to the Council of Ministers in November 2000, to find a way of making progress. I was one of the team in the Directorate-General for Enlargement which prepared this paper, in which we developed the 'roadmap' for accession negotiations, a concept which subsequently structured the negotiations in a remarkably effective way – even more successfully than we initially expected.

Although it was not a map in the geographic sense, but a timetable or 'action programme' similar in nature to many others invented by the Commission, I personally preferred the use of the term 'roadmap'. I confess that in advocating it I appreciated the paradox that this roadmap was not a map at all, but something else – in fact it was a scenario *with* dates. The fact that a cartographic label disguised its temporal nature perhaps contributed to its acceptance by the Council of Ministers.

What the Commission proposed was for the EU to commit itself to complete its 'common positions' for all of the remaining chapters in the accession negotiations over the next three periods of six months – that is, during three successive Presidencies of the Council. We tried to distribute the chapters over the three periods in a balanced way: although the 'ultimate' chapters of budget and institutional questions, which traditionally figure in the last stage of accession negotiations, were left until the third period, we also put some difficult chapters in the earlier periods. For example, the environment chapter, in which the applicant countries faced many problems and had requested long transitional periods, was put in the first six months of 2001.

The plan included no indication of timing for accession, but stated for the first time that the negotiations could be concluded 'by the end of 2002' with countries that made sufficient progress.[8] It did not commit the EU to closing chapters by the dates specified, only to presenting common positions; on receiving these positions the applicant countries would have to decide whether to accept them, or prolong the negotiations by further discussion. The concept thus maintained pressure on the applicant countries, but also gave them the hope that progress could be made within the time-frame proposed.

It has often been remarked that the most arduous and time-consuming part of an accession negotiation is not the negotiation with the applicant countries but the process of arriving at a common position of the EU member states – and this is not really surprising, since obtaining agreement on common positions among numerous member states is more complicated than decisions on positions by individual applicant countries who do not need (or want) to concert among themselves. In this context, the Commission's roadmap inserted an essential discipline into the accession negotiations by committing the member states to agree on positions by given dates. Within the Commission itself, the roadmap also provided a needed discipline, for the task of preparing proposals for all the chapters of the negotiations required important technical and political input from the Commissioners and services responsible for the areas concerned.

In finalizing our proposal we consulted the other Commissioners and services of the Commission, but we did not have time to consult informally the member states, and in particular the three states who would take over the Presidency of the Council in the period covered by the roadmap. Personally I expected problems as a result of this non-consultation, and I thought that the proposal would be modified and probably diluted in discussions in the Council. But I was wrong. The only significant hesitations came from Spain, which was concerned that the roadmap included for its six-month Presidency some difficult dossiers such as regional policy in which Spain had particular national interests. But these hesitations in Madrid were brief, and the Council gave its agreement to the roadmap without change in December 2000. This rapid approval of the roadmap was an important step forward in the enlargement process; the Commissioner for Enlargement Günter Verheugen declared it to be 'the best day since he came to office'.

Although there was later some slippage in the programme, particularly in the first half of 2002, the roadmap successfully structured the accession negotiations and ensured that they concluded within the next two years. The positioning of the budgetary chapter in the last phase of the roadmap – the first half of 2002 – was a significant element in mobilizing the 'end-game' of the negotiations, for it obliged the EU to bring on to the table a concrete date for accession. The reason why the budgetary chapter is handled towards the end – sometimes at the very end – of accession negotiations is not only because financial questions are of capital importance, but also because budgetary receipts and payments have a 'temporal' character. Whereas most chapters of an accession negotiation can be discussed – or even closed – without commitment to a specific date of accession, negotiators cannot seriously address the budgetary questions without using a concrete date of accession, at least as a working hypothesis, for calculating the budgetary impact of enlargement. Once that date is on the table, it is likely to trigger the conclusive phase of negotiations. Thus the budgetary chapter placed at the end of the roadmap acted as a kind of delayed-release detonator or 'time-bomb' for the conclusion of the negotiations.

A particularly effective aspect of the roadmap was that it gave a sense of 'ownership' to successive Presidencies: the contents of the roadmap became part of their own agenda, motivating them to complete it by the end of their six-month period. 'Action programmes' typically define targets on an annual basis, or over longer periods, but in this case the decision to divide the programme into periods of six months was inspired, for it gave each successive Presidency, as a principal actor on the EU side, an incentive to push for progress. It became a matter of pride, and of friendly rivalry between Presidencies, to fulfil the roadmap's objectives.

3. THE DEMAND FOR A DATE

Here I consider the positions taken during the enlargement process by the applicant countries, on the one hand, and the EU, on the other hand, on the future date of accession. While the Central and Eastern European applicants frequently demanded an indication of the date, the EU – or at least the EU's Council of Ministers – consistently refused to give it.

Romano Prodi, when he took office as President of the Commission in September 1999, declared that one of his principal aims was to ensure that the first accessions took place before the end of his Commission's mandate (scheduled for January 2005), an aim to which he contributed as President by supporting the enlargement process. Within the Commission he consistently supported the work of his Enlargement Commissioner, Günter Verheugen, who said presciently in September 1999 that 2004 was 'the most reasonable and realistic date for the first accession'.

Nevertheless, the EU's Council of Ministers refused to confirm any date, and the Commission prudently expressed itself in terms of aspiration rather than commitment. The applicant countries often argued that in the absence of a clear date for accession they could not be expected to implement difficult and costly parts of the *acquis*, and that a firm date was necessary to oblige their domestic ministers and ministries to take the necessary action.

I recall several occasions when, as a representative of the Commission, I was confronted by pleas and reproaches, in public and in private, from applicant countries on the theme 'you must give us a date'. I replied that, while I sympathized with their argument for a date to drive forward the domestic preparation for membership, my practical experience of public administration led me to believe that the contrary would be the result. In response to a date for accession announced by the EU, even an 'indicative' date hedged by all sorts of qualifications, the authorities of an applicant country would normally relax, rather than reinforce, their efforts of preparation.

It may seem counter-intuitive that the setting of a clear date and timetable would cause an applicant country to relax, while uncertainty would cause it to try harder to meet the EU's requirements. But game theory provides confirmation that in a bargaining situation the strategic use of uncertainty by one actor can cause another actor to concede more than he wants. From the point of view of the applicant countries, the continuing uncertainty concerning the date of accession posed a threat which according to game theory could be interpreted in different ways: when the EU fixed a date, would it be too near, or too distant, or alternatively would it never fix a date? Of these three possibilities, the first and the last could be considered rather unlikely. On the one hand, the concerns of the EU's existing members about the budgetary cost of enlargement, and about the economic and social consequences of accepting inadequately prepared new members, made them much more prone to delay than to accelerate the timetable. On the other hand, they had already made a sufficiently clear political engagement to the principle of enlargement to make indefinite delay unrealistic. So neither the threat of being admitted too soon, nor the threat of never being admitted, was pertinent.

The most credible threat for an applicant country, in case of non-compliance with the EU's requirements, was that the date of its accession would be delayed until after the accession of another applicant country; in other words, that it would not be in the 'first wave' of enlargement. The often-repeated principle of 'differentiation', according to which each country's path to membership depended on its progress in meeting the criteria, and the competitive nature of the process involving 12 applicant countries, was thus an important factor. The absence of any predetermined grouping for accession, on political or geographic grounds, meant that none of the applicants could be sure that they would not be left behind.

Speculation on the date of enlargement was naturally linked to the question of which group of countries would be included in a first wave. Among the member states, the idea of a rapid enlargement to include a small group of well-prepared countries – perhaps as few as three – was sometimes mentioned, for example by Austria. The applicant countries who were most confident of their good preparation, such as Hungary, Slovenia and Estonia, gave quiet support to this scenario, while commentators often saw Poland as being at risk of being left behind; it was believed by some that Poland had sought and even obtained an assurance from its powerful neighbour Germany that there would be no first wave without them, but the Poles denied this. Although the press was already speculating by the end of 2000 on a 'big-bang' scenario for enlargement to bring in as many as ten countries in 2005 or 2006, the EU institutions argued that it was premature to decide, and that the choice would be made on objective criteria.[9] This official uncertainty on the part of the EU concerning the date and composition of the future enlargement had the effect of maintaining pressure on the applicant countries.

This question of when and how the date of accession is fixed is crucially important for the exercise of the conditionality of enlargement. It lies at the heart of the 'magic' employed by the accession process in driving change and reform, and in enabling the EU's 'transformative power'. To what extent and in what way should the EU give a promise of accession? On the one hand, unless the EU maintains the credibility of the accession perspective, its conditionality is ineffective; on the other hand, if it gives a promise (or is believed to give a promise) of a specific date, the conditionality is diminished. How to ensure that the question is not '*whether* the applicant country will join' but '*when* it will join', without actually giving an answer to the question *when*? What is the correct solution to this puzzle of temporality?

The EU solved the puzzle rather well during the accession process with the Central and East European countries. It gave sufficient reassurances – first by the 'working hypothesis' of 2002 used in the Opinions, which drove timetables for domestic preparation by the applicant countries, and then by the 'roadmap', which became the timetable for the accession negotiations – but it never officially conceded a date for accession until the last stages of the process.[10]

Interestingly, it was another EU institution – neither Commission nor Council – which was the first to take a clear position in favour of 2004. The European Parliament is normally kept distant from the quintessentially intergovernmental activity of enlargement, but it entered the arena in the autumn of 2000 by voting in favour of the accession of new members in time to take part in the next elections to the Parliament in June 2004.

For a long time the Council continued to refuse to be drawn into precision on the date of accession, relying on the Delphic formula that the Union would be 'ready to welcome new members from 2002 onwards'. In January 2002 the Commission proposed a financial package for the accession negotiations based on the hypothesis that ten new members would join on 1 January 2004, but this remained a hypothesis for discussion, not a common position, and it was only in November 2002 that the Council took a clear decision in favour of a date. At this point the idea emerged that the date could be delayed by four months to 1 May 2004: this delay was ostensibly to allow more time for ratification of the Accession Treaty, but in reality it was part of the solution devised for the budgetary chapter, for it allowed the new members to pay less into the budget in their first year of membership (payments for only eight months) but to obtain receipts corresponding to a full 12 months.[11]

Thus it was decided that the EU's enlargement from 15 to 25 members would finally take place on 1 May 2004. I conclude this section with a personal anecdote of a temporal nature. The process of enlargement to Central and Eastern Europe was not often marked by humour, so the rare moments of amusement were particularly appreciated by those involved. In a speech at a conference in Hungary's Parliament in Budapest in 1996 I declared that, after consulting my crystal ball, I could announce the date when Hungary would join the EU. 'It will be,' I said, 'on the first of January: you can be sure of that, because every accession before now has taken place on the first of January.' After a pause I continued, 'but if you want to know the year, you will have to wait a bit longer.' Knowing the Hungarian genius for science and mathematics, I was not surprised when one of my Hungarian friends retorted: 'Of course we know perfectly well when our accession will take place. We are going to join the EU in five years' time. We Hungarians are *always* going to join the EU in five years' time.' Finally, the accession of Hungary took place on 1 May 2004, so in the end the joke turned against me.[12]

4. CONCLUDING REMARKS

Such were the uses of time and 'temporality' in the sequence of events which led to the EU's enlargement of 2004. The EU institutions used time-factors in such a way that both the existing members and the applicant countries were mobilized to reach a timely conclusion. However, they also maintained a prudent room for manoeuvre, since experience with timetables shows that, although they can mobilize the decision-making process, they can have a negative impact if events in the real world cause deadlines to be missed, with resulting disappointment and loss of credibility.

Many other aspects of temporality merit examination in the context of the EU's enlargement process. For example, the nature, significance, and relative importance of the various 'transitional measures' agreed between the EU and the applicant countries – after all, such temporal measures are the principal subject-matter of accession negotiations. Another question is the relative length of time needed for enlargement. In the case of the 2004 enlargement, the overall process from application to accession[13] occupied ten years and one month, of which the accession negotiations occupied four years and ten months. Was this duration justified (too short? too long?)? How can it be compared with other enlargements? These are interesting questions, but adequate analysis of them would require another paper.[14]

I conclude therefore with:

- a remark on 'temporality' in the current round of accession negotiations with Croatia and Turkey;
- a brief reflection on how the three cases described in this paper may contribute to a theoretical analysis of the EU timescape.

Current accession negotiations

If we consider the current accession negotiations, we see that there is (as yet) no roadmap for Croatia or Turkey, and a marked reluctance on the part of the EU to introduce the dimension of 'temporality' into the process. The only date of accession in public discourse has been the self-determined aim of Croatia to join the EU by mid-2009, in time to participate in the next elections for the European Parliament. However, in the light of progress in the accession negotiations, this date is no longer feasible.

As for Turkey, the statements made at the opening of their accession negotiations in 2005, that the negotiations are 'open-ended' and could last 10–15 years, show that the concept of 'temporality' for this applicant country is of a different nature from any preceding case. Indeed, the credibility of the traditional method of enlargement is put in question by the case of Turkey, since – taking up the analysis from game theory discussed in an earlier section of this paper – one can see that the incentive for Turkey to meet the EU's requirements for membership is severely reduced by the risk that the EU may never concede a date for Turkey to join.

Theoretical aspects

Viewed from the perspective of theory, what lessons can be learned from the three cases discussed in this paper? What do they tell us about the categories 'performance, power, and legitimacy' proposed by Goetz and Meyer-Sahling (2009) for analysis of the EU's timescape?

Clearly, the uses of time in the EU's enlargement process discussed in this paper had little to do with legitimacy, and were mainly related to the dimension of performance. They were designed to drive the process of enlargement by encouraging the different actors (national governments and EU institutions) to perform in various ways.

By employing the 'medium-term' time-frame in its Opinions on the applicant countries the Commission introduced a temporal dimension into the interpretation of the Copenhagen criteria, and created a first working hypothesis for the date of accession – implicitly, the year 2002. Although this date was never adopted as an official target on the EU side, and the technical nature of the time-frame was underlined in the Opinions, it nevertheless served as a proxy for a target date, and induced the applicant countries to base their initial planning for implementation of the *acquis* on the same time-horizon. It thus helped to mobilize national administrations to prepare for EU membership in a practical and concrete way. Despite the fact that a different date – 2004 – was finally decided for enlargement, the working hypothesis of 2002 was undoubtedly effective in terms of performance, for it facilitated effective planning and co-ordination on the part of the applicant countries.

By contrast, the 'roadmap' employed in the accession negotiations was designed as a timetable to commit the EU Council of Ministers to reach agreement on common positions by certain dates. Since it was officially and publicly endorsed by the Council, it operated as a self-discipline for the EU side, and its effectiveness in terms of performance was reinforced by the way in which it encouraged successive Presidencies to respect the timetable. It thus effectively facilitated planning and co-ordination on the part of the EU institutions – not only the Council, but also the Commission.

The refusal of the EU to concede a date for accession until the final stage of the negotiations was likewise linked to performance, in the sense that – as explained in this paper – the uncertainty of the date was essential to the logic of conditionality and differentiation underlying the enlargement process. Following the EU's endorsement at Copenhagen in 1993 of the ultimate aim of bringing in the countries of Central and Eastern Europe, the basic question remaining was not whether these countries would join, but when. The aim of the applicant countries can be summarized as 'the sooner the better' since for political and economic reasons they wanted to join the EU as soon as possible. But this was not the position of the existing members, who feared that the EU's functioning would be disrupted if it admitted countries which did not comply with the Copenhagen criteria for membership – criteria which had been designed mainly for reasons of prudence (protection of the EU from risks of premature enlargement) rather than altruism (improvement of conditions in the acceding countries). The EU's aim can thus be summarized as 'better a well-prepared accession than a rapid one', and from this point of view it can be seen that, although the temporal instruments served to drive the enlargement process, they did not necessarily accelerate it.

These reflections on the performance-related aspects of the use of time in the enlargement process also demonstrate that the dimension of power was always present. Throughout the process, the timetable and other temporal elements were largely controlled by the EU, rather than the applicant countries. Of the three cases examined, only the 'roadmap' afforded a degree of temporal power to the applicant countries, in the sense that it constrained the EU side to comply with a timetable that assisted the applicants' aim of concluding the accession negotiations within a reasonable time. But even in this case, the EU took care to define the temporal rules in such a way that its obligation under the timetable was limited to presenting its negotiating positions for certain chapters by certain dates; there was no obligation for the EU to conclude agreement with the other side on these chapters, so that once the EU had tabled its positions, the pressure was on the applicant countries to make concessions.

This overview of the power dimension shows that the timescape was subject to the general rule that the process of enlargement, and particularly of accession negotiations, tends to be asymmetrical in nature – a feature which follows from the fact that it is not the existing members, but the prospective members, who are applying to join the club. The clearest example of this asymmetry is that in accession negotiations an applicant country is asked to accept and apply all the EU's rules, without exception or modification, and the scope of negotiations is limited to agreement on possible delays of application or 'transitional measures'. For the temporal aspects of the enlargement process, the distribution of power between the existing members of the EU, on the one hand, and the applicant countries, on the other hand, means that it is the EU that normally determines the parameters of the timescape.

Biographical note: Graham Avery is Honorary Director General of the European Commission[15] and Senior Member of St Antony's College, University of Oxford, UK.

NOTES

1 During my career in public service I was involved in successive enlargements: on the British side I worked in London in the Ministry of Agriculture, Fisheries and Food as a junior member of the team for the accession negotiations (1969–72), and later in Brussels I served in various capacities in the European Commission (1973–2006) including as Director of the Task Force for Enlargement in DG I which prepared a report for the Lisbon European Council (1992), Director for Relations with Austria,

Sweden, Finland, Norway, Iceland and Switzerland in DG I (1992–93), Director and Negotiator with Austria in the Task Force for Enlargement (1993–94), Chief Adviser for enlargement in DG IA responsible for co-ordinating the Opinions on the applications for membership from ten Central and East European countries (1996–98), Chief Adviser for strategic questions in the DG for Enlargement (2000–02), and then as Fellow at the European University Institute, Florence (2002–03) where I piloted the report of Wim Kok on EU enlargement.

2 I take this occasion to pay a personal tribute to the work of Françoise Aubier-Gaudenzi, later the European Commission's negotiator with Poland, who died in March 2004 just before the enlargement of which she was an architect.

3 'Poland and Hungary: Assistance for the Reconstruction of the Economy' – an English phrase giving the acronym PHARE which means 'beacon': an elegant example of a multilingual acronym.

4 I also co-ordinated the preparation of the draft Opinion on Switzerland's application for EU membership, but it never saw the light of day because the Swiss application was withdrawn after the 'no' in their referendum on the European Economic Area.

5 How the criteria were decided at the European Council in Copenhagen in 1993 – on the basis of what preparation, and from what sources – is a question that merits fuller research by historians of enlargement. Another episode in the history of enlargement that has not attracted the research which it merits is the 'application for membership' made by Morocco's King Hassan in a letter to the European Community's Council of Ministers in 1987.

6 The choice of five years did not result from any sophisticated political or economic reasoning: it simply seemed a reasonable period to choose, being longer than a 'short term' of two to three years (unrealistic as a hypothesis for the prospective accessions) and shorter than a 'long term' of ten years (impractical for the evaluation of the criteria).

7 Within the Commission these were described irreverently as 'Mickey Mouse positions'.

8 When this position of the Commission was finally confirmed a year later by the European Council at Laeken in December 2001, the way was opened for the end-game of the negotiations.

9 See Avery (2004: 51–2) for an analysis of the situation of the 'laggard' Poland and the 'front-runners' such as Hungary.

10 Subsequently, the European Council in December 2006 confirmed the principle that the EU should not concede a date for accession until the last stages of the process; it stated that 'target dates for accession will not be set until negotiations are close to completion'. Since this principle was followed implicitly in the negotiations for the 2004 enlargement, its explicit articulation by the European Council can hardly be construed as a novelty; it was rather a self-criticism of the conduct of the negotiations for the 2007 enlargement, in which the conditionality for Bulgaria and Romania was weakened by giving the EU's premature promise of accession in 2007, coupled with the (ineffective) threat to delay it to 2008.

11 Preceding and subsequent accessions all took place on 1 January, a date which accords better with the EU's institutional and budgetary timetable: it was commonly believed that the technical and political difficulty of negotiating a subdivision of the annual budget into two periods (pre-accession and post-accession) rendered any other date impossible. But this difficulty was ingeniously avoided by the arrangement devised for 2004 in order to improve the budgetary cash-flow of the new members.

12 Another source of humour in the enlargement process was the 'Candy letters', written by an anonymous Brussels insider and published in Poland by Unia-Polska; see Anon. (1999, 2000).

13 The periods quoted here refer to Hungary and Poland, the first countries to submit their applications; for the other countries which acceded in 2004, the periods were shorter.
14 See, however, the brief commentary in Avery (2004: 59–60 together with the chronology at p. 37).
15 The views expressed here are my own, and not necessarily those of the European Commission.

REFERENCES

Anon. (1999) 'European love letters', *Unia-Polska*, February (available in English at http://www.unia-polska.pl/archive/98-99/9902_2/06_22i.html).

Anon. (2000) 'Candy', *Unia-Polska*, February (available in English at http://www.unia-polska.pl/index.php?id=4&q=116).

Avery, G. (2004) 'The enlargement negotiations 1998–2003', in F. Cameron (ed.), *The Future of Europe: Integration and Enlargement*, London: Routledge, pp. 35–62.

Avery, G. and Cameron, F. (1998) *The Enlargement of the European Union*, Sheffield: Sheffield Academic Press.

Goetz, K.H. and Meyer-Sahling, J.-H. (2009) 'Political time in the EU: dimensions, perspectives, theories', *Journal of European Public Policy* 16(2): 180–201.

Policies, institutions and time: how the European Commission managed the temporal challenge of eastern enlargement

Katja Lass-Lennecke and Annika Werner

ABSTRACT This article examines the relation between policies, institutions and time by addressing the case of eastern enlargement policy and the European Commission. Our main question is how the special challenges and requirements of EU eastern enlargement policy impacted on the administrative level of the Commission, i.e. the level in charge of structuring, monitoring and steering the policy's implementation. We provide empirical data on institutional change in the Commission from the mid-1990s until 2004 and examine temporal categories at both the policy level and the institutional level. This analysis shows that – especially the temporal – requirements of enlargement policy drove the Commission to adapt its internal organization and time management; internal structures and procedures changed; actors were bound in a temporal grid. This allowed the mobilization of the actors and the in-time synchronization of their input. On the whole, our results open a new perspective on institutional change and time in the context of European governance.

1. INTRODUCTION[1]

Analysing the triangle of policies, institutions and time is a novel approach with potential to broaden our understanding of the connection between policies, institutions and institutional change. Our paper applies this perspective to the study of the interdependence of policies and institutions at the level of the European Union (EU) and shows how time, in particular time management, can be a helpful tool to identify the mechanisms of change that are involved.

When thinking about the connection between policies and institutions, the widely analysed direction of cause and effect goes from institution to policy. The reverse approach – analysing the impact of policies on institutions – is still rarely used (one of the few exceptions: Heidbreder 2007). The aim of this paper is, therefore, to find out more about how policies – their goals, requirements and instruments – influence the institutions that are involved in their implementation.

In this inductive case study, we show that the pre-accession policy of the EU's fifth enlargement round in 2004–2007[2] had a distinct effect on the institutional make-up of the Commission. The effect resulted from the enormous policy task at hand. Enlargement towards twelve new member states, ten Central and Eastern European countries (CEECs) and two Mediterranean ones, created major challenges for the candidate countries, the member states and the EU institutions. It required the development and implementation of a comprehensive and integrated policy to manage the task. At the heart of this policy was the European Commission, which had a central role in the preparation and implementation of enlargement policy.

Since the Commission administration was in charge of preparing and implementing enlargement policy (Avery and Cameron 1998), it is made the focus of our analysis of institutional change. In contrast to the widespread focus on the political level – the College of Commissioners and their cabinets – we investigate the administrative level of the Commission. More explicitly, we focus on the reorganization of the internal structures and procedures resulting from the implementation of enlargement policy.[3] For the empirical analysis, we mainly draw on interviews with former and present officials of the Commission who were involved in the enlargement preparations at the level of Heads of Unit, staff of the Co-ordination Unit, country and policy specialists and political advisers.[4]

With a focus on the Commission's administrative level, our analysis is located in the field of literature that deals with network patterns of Commission officials (Suvarierol 2007), general bureaucratic change (e.g. Nugent and Saurugger 2002; Balint *et al.* 2008) and administrative reform (Egeberg 2002; Kassim 2004; Ellinas and Suleiman 2008). Our investigation of administrative change in the Commission in the context of eastern enlargement also complements discussions of the effects of enlargement on the EU institutions *after* the accession, including the internal transformation of the Commission (Best *et al.* 2008). We show that the internal transformation of the Commission had already started during the pre-accession phase due to the policy tasks involved in the preparation of this enlargement round. A similar point is made by Heidbreder (2007) who shows that the Commission expanded some of its policy-making competences by extending enlargement-specific policy instruments such as conditionality to certain fields of general policy-making.

In our analysis, we focus on time-related issues of enlargement policy and regard changes in the Commission's internal time management as a sign of institutional change. 'Time' as a general category has so far received little attention in political science research. Most work concentrates on 'politics in time' (Riescher 1994; Pierson 2004) or addresses time constraints in democracies (Linz 1998; Schedler and Santiso 1998). Time management has been neglected in political science analyses but it is more prominent in the field of business management (Das 1991). Change in patterns of time management, however, is a promising focus for the observation of institutional change in the case of the Commission and eastern enlargement policy because time played a central role at the levels of both the policy and the institution. The policy comprised several temporal challenges such as the in-time mobilization of actors and the temporal synchronization of their actions. To deal with them, the Commission referred to a large extent to means of managing time.

The paper is structured as follows. The next section introduces the independent variable enlargement policy, its embedded challenges and requirements for the Commission. The focus will be directed at the temporal aspects of enlargement policy. The third section addresses the dependent variable, concentrating on the impact of the temporal policy challenges and requirements on the institution. The changes in the Commission's internal structure and procedures between the mid-1990s and 2004 are investigated and assessed in connection with the overall question. The final section discusses the implications of our findings for the study of the 'EU timescape' (Meyer-Sahling and Goetz 2009) and for theories of institutional change.

2. THE TEMPORAL CHALLENGE OF EU EASTERN ENLARGEMENT

The preparation of eastern enlargement presented a complex and far-reaching task. It was not only demanding for the countries seeking to join, but also for the EU itself (Mayhew 1998; Grabbe and Hughes 1998; Avery and Cameron 1998; Nugent 2004). Several challenges had to be dealt with by the EU institutions.

Most of these challenges arose from the characteristics of the candidates. First, the sheer number of candidates reached a new level. The EU had to monitor and steer accession preparations of 12 candidate countries at the same time. This process took more than ten years and posed high demands on the EU to structure and to set clear rules for the involvement of all actors in each phase. Another difficulty was the considerable discrepancy between the candidate countries and the EU-15 concerning their level of development (Phinnemore 1999). For the EU, it required high capacity and new procedures to monitor reform progress and to encourage the candidates over time. This was also a temporal challenge for the EU institutions and their internal organization because they had to deal with a process that needed – at times – fast interventions and co-ordinated answers.

There were additional issues that created major challenges for the EU institutions. The EU-15 had set two obligations 'to ensure that no applicant would enter the EU unless it met demanding entry terms' (Nugent 2004: 46): the fulfilment of the political accession criteria of the Copenhagen Council 1993 and the complete transfer of the body of EU law, the *acquis*. The progress of the candidates in meeting these obligations had to be continuously monitored and assured by the EU institutions. However, the political criteria were rather vague and lacked comparable measurement standards.

Moreover, the legal body of the EU had grown vastly in the course of European integration, especially in the 1990s. The *acquis* comprised some 80,000 pages (Grabbe 2002: 252), which had to be structured, transferred and supervised to be legally implemented in the candidate countries.[5]

Furthermore, the EU had no overall plan or timetable for enlargement. Enlargement preparations were constantly accompanied by political quarrels and a lack of consensus at the EU's political level. For example, several European Council summits were not able to bring about an agreement on major institutional and policy reforms that many experts agreed on as being necessary (Grabbe and Hughes 1998: 103ff.; Nugent 2004: 47ff.). Thus, various time-related conflicts arose in the day-to-day policy process, where the timing, sequence, speed and duration of the single steps on the path to accession were the result of 'intense conflict, bargaining and negotiations' (Goetz 2009). Issues such as the timing and sequencing of the opening of negotiation chapters; timetables for the transposition of EU law; or the time and speed of domestic institutional and policy reforms arose constantly. Those issues had to be solved – despite the missing specifications from the political level. To reach progress at the practical level, adequate concepts and a plan of successive steps were needed.

Taken together, these circumstances presented an enormous challenge for the EU, in particular a temporal challenge to manage a complex process over time and to activate and synchronize all relevant actors. It required an effective approach of all EU institutions in terms of internal organization, communication and co-ordination with internal and external actors, and the monitoring and steering of the process. The policy had to be highly structured, especially in terms of time, and a clear time-frame was needed to drive the process forward.

The Commission was the main EU institution faced with these tasks. The European Council, the Council of Ministers and, to a lesser degree, the European Parliament took the grand political decisions. Yet the Commission was in charge of all technical preparations and had to manage the day-to-day policy process (Cameron 1997; Christoffersen 2007; Vassiliou 2007; Avery 2009). Thus, it had to deal with the above mentioned challenges and find adequate answers.

These answers had to be open to decisions of European Council summits, which influenced the Commission's agenda for pre-accession policy. The most relevant Council decisions were taken, first, at the Copenhagen summit 1993, which defined accession criteria impacting on the direction and speed of the whole accession process; then the Luxembourg summit of 1997 decided to open accession negotiations with six candidate countries; and the Helsinki summit of 1999 added the negotiations with further six candidates; finally, the Rome summit of 2003 officially ended the negotiation process with the signing of the Acts of Accession. All of these decisions set a framework for the actions of the Commission by continuously defining new conditions that the Commission had to deal with in the day-to-day policy process.

What did the Commission do? It translated the policy requirements into concrete policy devices and thereby tried to make the temporal challenges of the pre-accession phase manageable. These devices comprised: the medium-term perspective; the regular progress reports; the roadmap; no precision on an accession date; and transition periods for the implementation of the *acquis*. All of them included strong temporal components. However, their purpose differed. The first three instruments were set up to steer the enlargement process and to create certainty for the involved actors. By contrast, the latter two served to use time flexibly in order to solve some of the main problems of enlargement. Time was thus a major resource of the Commission in the enlargement process (Goetz and Meyer-Sahling 2009).

How did the Commission's devices work? The starting point for all following instruments was the 'medium-term perspective' in the Commission's formal Opinions on EU membership of the candidates in 1996 (published in 1997). By defining 2002 as a technical working hypothesis for accession, it gave a first time-frame for the upcoming five years of enlargement preparations. The advantages were twofold. On the one hand, the time perspective offered the Commission's administration a first temporal parameter for the evaluation of the accession criteria that the European Council had defined in 1993. On the other hand, it encouraged the candidates to 'develop a realistic time-horizon for their accession, and to construct a calendar' for their activities and it 'obliged [the national] administrators and legislators to prepare for accession in a concrete way' (Avery 2009: 255).

As a second instrument with strong time components, the Commission introduced 'regular reports' on the progress of each candidate country in 1999. They annually assessed the candidate's achievements in meeting the Copenhagen criteria and included explicit and implicit timetables for single policies and their implementation. The results of these reports became quite influential; they laid the ground for the political decisions of the December European Councils and supported the EU in identifying its priorities and in monitoring their implementation in the candidate states. Thus, the reports became a 'key mechanism' for the 'soft conditionality power' of the EU towards the candidates (Grabbe 2002: 261). They stimulated a competition for progress between the candidates (Grabbe 2002: 262) and generated political debates (Grabbe and Hughes 1999), where especially opposition parties could attack undemocratic government practices on the basis of the reports (Barysch and Grabbe 2002: 10).

Third, in 2000 the Commission proposed a 'roadmap' (*feuille de route*) to structure the accession negotiations until 2002. After repeated requests from the first six candidates in negotiations since 1998 not to delay the process after the decision of the 1999 Helsinki European Council to enlarge the group to 12 from 2000 on, the Commission developed a timetable for the completion of all remaining chapters until mid-2002. In a Strategy Paper for the Council of Ministers in November 2000, it provided a 'scenario with dates' (Avery 2009) for the negotiations, which was 'the first real attempt to guide the negotiations towards a conclusion in a not too distant future' (Mayhew 2000: 42). This was necessary at this point to maintain the speed of the negotiation process, which had started to slow down (Inotai 2003: 89).

Installing a roadmap helped to bring 'an essential discipline into the accession negotiations by committing the member states to agree on positions by given dates.'(Avery 2009: 256) It forced them to complete their Common Positions for all remaining chapters during the three following Council Presidencies and provided a clear timetable for the Commission's preparation of the Draft Common Positions for the Council meetings. As a further accelerating momentum, the plan gave 'a sense of "ownership" to the successive Presidencies: the contents of the roadmap became part of their own agenda, motivating them to complete it by the end of their six-month period' (Avery, 2009: 258).

In sum this group of policy devices helped the EU institutions to steer the pre-accession process and provided a grid for the actors to plan their actions. The roadmap in particular contained a momentum of flexibility, laying out a plan – with fixed sequences – for the accession negotiations, but no detailed timetable in order to give the EU some leeway as to when exactly to open and close chapters. This gave the EU some discretion in the process.

A second group of instruments was more explicitly characterized by providing flexibility and the possibility to use time strategically. The first tool can be described as 'no precision on an official accession date' by the EU until the last stages of the negotiation process. The candidate countries continuously demanded such a date and argued that a higher degree of certainty would considerably facilitate the implementation of difficult parts of the *acquis* (Mayhew 2000: 45). The Commission, however, was worried that any precise date would weaken the EU's conditionality power and that 'the authorities of an applicant country would normally relax, rather than reinforce, their efforts of preparation' (Avery 2009: 256). Hence, time was used by the superior side to maintain incentives for the inferior side and to enhance its conditionality power (Schimmelfennig and Sedelmeier 2004). Following this logic, the Council officially gave the accession date of 2004 only in November 2002, being aware that this commitment diminished the effectiveness of EU conditionality.[6]

The last temporal instruments examined here are the so-called 'transition periods' which delayed the obligation for the new member states to apply the full EU *acquis* at the moment of accession. Transition periods were individually negotiated for difficult policy areas and included a timetable for implementation after accession (Homeyer *et al.* 2000: 349f.). They were crucial to allow the accession of ten candidate countries at the EU's political target date in 2004. Without this temporal flexibility, the pre-accession stage would presumably have lasted much longer and contained more difficult negotiations.[7]

As this overview shows, the policy instruments helped the Commission in the pre-accession phase to address the challenge of steering the enlargement process and of mobilizing and synchronizing all relevant actors. Their strong time components supported the Commission in its task to structure, monitor and control progress, and to preserve the power of conditionality. At the same time, the instruments imposed a clear structure and temporal rules on both the candidates and the EU institutions. But how did this impact on the Commission administration itself? This is examined in the following section.

3. MANAGING TIME IN THE COMMISSION

As the last section demonstrated, eastern enlargement preparations comprised specific challenges with regard to the management of time. These conditions required temporally tightly structured policy means and also profound organizational answers of the EU's administration, especially the Commission. It had to adapt in order to meet its policy goal: the successful accession of all candidate countries. This section shows that the resulting changes were both structural and procedural.

The Commission normally deals with new tasks, as one would expect from a bureaucracy with established administrative structures and routines: by using existing structures and procedures (Balint *et al.* 2008: 678). Resistance to change is common in most, if not all, administrations and is promoted by a preference for bureaucratic stability. It is not surprising to see a similar development in the Commission, at least until the downfall of the Santer Commission in 1999 and the subsequent Kinnock reforms (Bauer 2008: 628ff.). Until then, the Commission bureaucracy was rooted in institutional choices of the 1950s (Balint *et al.* 2008: 677) and its track record of institutional reform was poor (Bauer 2008; Peterson 2008).

The reluctance of the Commission to make lasting changes also applied during earlier enlargements. Until 1999, the Commission customarily established an internal temporary task force. It consisted of staff from the 'line Directorate-Generals (DGs)', i.e. the DGs dealing with special policy fields like DG Agriculture, DG Transport, etc. After the task was completed the members of the task force went back to their respective DGs (Interview 6). The tasks at hand were addressed by turning to procedures that were well established in the Commission or by adopting ad hoc measures, which did not become lasting routines. As a result, previous enlargements did not cause enduring structural and procedural change. This was different in the case of eastern enlargement.

Parallel to the preparation of the eastern enlargement, the Kinnock reforms proceeded and profoundly changed the Commission. But the changes that we are tracing here to enlargement policy are not connected to this reform programme. Neither the attempt of the Kinnock reform to develop the Commission towards a 'culture based on service', nor the attempt to effectively allocate and use resources on prioritized policy outputs, improve financial management or modernize human resource policy (Ellinas and Suleiman 2008: 710f.) can explain the changes that are assessed in this article.

Structural changes within the Commission: the Directorate-General for Enlargement and the 'matrix system'

When the Commission started to deal with eastern enlargement in the early 1990s, it had experience with similar projects and had a tried and tested workflow, which was initially also applied in this case. During the course of the 1990s, however, the Commission had to change its structure to deal with the challenges inherent to the task at hand and to provide the structural means for efficient time management.

After the Commission created some dispersed internal structures to deal with the CEECs in the early 1990s, several single units were combined in DG 1A in 1995. This DG was responsible for financial assistance as well as the negotiations and management of bilateral agreements. Then the European Council in Luxemburg 1997 decided to set up a separate task force to start the preparations for enlargement following the traditional approach of all previous enlargement rounds. The logic behind this step was not to mix politics and finance. 'When the negotiations were opened, we preferred to see the two processes separated. One which was . . . to pursue the relationship linked to aid and to the reconstruction of the economies of these countries. And then the classic enlargement negotiations . . .' (Interview 3).

However, some Commission officials would have preferred the creation of a special DG that covered both aspects already in 1997, for two reasons (Interviews 3, 7). First, the separate structures demanded a high level of co-operation and co-ordination. It quickly emerged that '[i]ntra-organisational conflict gave the impression of sub-optimal preparation' (Bellier 2004: 140). Second, it turned out that the potential additional advantages of connecting negotiations and financial assistance were extensive. The complexity of the process demanded an integrated organization. 'The challenge of the enlargement to CEE was that . . . the whole legal, administrative and the economic structure had to change' (Interview 7). Therefore, the assistance needed to be streamlined to support reforms in the candidate countries and to promote negotiations. For these reasons and because of the Helsinki decision to open negotiations with six additional countries, which again raised the complexity of the task, the Commission adapted its structure by setting up the Directorate-General Enlargement (DG ELARG) in 1999. The changeover from the Santer to the Prodi Commission was regarded as a good opportunity to introduce a new structure (Interview 3). In other words, the creation of DG ELARG reflects the influence of policy requirements on the Commission administration's internal structure.

An additional structural reaction to the need to adapt the institution was the invention of the so-called 'matrix system'. This system was a novel way to distribute responsibilities at the level of a DG's units and was introduced to deal with the complexity of the eastern enlargement task: the large number of countries and policy areas and the interrelated need to mobilize and co-ordinate the necessary expertise. For every candidate country one unit was set up in which one group of officials was responsible for that particular country. For instance, within unit 'Cyprus' a team dealt with the accession of Cyprus. This team, the so-called 'country desk', monitored the development of all chapters within the respective candidate and was in direct contact with national actors. At the same time, these units also contained one to three 'chapter desks', depending on the size of the negotiation chapters to be supervised. The chapter desks were responsible for monitoring the developments of their respective negotiation chapter, i.e. policy field, in all candidate countries. The unit for Cyprus, for instance, included the team that dealt with the free movement of services (Interview 5).

The advantage of this structure was seen in the co-operation of country and chapter desks when it came to the preparation of regular reports and Draft Common Positions (DCPs) for the accession negotiations (for the detailed DCP procedures see Mayhew 2000: 70). As Figure 1 illustrates, the double-heading allowed the combination of two views: one with expertise on the candidate country and one with expertise on the individual chapter. For the preparation of the regular reports, the responsible country and chapter desk met under the heading of the country desk. For the creation of the DCPs, the chapter desk exchanged views with all those officials responsible for the respective chapter in the country desks.

In relation to other parts of the Commission, this new system increased the independence of DG ELARG from the line DGs. 'The idea is that you have in each geographical unit within DG Enlargement one person who has more expertise than the general external relations knowledge' (Interview 6). During the process of preparing the regular reports and the DCPs, DG ELARG still had to rely on contributions from line DGs but had a stronger position in case of disagreements since it had its own policy experts (Interview 6).

In general the 'matrix system' is different from the normal working style within the Commission. Regular working routines are similar to other bureaucracies, with folders moving up and down the internal DG hierarchy and with inter-DG co-ordination at higher (and informally also at lower) levels (Cini 1996; Nugent 2001). Therefore, what was established in DG ELARG

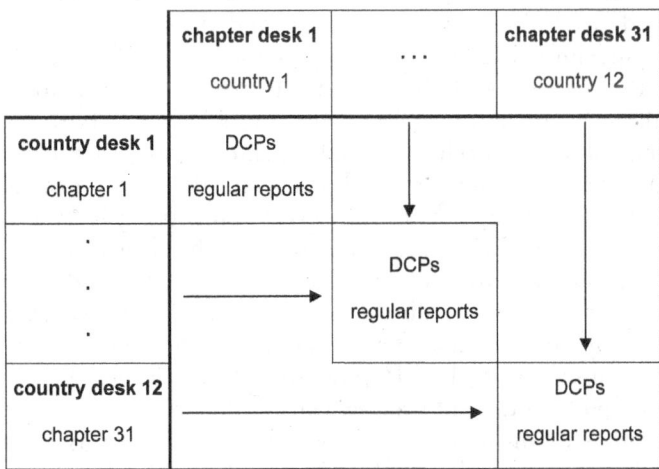

Figure 1 Co-operation between country desks and chapter desks for preparation of Draft Common Positions and regular reports
Source: Authors' compilation.

was an effective way of combining specialization and co-ordination of expertise. The future will tell whether this model will be exported to other parts of the Commission or remain a policy-specific experiment.

Procedural changes: management by temporal grid

In addition to the structural changes, the Commission also introduced new procedures to meet the special demands of eastern enlargement policy. To fulfil the task of mobilizing all actors within the Commission's services and to ensure the right timing of their input, procedures with strong time components were established. They created a 'temporal grid' of strict timetables, sanctioned deadlines and fixed sequences for the different internal and external inputs.

The internal procedures for the preparation of the annual regular reports are a good example of changes which were a response to particular policy requirements. The reports were one of the main pre-accession policy instruments and their preparation was one of the central tasks of DG ELARG. The reports influenced the speed and timing of opening and closing chapters in the accession negotiations and prepared the political decisions at the European Council's December summits. Thus, they had to be comprehensive and coherent. Moreover, they had to be delivered at a particular time: every year in the middle of November. Given these demands, this policy tool illustrates well how the requirement of the policy for successful time management impacted upon the Commission's internal temporal setting.

An innovation in enlargement policy, the procedures for the regular reports were established in 1999 and have changed only marginally up to today (Interviews 7, 11).[8] The procedures were fixed in detailed internal 'Guidelines for the Regular Report', which were developed by the Co-ordination Unit of DG ELARG and determined the sequence of and deadlines for the individual steps. The guidelines listed the accession criteria and different sub-headings of the *acquis* that had to be dealt with and their main task was to schedule all stages in the work process and list all the actors involved. Furthermore, they set temporal rules for mobilization and synchronization, especially deadlines, and thereby created a strong temporal pattern for the work on eastern enlargement. The time planning took place each year in the spring and was a backward counting process: the Commissioner would set the final deadline when the reports had to be forwarded to the Council and from this date on the Co-ordination Unit set exact deadlines (Interviews 3, 10). These deadlines were strict cut-off days and sanctioned any delay with a loss of influence.

The process usually started on 15 June when the candidates' governments had to submit a report about their achievements in the previous 12 months. At the same time, the Commission's delegations had to send their assessments based on their own monitoring using local, regional and national sources. At the Commission's headquarter, in Brussels, the country desks started to prepare first drafts of the respective reports on the basis of these inputs and their own knowledge. The country desks' drafts were then confronted with every chapter desk within DG

ELARG. They had to make sure that they were technically correct and consistent in their policy area. In the end, the drafts were revised by the Co-ordination Unit, to ensure coherence in both content and language (Interviews 3, 10).

In July, the Commission officials consulted third parties who offered further detailed information. On the political criteria they met with the Council of Europe and non-governmental organizations (NGOs) (Amnesty International, Human Rights Watch, etc.) and with the respective ones on the economic part (International Monetary Fund (IMF), the World Bank, the Organization for Economic Co-operation and Development (OECD), the European Bank of Reconstruction and Development (EBRD) and the European Investment Bank (EIB)). The aim was to get a picture that was as complete as possible. Besides that, the candidate countries had the opportunity to update their input until a previously set cut-off date in September (Interview 3).

By early September, the Commission had much more advanced drafts, which were harmonized within DG ELARG and reached a certain level of consistency. The drafts were then sent to all line DGs of the Commission for the so-called 'inter-service consultations'. 'To maintain confidentiality' (Interview 9), however, the line DGs did not receive the whole text but only the individual chapters concerning their field and had a pre-assigned time-frame of ten days to make comments (Interview 3). After the Co-ordination Unit in DG ELARG had received all the responses, a final reading and adjustment was done until the end of September as the final internal deadline.

In the first half of October, a short bilateral meeting with each applicant took place in Brussels where Commission officials presented the central points of the report, 'not to give them our conclusions, but a flavour of what they can expect' (Interview 10). Afterwards, the reports left the administrative level within the Commission and approached the political one. After inter-cabinet consultations and the adoption by the Commission's College – between the second half of October and the first half of November – the final version was submitted to the Council and then officially adopted by the European Council in December.

These procedures mirrored the complexity of the task of involving several internal and external actors and delivering up to 12 reports a year. In order to manage this task, the establishment of a clear temporal pattern with fixed deadlines and a developed time-frame was central. This pattern generated a 'temporal grid' for all stages and actors: providing guidance on what to do, and when, for all involved parts of the Commission and for external actors.

Regarding the Commission, the implications of the procedural changes for the reports were, however, more far-reaching than just increasing capacity to deal with the policy. From an overall perspective, the newly installed temporal grid had an impact on the temporal setting of the whole institution. All line DGs were influenced by the temporal requirements of eastern enlargement policy. They all had to deliver their input on fixed dates and, therefore, had to mobilize their institution at particular times.

On the basis of managing its own time, the Commission was also partially able to manage the time of other actors. The influence of the Commission's timetable on the candidate countries is particularly obvious. By setting up the roadmap, and by giving advice on the candidates' preparations for the negotiations, the Commission secured a definite influence over the candidates' timetables. The regular reports constituted a recurring evaluation that the candidate countries could influence the better they met the deadlines. Furthermore, the candidates tried to improve their individual assessments by introducing a large number of laws just before the regular reports (Interview 6). Deadlines and regularity clearly had an accelerating effect at this point.

It is much harder to assess whether the Commission was able to influence the timetable of the Council or the European Parliament in eastern enlargement policy. The role that time and time management played, and still plays, in inter-institutional relations is generally an under-researched field and could constitute an interesting topic to broaden our understanding further on this matter.

4. CONCLUSION

This paper has analysed the triangle of policies, institutions and time in the case of EU eastern enlargement policy and its impact on the Commission. The main question was how the special challenges and requirements of eastern enlargement policy influenced the administrative level of the Commission. To find answers, we addressed empirical data on organizational change in the Commission's internal structures and procedures, and used a special focus on time and time management. Temporal categories were investigated in both the policy and the institution and then connected to each other. This approach revealed the effects of the policy's temporal requirements on the institution's temporal setting. In short, institutional structures and procedures were adapted as a reaction to policy demands.

There are, of course, some characteristics of enlargement policy that support the influence on the institutional environment. The most compelling are: (a) the great complexity of the policy tasks; (b) the long duration of the process of formulating and implementing the policy; and (c) the large number of actors that had to be systematically and continuously involved in the process. Under these conditions, the institutional actor in charge of managing the policy should have high incentives to introduce means that tightly structure the policy process and provide a clear time-frame. The means can comprise timetables, deadlines and fixed sequences for internal and external inputs, and can relate to both the policy devices aimed at actors outside the institution as well as the rules for the internal organization of the institution itself. Whether this mechanism is indeed unique to the case studied here, or whether similar conditions have similar effects in other policies and institutions, are questions for further investigation.

As the empirical results show, the installation of a 'temporal grid' with strict time rules for all actors and procedures offers several advantages but it has additional, potentially unintended, consequences for the institution applying it. On the one hand, policy devices with strong time components and clear time rules ensure the in-time mobilization of the different actors and the temporal synchronization of their actions. On the other hand, the temporal mechanisms also affect the institution applying them. By demanding the establishment of new procedures, they modify the existing temporal setting of the institution as a whole, and can lead to a new balance of power between the component actors. Thus, the temporal grid is a distinct device that is promising for research in other cases.

In addition to testing a time-centred analysis for the relation of policies, institutions and institutional change, we offer new insights that contribute to the body of literature on the Commission. Our results show that administrative change in the Commission can be generated by policies, in this case by a complex policy task that demanded adaptation, despite a traditionally high level of resistance (Bauer 2008). This confirms a relatively new tendency. The Commission was able to avoid modernization for a long time; it only started to modernize in the late 1990s, 'given the new public management prominence of public sector reform in most of its national constituencies' (Bauer 2008: 691). Balint *et al.* (2008: 689) see two challenges for the Commission that trigger reforms: the increase in the Commission's tasks and duties 'caused by the intensifying and deepening of the European integration process' as well as the 'vast and growing "management gap" ... resulting from the lack of organisational adjustments' (Balint 2008: 689). The task to manage enlargement processes is an additional driver of change.

Thus, we agree with Peterson (2008) who regards eastern enlargement and the Kinnock reforms as the two biggest organizational challenges recently confronted by the Commission. Although we examined the *pre*-accession phase and not the changes *after* enlargement, the findings presented in this article add to the overall perspective on institutional development following the concept of 'functional adaptation' (March and Olsen 1995), which refers to change caused by new tasks. Still, the adaptation for enlargement has to be separated from that caused by the Kinnock reforms in the early 2000s which differed in scope and direction. The changes examined in this paper are about dealing with policy challenges and not about avoiding mismanagement or fraud. Of course, it is possible that these two reforms, which took place largely in the same period of time, influenced each other. At least, the readiness to reform and to install new structures and procedures could have risen by the mutual effects of different reforms in the same administrative environment – another field that offers interesting questions for further investigation.

In sum, analysing the triangle of policy, institution and time is an approach that broadens our understanding of institutional change. The inquiry into temporal categories of policies as well as institutions allows the tracing of institutional change in complex environments. It opens a new perspective on institutions in the context of European governance and the analysis of institutions in general.

Biographical notes: Katja Lass-Lennecke and Annika Werner are research fellows and Ph.D. candidates at Potsdam University, Germany.

ACKNOWLEDGEMENTS

We would like to thank Simon Bulmer, Klaus H. Goetz, Bart Kerremans, Thomas König, Jan-Hinrik Meyer-Sahling, Louise van Schaik and the anonymous reviewer for their helpful comments on an earlier draft of this paper. Furthermore, we would like to thank all EU officials for their time and assistance.

Interviews

Interview No. 1, 14.01.2008, European Commission, Staff
Interview No. 2, 14.01.2008, European Commission, Head of Unit
Interview No. 3, 14.01.2008, European Commission, Director
Interview No. 4, 15.01.2008, European Commission, Head of Unit
Interview No. 5, 15.01.2008, European Commission, Staff
Interview No. 6, 15.01.2008, European Commission, Head of Unit
Interview No. 7, 15.01.2008, European Commission, Director, former Head of Delegation
Interview No. 8, 16.01.2008, European Commission, Director
Interview No. 9, 16.01.2008, European Commission, Head of Unit
Interview No. 10, 16.01.2008, European Commission, Head of Unit
Interview No. 11, 17.01.2008, Political Advisor
Interview No. 12, 18.01.2008, Political Advisor
Interview No. 13, 17.01.2008, Council Secretary, Head of Division

NOTES

1 This paper is part of the project 'The Politics of Time: The Temporality of EU Enlargement and Europeanization', funded by the German Research Foundation (DFG) and directed by Professor Klaus H. Goetz, University of Potsdam, Germany.
2 We refer to this EU enlargement round as 'eastern enlargement' owing to the high number of candidate countries from Central and Eastern Europe whose accession preparations dominated the process.
3 However, we do not consider social norms, rules of behaviour or cultural aspects in our work even though they could also be fruitful for analysis (see, e.g. Cini 1996; Héritier 2007).
4 The authors conducted 13 interviews about the management of eastern enlargement policy within the Commission's services in January 2008.
5 Besides the *acquis*, the candidates had to take on the EU's 'soft law' of non-binding resolutions and recommendations. This made the legal body broader for this enlargement compared to previous rounds (Grabbe 2002: 253).
6 An assumption that proved right in the case of Bulgaria and Romania who received an early promise for accession in 2007, coupled with the '(ineffective) threat' to delay it to 2008 (Avery 2009; Barysch and Grabbe 2002: 7; Pridham 2006: 382), and maintained an enormous deficit in fulfilling the membership requirements.
7 Furthermore, in the post-accession phase, the transition periods enabled the EU to bind and control the new members after accession by giving them 'only some flexibility over the timing of the implementation' of the EU *acquis* and for 'a limited number of acts' (Pridham 2006: 391; see also Mayhew 2000: 48).
8 The following explanations only deal with the third, major, part of the reports. The two other parts, the political and the economic ones, were composed solely by the country desk head officer and by DG ECOFIN, respectively.

REFERENCES

Avery, G. (2009) 'Uses of time in the EU's enlargement process', *Journal of European Public Policy* 16(2): 252–65.

Avery, G. and Cameron, F. (1998) *The Enlargement of the European Union*, Sheffield: Sheffield Academic Press.

Balint, T., Bauer, M.W. and Knill, C. (2008) 'Bureaucratic change in the European administrative space: the case of the European Commission', *West European Politics* 31(4): 677–700.

Barysch, K. and Grabbe, H. (2002) *Who's Ready for EU Enlargement?* London: Centre for European Reform Working Paper.

Bauer, M.W. (2008) 'Introduction: Organizational change, management reform and EU policy-making', *Journal of European Public Policy* 15(5): 627–47.

Bellier, I. (2004) 'The European Commission between the aquis communautaire and enlargement', in D. Dimitrakopulos (ed.), *The Changing European Commission*, Manchester: Manchester University Press, pp. 138–52.

Best, E., Christiansen, T. and Settembri, P. (2008) *The Institutions of the Enlarged European Union: Continuity and Change*, Cheltenham and Northampton, MA: Edward Elgar.

Cameron, F. (1997) 'The European Union and the challenge of enlargement', in M. Maresceau (ed.), *Enlarging the European Union: Relations Between the EU and Central and Eastern Europe*, London/New York: Longman, pp. 241–51.

Christoffersen, P.S. (2007) 'Organization of the process and beginning of the negotiations', in G. Vassiliou (ed.), *The Accession Story. The EU from Fifteen to Twenty–Five Countries*, Oxford: Oxford University Press, pp. 34–50.

Cini, M. (1996) *The European Commission: Leadership, Organisation and Culture in the EU Administration*, Manchester: Manchester University Press.

Das, T.K. (1991) 'Time: the hidden dimension in strategic planning', *Long Range Planning* 24(3): 49–57.

Egeberg, M. (2002). 'An organisational approach to European integration – what organisation tells us about system transformation, committee governance and Commission decision-making'. Paper presented at the ARENA Seminar, Oslo, April, 2002.

Ellinas, A. and Suleiman, E. (2008) 'Reforming the Commission: between modernization and bureaucratization', *Journal of European Public Policy* 15(5): 708–25.

Goetz, K.H. (2009) 'How does the EU tick? Five propositions on political time', *Journal of European Public Policy* 16(2): 202–20.

Goetz, K.H. and Meyer-Sahling, J.-H. (2009) 'Political time in the EU: dimensions, perspectives, theories', *Journal of European Public Policy* 16(2): 180–201.

Grabbe, H. (2002) 'European Union conditionality and the *acquis communautaire*', *International Political Science Review* 23(3): 249–68.

Grabbe, H. and Hughes, K. (1998) *Enlarging the EU Eastwards*, London: Royal Institute of International Affairs.

Grabbe, H. and Hughes, K. (1999) 'Central and East European views on EU enlargement: political debates and public opinion', in K. Henderson (ed.), *Back to Europe: Central and Eastern Europe and the European Union*, London: UCL Press, pp. 185–202.

Heidbreder, E.G. (2007). 'The impact of implementing eastern enlargement: execution of policies as sources for new policy-making in the Commission'. Paper presented at the Congress of the Societá Italiana de Scienza Politica, Catania/Italy, September, 2007.

Héritier, A. (2007) *Explaining Institutional Change in Europe*, Oxford: Oxford University Press.

Homeyer, I., Carius, A. and Baer, S. (2000) 'Flexibility or renationalization: effects of enlargement on EC environmental policy', in M.G. Cowles and M. Smith (eds), *The State of the European Union – Risk, Reform, Resistance and Revival*, Oxford: Oxford University Press, pp. 347–368.

Inotai, A. (2003) 'The "eastern enlargements" of the European Union', in M. Cremona (ed.), *The Enlargement of the European Union*, Oxford: Oxford University Press, pp. 79–104.

Kassim, H. (2004) 'A historic accomplishment? The Prodi Commission and administrative reform', in D. Dimitrakopoulos (ed.), *The Changing European Commission*, Manchester: Manchester University Press, pp. 33–62.

Linz, J. (1998) 'Democracy's time constraints', *International Political Science Review* 19(1): 19–37.

March, J.G. and Olsen, J.P. (1995) *Democratic Governance*, New York: Free Press.

Mayhew, A. (1998) *Recreating Europe: The European Union's Policy Towards Central and Eastern Europe*, Cambridge: Cambridge University Press.

Mayhew, A. (2000) 'Enlargement of the European Union: an analysis of the negotiations with the Central and Eastern European countries', *Sussex European Institute Working Paper* 39.

Meyer-Sahling, J.-H. and Goetz, K.H. (2009) 'The EU timescape: from notion to research agenda', *Journal of European Public Policy* 16(2): 325–36.

Nugent, N. (2001) *The European Commission*, Basingstoke: Palgrave.

Nugent, N. (2004) *European Union Enlargement*, Basingstoke: Palgrave.

Nugent, N. and Saurugger, S. (2002) 'Organizational structuring: the case of the European Commission and its external policy responsibilities', *Jounal of European Public Policy* 9(3): 345–64.

Peterson, J. (2008) 'Enlargement, reform and the European Commission. Weathering a perfect storm?' *Journal of European Public Policy* 15(5): 761–80.

Phinnemore, D. (1999) 'The challenge of EU enlargement: EU and CEE perspectives', in K. Henderson (ed.), *Back to Europe: Central and Eastern Europe and the European Union*, London: UCL Press, pp. 71–88.

Pierson, P. (2004) *Politics in Time. History, Institutions, and Social Behaviour*, Princeton, NJ: Princeton University Press.

Pridham, G. (2006) 'European Union accession dynamics and democratization in Central and Eastern Europe: past and future perspectives', *Government and Opposition* 41(3): 373–400.

Riescher, G. (1994) *Zeit und Politik. Zur institutionellen Bedeutung von Zeitstrukturen in parlamentarischen und präsidentiellen Regierungssystemen*, Baden-Baden: Nomos.

Schedler, A. and Santiso, J. (1998) 'Democracy and time: an invitation', *International Political Science Review* 19(1): 5–18.

Schimmelfennig, F. and Sedelmeier, U. (2004) 'Governance by conditionality: EU rule transfer to the candidate countries of Central and Eastern Europe', *Journal of European Public Policy* 11(4): 661–79.

Suvarierol, S. (2007) *Beyond the Myth of Nationality: A Study on the Networks of European Commission Officials*, Delft: Eburon Academic Publishers.

Vassiliou, G. (2007) *The Accession Story. The EU from Fifteen to Twenty-Five Countries*, Oxford: Oxford University Press.

The evolving timescapes of European economic governance: contesting and using time

Kenneth Dyson

ABSTRACT This article examines the ambivalent character of time in European economic governance and how it is conceptualized, especially by its constituent expert élites. On the one hand, it serves to rationally order and stabilize power relationships; on the other, it provokes contest about its appropriate use, focused on fiscal and economic reform policies. The article also highlights the different functional specificities in temporal governance in monetary, fiscal, financial stability and economic reform policies and the differences in potential of issues to mobilize political opposition and to produce problems of synchronization. In particular, monetary union forms an inner circle within European economic governance. Its discursive, regulative and strategic effects radiate with varying results into its other circles. Nevertheless, European economic governance is not a single 'time-rule' exercise. Finally, the article examines how, through its 'compression' effects on European states, European economic governance raises serious issues about the quality of modern democracy.

INTRODUCTION

Contest about the nature, organization and use of time pervades European economic governance. Its centrality in this policy sector owes a great deal to the dominance of 'time-inconsistency' in modern theoretical literature on inflation, which contrasts a linear conception of 'sustainable' economic growth with the 'boom and bust' generated by the short-term politics of domestic electoral cycles. The focus on linear political time in 'time-inconsistency' literature fits into the way in which political time is organized at the European Union (EU) level (Goetz 2009). It creates a powerful disposition to resort to temporal governing devices like roadmaps and timetables in the attempt to mobilize and synchronize an altered approach to organizing domestic political time. These devices promise to deliver credibility of commitments to economic stability. At the same time they remain acutely vulnerable to ongoing inter- and intra-institutional negotiation over time-setting. European economic governance has shifted the underlying temporal parameters and assumptions within which national economic policies are debated, though in ways that are difficult to disentangle from the more general influence of 'time-inconsistency' literature across Organization for Economic Co-operation and Development (OECD) and International Monetary Fund (IMF) economies. However, other than in monetary policy, where one can speak of time-setting 'from above', the intrusion of domestic electoral cycles means that European economic governance retains a fragile character. This article examines the ways in which the contest about time manifests itself in this sector.

Within European economic governance time expresses itself in variable ways (Schedler and Santiso 1998; Schmitter and Santiso 1998). In policy issues related most closely to monetary union, and securing the public good of price stability, deadlines and roadmaps have been central instruments for mobilizing actors, securing compliance and synchronizing action. An example is Euro Area entry (Dyson 2006). The distinctive character of European economic governance, the nature of its evolving institutionalization, and the missionary self-confidence and persuasive power of its practitioners derive from the elaborate, theoretically coherent temporal discourse in monetary policy and the underlying conception of price stability as an indivisible public good (Dyson 2000). This 'time-inconsistency' discourse reveals a strong preference for high institutional autonomy to safeguard long time-horizons and lock-in long-term expectations of inflation consistent with price stability and for clear, firm temporal rules.

Nevertheless, European economic governance is not a single 'time-rule' exercise. It reflects different functional specificities and differences in potential of issues to mobilize political opposition. The underlying assumption remains: 'One time does not fit all.' Consequently, the variety of clocks in European economic governance throws up an internal challenge of their synchronization (Umbach, forthcoming). Time also has an ambivalent character. On the one hand, it serves to rationally order and stabilize power relationships; on the other, it provokes contest about its appropriate use (Adam 2004; Riescher 1994). Though this ambivalence pervades European economic governance, it is more concealed in monetary policy.

This ambivalence is demonstrated in how member state governments respond to the incentives and pressures to synchronize fiscal, employment and macroeconomic co-ordination clocks with the clock of European monetary governance and to the consequent 'squeeze on the national present' (Ekengren 1997, 2002). As seen most clearly in the Lisbon strategy, threats of constraints on member states' capacity to act as time-setters in economic reforms from domestic electoral time-rules induce governments to evade commitments that 'bind their hands' and to avoid delegating power to the European Commission. In consequence, disincentives to free-riding are weak, domestic ownership of European processes problematic, and non-compliance difficult to establish in the context of vague commitments. This 'squeezing of the national present' has, however, deeper structural roots that are examined below, that give it an extra momentum, and that raise serious issues about effects on the quality of European democracy, which remains state-based (Collignon 2003; Eder 2004; Goetz 2009).

Monetary union forms an inner circle within European economic governance, and its discursive, regulative and strategic effects radiate with varying results into its other circles. In the first place, the privileged, if contested temporal discourse of monetary policy includes norms about medium- to long-term time-horizons, time-consistent behaviour based on clear rules, and sustainable convergence. These norms shape conceptions of commitment and compliance, institutional independence, inter-institutional co-ordination and policy synchronization. Secondly, a complex, evolving set of institutional and policy time-rules anchor these norms in European economic governance. They define who does what, when, how, and over timescales that do not equate with domestic electoral cycles.

Finally, European economic governance is an arena whose expert élites – central bankers and finance ministry officials – are intensely practised in the arts of the strategic use of time. They seek to reinforce their autonomy and to mobilize action by governments and by market players on behalf of their Treaty-based agenda of stability-oriented policies. Their temporal discourse derives from a belief in the need to pre-commit both themselves and political and financial market élites and thereby to exert discipline, gain insurance against non-compliance and build credibility. As these three aspects of the temporal ordering of European economic governance have evolved to become more formalized and synchronized over time, they have shifted the parameters of the domestic management of political time.

This article offers a broad map of the complex and evolving timescape of European economic governance, highlighting the specificities of its temporal discourse, time-rules, and use of temporal devices (see Meyer-Sahling and Goetz 2009 for a discussion of the notion of 'timescape' in the EU context). It provides a story of the evolution of 'internal' or 'proper' time (*Eigenzeit*) (Nowotny 1994). Seen 'from outside-in' (that is, in comparison with other EU policy areas), European economic governance represents a very distinctive temporal world. Seen 'from the inside', it is a set of overlapping circles, in which attitudes towards time and its strategic use vary across monetary, fiscal, structural reforms and macroeconomic co-ordination policies. Yet, seen as a whole, they are distinctive because of the radiating effects from monetary governance. European economic government is a temporal world faced with the challenge of synchronizing a complex set of administrative clocks. They operate differently across its component policy areas. These variations reflect differences in functional specificities and in degree of exposure to the multi-level system of EU governance and its domestic political rhythms.

Despite this variation the administrative clocks of European economic governance have in common a distinctive length of time-horizons compared to EU member states, where domestic electoral time-rules serve as political incentives to shorten horizons. These time-horizons serve to hold up an unflattering mirror to domestic electoral opportunism, providing benchmarks to assess the credibility of promises. The temporal clocks of European economic governance are distinctive in a second sense. In contrast to other EU policy areas, European economic governance is characterized by the elaborate, coherent and robust temporal discourse in which it is embedded. In this respect its temporal world is more akin to the evolving world of domestic economic governance across OECD economies, where long time-horizons and clear rules are seen as preconditions of economic and financial stability. In short, monetary policy discourse imparts to European economic governance a distinctive 'internal time' or sense of 'proper time'. This 'internal time' has its origins in the renaissance of monetary economics since the 1970s and in the associated empowerment of central banking. More fundamentally, it derived from the post-Bretton Woods experience of explosive financial market changes and the search for clear time-rules to offer states insurance against unprecedented financial, monetary and exchange-rate volatility and the frequency and severity of financial crises (Moran 1991; Kindleberger 2005).

The pervasiveness of time manifests itself *inter alia* in the three 'stages' of economic and monetary union (EMU) – 1990 for stage one, 1994 for stage two and, above all, the final deadline of 1 January 1999 for stage three; the reference periods for European Commission and European Central Bank (ECB) assessment of whether EU member states with a derogation have met the Maastricht convergence criteria for euro entry (one year for inflation and long-term interest rates and 'at least two years' for the exchange rate); the roadmaps and self-defined dates in domestic Euro entry plans of new EU member states; the medium-term focus of ECB monetary policy strategy; the detailed timetable governing the operation of the excessive deficit procedure, spelt out in the Stability and Growth Pact (SGP) (including dates for achieving 'close to balance' in fiscal policy); the dates attached to the negotiation and implementation of the TARGET2S securities settlement system and to the stages of the Single Euro Payments Area (SEPA); and the evolution in temporal synchronization of the various EU macroeconomic co-ordination exercises from 2005. Attitudes to, and practices of, the strategic use *of* time have evolved *in* time, without formal Treaty amendment. Above all, time-rules have been seen as central to mobilizing political and market action, gaining commitment and securing compliance, and synchronizing action.

More fundamentally, European economic governance exemplifies the most intensive 'time–space compression' in European integration (Harvey 1990). The experience of time amongst central bankers and finance ministry officials has been radically transformed since the late twentieth century. The chief causes include their direct exposure to the effects of financial market globalization and its accelerated speed of contagious volatilities and crises; the instantaneous communications made possible by new technologies like email and video-conferencing; and cheaper and faster travel, along with the fuller travel schedules created by the evolving administrative clocks of European economic governance. In consequence, the spatial co-ordinates of central bankers and finance ministry officials have shifted away from the domestic arena to European and to global forums. They have been catapulted into an 'internal time' of instantaneous European and global contacts.

The resulting identity shift of officials from domestic to European and global levels can be plotted in the two key committees of European economic governance: the Economic and Financial Committee (EFC) and the Economic Policy Committee (EPC). They prepare the work of the Economic and Financial Affairs Council (ECOFIN) and the Euro Group and act as their 'brain trusts'. From the inception of the European community (EC) Monetary Committee (the predecessor of the EFC) in 1959, it has had a reputation for its independence and club-like and technocratic character as a body of experts. Its shared identity and co-operative, consensus-seeking style were strengthened by three factors that distinguished it from the EPC: its long, direct experience of crisis management, above all in the old exchange-rate mechanism (ERM); its sense of responsibility for the Maastricht Treaty commitments on EMU; and its immersion in the time-discourse of monetary economics through the greater proximity of its work to monetary union (e.g. in financial stability issues and the creation of financial infrastructure). The survey of EFC and EPC members by Dyson and Quaglia (2008) shows the high frequency of contacts, the high level of attachment to the EU level, which is seen as having become more important compared to member states, and the importance attached to the creation of a European identity. EFC and EPC are both institutional expressions of, and vehicles for, the intense 'time–space compression' in European economic governance.

THE FUNCTIONS OF TIME IN EUROPEAN ECONOMIC GOVERNANCE

Time is central to European economic governance in three ways. First, the development of EMU, especially monetary union, has depended on its historical legitimacy within the larger political project of European union. Its sequencing and 'timeliness' within this larger project have been rationally contested (Adam 2004). For 'coronation' theorists of EMU, monetary union should come at the end of a process of economic union and of political union (Dyson 2000). Its success depends on prior conditions of economic convergence and of shared political identity, on being embedded in a 'community of solidarity' represented by a European fiscal union and reflected in cross-national labour mobility. In contrast, 'monetarists' saw an early shift to monetary union as a catalyst for closer economic and political union. It would drive mutually interacting processes of formal and informal integration (Dyson 2000). In compensation for an historical evolution of European monetary union that was inconsistent with both 'coronation' and 'monetarist' theories, the ECB attached prime importance to domestic compliance with firm and clear time-rules in fiscal and wages policies and in structural economic reforms. This contest about the appropriate temporal logic in the design of EMU highlights how much its legitimacy is bound up in bigger issues about sequencing and timing in European integration (Goetz and Meyer-Sahling 2009).

Secondly, time has figured in issues of rule formulation and application across the diverse areas of European economic governance. Time-rules offer a method of securing compliance by pre-commitment through 'binding hands': for instance, in monetary policy, the excessive deficit procedure, and procedures for macroeconomic co-ordination like the Integrated Guidelines (see below). They serve to mobilize actors behind policies to meet the Treaty commitment to sustainable, non-inflationary growth; to endow European economic governance with a high degree of autonomy; and to synchronize action. By compliance with time-rules that minimize inflationary risks, domestic governments can improve their reputation for economic competence (Giavazzi and Pagano 1988). Not least, time-rules enable actors to be held accountable for meeting a set of common standards and make more transparent the motives behind their behaviour. Examples include fiscal rules 'over the cycle', the medium-term ECB monetary policy framework, and euro entry dates with associated road-maps for individual states. Non-compliance involves costs to reputation.

The time-discourse and time-rules of European economic governance provide the context within which actors use their scarce time-budgets strategically. Time-budgets vary. They are least scarce in monetary policy and policies related to financial stability, like euro payment and settlement systems. Responsibility for these policies lies with the ECB directorate and national central bank governors in the Governing Council. They enjoy lengthy periods of office: eight years (non-renewable) for the former and 'at least five years' for the latter. In addition, their retirements are spread over time so that there are no time-points of sharp transition. Correspondingly, Euro Area central bankers' view of time is linear and long-term.

If time is a more limited resource for European Commissioners for Economics and Finance, it is much scarcer for national heads of state and government in the European Council and for finance ministers in ECOFIN and the Euro Group. They are elected, not appointed and face shorter-term, potentially variable electoral time-rules. This constraint induces them to 'play for time' by seeking flexibility and discretion, for instance over the timing of euro entry, of meeting obligations under the SGP, or of completing economic reforms as part of the Lisbon strategy.

Nevertheless, because domestic political élites are bound up in the continuously ticking global financial market clock, and the daily accountability to its market actors, they remain dependent on compliance with central bankers' time-rules in order to provide them with credibility. Compliance with an 'internal time' of European economic governance that is rooted in the long, linear temporal logic of monetary economics and central banking provides insulation from the high risks and uncertainties of market volatility.

Above all, time is a resource that actors can deploy strategically in order to firmly anchor, align and manage the expectations of a range of relevant economic and political actors. Its strategic use can accelerate change and reduce its costs by inducing co-ordinated behaviour. For instance, a medium-term orientation in ECB monetary policy provides a means to signal a determination not to accommodate short-term political pressures. Finance ministers use EU fiscal rules as an external discipline to empower themselves in domestic political battles over fiscal consolidation. European Commissioners seek to gain acceptance for clear timetables to accelerate co-ordinated market adjustment to new instruments for creating a Single European Payments Area.

The historical specifics of the early temporal sequencing of European monetary union have profoundly affected the functions of time in European economic governance. The high sunk costs in this early transition to monetary union (1990–99) and the Treaty-based obligations at stake – including the final date for stage three – made the viability of the European monetary union into a fundamental collective commitment. It was framed as a shared vital national interest. In consequence, monetary union has been pivotal to the evolution of time-discourse and time-rules across European economic governance. It provided a strong collective incentive to resist short-term individual inducements to freeriding in fiscal and macroeconomic policies. In the process domestic time has been 'squeezed'.

EXPLAINING 'INTERNAL' OR 'PROPER' TIME IN EUROPEAN ECONOMIC GOVERNANCE

Explaining 'internal' or 'proper' time in European economic governance raises four questions that can be addressed by using different theories of European integration. The first question involves the bargaining power that shapes the content of its time-rules and is illuminated by the theory of liberal intergovernmentalism (Moravcsik 1998). Above all, monetary time-rules reflect the imprint of Germany, more specifically the Bundesbank, consequent on the underlying asymmetrical interdependence in European exchange-rate and monetary policies (Dyson and Featherstone 1999). The Bundesbank sought to ensure the credibility of inter-state commitments to a stable euro, to deter non-compliance, and hence to secure the predictability of behaviour of others, through rules to entrench central bank independence, through an ECB monetary policy strategy that would focus on the medium- to long-term, and in 1995–97 through the SGP. The increased intensity of interdependence in trade and finance within monetary union would create stronger incentives to comply over time. Crucially, however, the initial imprint derived from a German desire to make the behaviour of others more predictable. This predictability was achieved by the uploading of a rules-based attitude to securing an EU 'stability community' through long time-horizons in economic governance.

The second question involves the evolution of time-rules in European economic governance and is illuminated by the concepts of 'spillover' in neo-functionalism and of 'path dependency' in historical institutionalism. These concepts throw light on European economic governance as a phenomenon in time. 'Spillover' highlights the temporal links between the single European market and monetary union (in the notion 'one market, one currency'). It shows how, in turn, European monetary union creates new incentives to develop time-rules to lock in supportive fiscal behaviour and the co-ordination of macroeconomic policies and structural reforms. Once monetary union had been agreed in the Maastricht Treaty, a broad academic and official consensus evolved on the need for precautions against negative fiscal externalities, especially once financial market discipline was gone in a currency union, and for pre-commitments to structural economic reforms. These precautions involved the strengthened role of the European Commission in ensuring compliance in both these areas through explicit, clear time-rules and autonomy in enforcing them.

The SGP, the Broad Economic Policy Guidelines (BEPGs), the Lisbon strategy and the employment guidelines and national action plans threw up a series of clocks for reporting, monitoring and peer review. Institutional evolution was marked by a spread of time-rules and new challenges of synchronization of different clocks. Similarly, monetary union spilled over into timetables for developing electronic wholesale payments and settlement systems (TARGET, TARGET2 and TARGET2S) and for the SEPA. This process of institutional evolution throws into sharp relief the strategies of the European Commission, the EFC, the EPC, and the ECB/European System of Central Banks (ESCB) to carve out more autonomous roles in mobilizing action and monitoring compliance. It also highlights a path-dependent development from its origins in the Maastricht monetary constitution.

The third question involves the motives of states in designing or assenting to particular time-rules, in complying with or reneging on these rules, and in seeking to renegotiate them. These motives are illuminated by approaches that focus on the domestic politics of European economic governance. German agenda-setting in negotiating the SGP in 1995–97 and in renegotiating it in 2003–05 had its roots in German domestic politics, especially intra-party and opposition party competition against the background of a difficult electoral calendar (Heipertz and Verdun 2005). In 2003–05 the Schröder government sought new time-rules in the SGP that would enable it to sequence costly structural reforms (Agenda 2010) before fiscal consolidation and avoid a future politically sensitive stage in the excessive deficit procedure before the anticipated 2006 federal elections.

However, domestic political élites do not have a one-dimensional view of the time-rules of European economic governance. In addition to seeking out flexibility and discretion in timing and pacing of fiscal and economic reforms, they have motives to embrace time-rules. Time-rules can be used to reframe domestic discourse (especially where the EU is highly valued), to secure power over policy and to minimize electoral vulnerability. Their use can also backfire. France offers an example of how the EMU timetable drove domestic electoral timing. Faced with the 1999 deadline, President Chirac called early Assembly elections in 1997 rather than wait till 1998. He sought to create political space to pursue appropriate domestic reforms. The consequent opposition party victory made Chirac more cautious both in reforms and in avoiding becoming a future hostage to EU deadlines. After the 2002 Presidential election he insisted on fulfilling his electoral mandate for tax cuts at the price of isolating France in the Euro Group over the SGP. In contrast, newly elected coalition governments in many small states, like Austria, the Netherlands, Portugal, and later Greece, used the SGP as an external discipline to accelerate fiscal consolidation. They worked closely with the European Commission.

This instrumental use of time-rules is clear in the euro entry plans of east central European states, which have a Treaty obligation to pursue entry but with no final date. Originally focused on an early date for entry (typically ERM II entry in 2004/05, euro entry 2007/08), these states have periodically revised dates to 2012, 2014 and even beyond (Dyson 2006). In the process the euro entry plans have lost credibility, and the roadmaps to euro entry have lost their capacity to mobilize and synchronize domestic policy action. One or more of three key factors have made for difficulties in meeting the Maastricht convergence criteria for entry. Each has a temporal dimension. Firstly, the short-term volatility of financial markets, especially consequent on high and variable levels of foreign direct investment, made the required two-year commitment to ERM II membership prior to entry too hazardous. Secondly, the speed of economic catch-up, and the political incentive to prioritize real convergence in living standards, made difficult the fulfilment of the low inflation criterion for entry. This problem has, in turn, made the ECB and the European Commission cautious about using a one-year assessment period for inflation as a test of sustainable convergence. This caution was signalled in 2006 when Lithuania was assessed as not ready. Thirdly, fiscal deficits have diverged from the convergence criteria consequent on the domestic political incentives to address difficult social policy issues thrown up by post-communist transition and to deliver prestigious infrastructure investments, not least by making effective short-term use of the EU Structural Funds through co-financing. These incentives are sharpened by domestic electoral timetables and the opportunistic behaviour that they induce. Euro Area outsiders have had to engage in difficult 'two-level' games of reconciling euro entry plans with domestic electoral timetables (Putnam 1988). The way in which this game is played and the nature of outcomes are shaped by the voluntary nature of the Euro Area entry timetable. Though under a Treaty obligation to enter, there is no EU-level timetable for entry (unlike for the entry into stage three on 1 January 1999). This lack of a final EU date reflects an underlying caution in Euro Area institutions about the appropriate timing for entry of states subject to the strains of economic catch-up.

The EU also has a group of semi-permanent euro outsiders who either have Treaty-based opt-outs or have abandoned euro entry plans with roadmaps and dates. In the cases of Britain, Denmark and Sweden domestic administrative clocks in economic governance retain a high degree of synchronization with the EU as they remain part of all processes other than monetary union. The 'internal' time in domestic economic governance of these outsiders also parallels that in other OECD/Euro Area states in its temporal discourse around modern monetary economics and central banking. Crucially, however, the lack of euro entry plans with dates means that they do not face the consequent domestic challenges of the mobilization of political and market actors, of synchronization of policy reforms, and of compliance.

The fourth question involves the detailed elaboration of time-rules in European economic governance and is illuminated by cognitive theories that focus on EU committee governance. The detailed content of time-rules derives above all from the technical experts, their autonomy at the EU level and their distinctive temporal discourse. The elaborate, sophisticated time-rules have evolved through processes of deliberation, socialization and learning amongst professional colleagues who focus on meeting Treaty obligations. They evolve in the expert world of the EFC, the EPC, the European Commission, Eurostat, the relevant services of the Council, and the ECB–Eurosystem–ESCB. In 1995–97 some 95 per cent of the text of the SGP was agreed in the EC Monetary Committee without further discussion at political level (Heipertz and Verdun 2005). Eurostat has been notably active in creating rules governing fiscal data for the excessive deficit procedure to ensure their reliability, comparability and timeliness (Savage 2005).

Despite a high degree of autonomy and technocracy, some of the most politically contentious issues in European economic governance are around time. In particular, the principle of 'automaticity' in the excessive deficit procedure, which was stressed by German officials in the SGP negotiations, would have taken time out of political hands. Political intervention, above all by President Chirac in 1996, ensured that political leaders were able to retain political discretion in this procedure. Two key areas of temporal discretion remained: over the successive steps in the excessive deficit procedure (its suspension in 2003 led to crisis); and over the date by which the medium-term fiscal objective of achieving 'close to balance or surplus' was to be achieved. This date was shifted in 2002 from 2004 to 2006 (to accommodate France, Germany and Italy) and then, in 2006, to 2010. Even then, in 2007, the newly elected President Sarkozy insisted that 2012 was more appropriate for France. Commission proposals for its own greater autonomy in the procedure and for a more precise date for the medium-term objective were rejected.

TIME DISCOURSE: THE EMBEDDED POWER OF CENTRAL BANKING

European economic governance exhibits contested rationalities of time. They reflect differing functional specificities and the varying extent to which its component policy areas – monetary policy, fiscal policies, economic reform, and macroeconomic co-ordination – are embedded in the multi-level EU governance structures. In particular, variation in exposure to domestic electoral calendars provides different opportunities for, and constraints on, the domestic partisan preferences and electoral opportunism of contending political élites to influence time-rules, how they evolve, and their strategic use (Dyson 2008). In consequence, the capacity to sustain commitments to longer-term time-horizons is more problematic in fiscal policies and structural reforms than in monetary policy. This variability is demonstrated in the fact that crises over time-rules have beset the SGP (2003–05) and the Lisbon strategy (2003–05) rather than the ECB. These contested rationalities of time reflect the well-known asymmetry at the heart of EMU. The supranational monetary union sits alongside 'hard' co-ordination of domestic fiscal policies and 'soft' co-ordination of EU macroeconomic co-ordination and domestic employment and structural reform policies (Dyson 2000).

The processes of European economic governance reflect a more general inbuilt bias to prioritize longer time-horizons, deadlines and roadmaps in European integration (Goetz 2009). The prime example was the historic commitment of Chancellor Helmut Kohl and President François Mitterrand to anchor a firm, final date for monetary union in the Maastricht Treaty. By binding their successors, they aimed to make the process of European unification irreversible (Dyson and Featherstone 1999). This use of a temporal commitment device to drive the *process* echoed the single European market '1992' programme, of which EMU was seen as a continuation and reinforcement.

However, the decision to accelerate monetary union in 1988–91 handed a distinct shaping power over the *content* of EMU to central bankers and, correspondingly, to the body of monetary economic concepts and theories that underpinned their work. Time is a central variable in the expert discourse of modern monetary economics and in explicit and tacit understandings of how financial markets work. It figures in debates about 'time-consistency', reputation and credibility in monetary and fiscal policies and in understanding of the key role of 'momentum' and timing in financial markets, for instance in creating and in managing asset price bubbles.

The significance of time-rules in modern monetary theory derives from four sources: the assumption of long-term stability in the demand for money; the recognition of long time-lags in the effects of monetary policy; the principle of the long-run neutrality of money with respect to growth and employment; and the role attached to forward-looking private-sector expectations and to the credibility derived from binding commitments in explaining, predicting and managing inflation (Lucas 1976). The fact that four of its leading theorists have won Nobel prizes in economics testifies to its prestige. According to monetary theory, the combination of long-term stability in the demand for money with time-lags in monetary policy make short-term activist use of monetary policy for counter-cyclical purposes counter-productive and support the value of long-term rules. Effective monetary policy requires policy-makers to firmly anchor and shape market expectations so that they are consistent with price stability and minimize the costs of disinflation. This requirement is met by earning credibility and gaining reputation in the markets. Credibility rests on the belief of economic agents that policy-makers will honour commitments to price stability. This belief is in turn a function of 'time-consistent' behaviour, which in turn depends on time-rules that provide no future incentive to renege (Kydland and Prescott 1977).

The problem is that political time-rules in democratic systems contain incentives to renege on commitments to price stability, thereby opening up a difference between *ex ante* and *ex post* optimality. This problem of 'time-inconsistent' behaviour has its roots in the theory of the political business cycle, according to which democratically elected governments are prone to subordinate economic policy to electoral time-rules (Alesina 1987; Rogoff 1987). They engage in short-term economic stimulation through lower taxes and/or higher public spending before elections and, in the process, undermine their commitments to price stability. The consequence is loss of confidence, long-term policy credibility and reputation and higher costs of disinflation.

The solution rests in time-rules that ensure binding commitments to the *ex ante* policy: through tying one's national currency to a 'hard' currency (as to the D-Mark in the old ERM or a currency board), much favoured by small open economies, and/or through central bank independence linked to inflation targeting or a money growth rule. In short, there is a need for institutional arrangements that embed long time-horizons into monetary policy. Credibility in monetary policy depends further on flanking 'time-consistent' behaviour in fiscal policies through rules that commit to sustainable fiscal positions over the long term. It also depends on more formulaic, biannual approaches to wages policies through 'productivity-plus' deals that abate inflationary expectations (Parsons and Pochet 2008). Monetary theory advocates clear time-rules in fiscal and wages policies that support a stability-oriented policy by reducing costs of disinflation.

In response to the power and volatility of financial markets in the post-Bretton Woods age, the theory and practice of modern monetary policy has come to rest on anchoring medium-term expectations of inflation at levels consistent with price stability. This shared rationale underpins the four main choices in European monetary policies: direct inflation targeting by central banks (as in Britain, Sweden, Hungary, the Czech Republic and Poland); exchange-rate targeting by tying hands to the euro through membership of ERM II (for instance, the Baltic States, Denmark and Slovakia); currency boards (the Baltic States and Bulgaria); and the two-pillar monetary policy strategy of the ECB. In particular, the ECB stresses the superior time-rules underpinning its strategy and the central role of its second monetary pillar in ensuring its medium-term orientation through the analysis of monetary aggregates. The economic pillar focuses on the short- to medium-term time-horizon, whilst the monetary pillar looks at the medium- to long-term horizon. In this way the ECB distinguishes itself from inflation targeting regimes, which highlight the central bank's short-term, uncertain and typically two-year economic forecast in relation to the inflation target as the basis for monetary policy decisions. The second monetary pillar provides a longer-term check on monetary policy decision-making by incorporating developments beyond this fixed time-horizon, notably in asset prices (Stark 2007). In contrast to all these European policy choices, monetary targeting involves a commitment to a specific and pre-announced rule about the rate of monetary growth. Some critics of the ECB, notably from the German Ordo-liberal tradition, stress the need for a firm monetary time-rule.

The ECB seeks to retain flexibility with respect to the precise time-frame of monetary policy. It does not offer a specific medium-term time-horizon, in part because the transmission mechanism in monetary policy operates with variable time-lags in affecting prices and hence there is some short-term volatility in inflation, and in part because policy must be calibrated to the nature and size of economic shocks (European Central Bank 2004: 54). The medium-term orientation signals a forwarding-looking monetary policy whose bias is to avoid excessive activism.

Consistent with historical institutionalism (Bulmer 2009), the leading edge role of the shift to monetary union in European economic governance has locked in this bias to long-term time-horizons and disciplinary time-rules. In consequence, European economic governance has evolved an inner circle of 'internal' time that rests on a distinctive and powerful time-discourse rooted in central banking and modern monetary economics. It not only endows the ECB with an extreme form of independence from its political environment (it defines its own price stability target). It also offers a powerful cognitive script that gives a distinctive missionary character to institution-building and policy development.

Two structural constraints create strong incentives for domestic political élites to discipline their political competition around this 'internal' time of central banking. Firstly, financial markets have become more powerful, globalized, opaque and volatile in the post-Bretton Woods age of floating exchange rates. Correspondingly, domestic political élites have had a greater incentive to enhance the credibility of central bankers as the most reliable guarantors of market stabilization. Hence they have bestowed a high degree of independence on central banks. Even when induced by short-term electoral competition to critique this independence, they have rapidly softened their positions in office (Dyson 2008). Secondly, the political pre-commitment to, heavy sunk costs in, and shared responsibility for, 'making the euro work' act as powerful constraints on both 'voice' and the threat of euro 'exit' as strategies (Hirschman 1970). The costs in reputation and policy of euro exit are sufficiently high and unpredictable to discourage threats of exit (Eichengreen 2007).

In consequence of these powerful systemic constraints on domestic political élites, the monetary policy time-discourse has pervaded European economic governance. Whether Euro Area 'insiders' or 'outsiders', EU member states have been made into time-takers by globalized financial markets and modern monetary economics and policy. As this distinctive 'internal' time radiates across European economic governance, domestic electoral cycles matter less in terms of their effects on macroeconomic policies. Central bankers matter more. The temporal distinctiveness rests in a dominant time-setting role for EU central bankers, coupled with a deeply entrenched idea of the linearity of time rather than its cyclical nature.

CIRCLES OF 'INTERNAL' TIME: 'ONE TIME DOES NOT FIT ALL'

Despite this distinctive inner circle, European economic governance lacks a single time-discourse and single time-rule, evident in variations in the use of deadlines and roadmaps. These variations reflect different functional attributes of monetary, fiscal, and economic reform policies and differences in the extent to which policy areas have a central and direct relevance to monetary policy. The closer that a policy issue is to monetary policy, and the more diffuse its effects, the more likely it is to be conceived as a public good requiring the use of deadlines and roadmaps. An example is the creation of European financial infrastructure and the integration of money and bond markets. Conversely, where policy issues are seen as involving direct, short-term, overtly redistributive and potentially costly effects on core political supporters and voters, the less likely it is that political élites will risk becoming hostage to detailed commitments. An example is the Lisbon strategy. In fiscal policy these two aspects of time-discourse and rules exist in a relationship of complex tensions. There are incentives to embrace time-rules to support monetary policy and incentives to avoid becoming hostage to them.

Within this two-level game of the hegemonic time-discourse in European monetary policy and the incentives of domestic electoral time-calendars, member states are continuously negotiating the time-rules of European economic governance. This process involves a complex calibration of risks from non-compliance of other states against domestic economic and political risks from binding hands too tightly. The outcome is inexorably a delicate balancing act that reflects functional attributes of policies and potential party and electoral costs. However, as stressed above, the larger context is the inducement to reduce vulnerability to more powerful and volatile financial markets by embracing and respecting the time-discourse and rules of monetary policy. The following three case studies of circles of European economic governance illustrate the different conceptions and uses of time.

Mobilizing market actors: financial market infrastructure

The European Commission and the ECB had a strong institutional self-interest, grounded in the logic of spillover, in using temporal devices of deadlines and roadmaps to complete the financial infrastructure of the single market and the Euro Area. In particular, the cost, speed and security of the financial infrastructure of payment and settlement systems were crucial to the monetary policy of the ECB. It illustrates the greater efficacy of dates and roadmaps as mobilizing devices, the closer a policy area is to ECB monetary policy.

At the same time the Commission and the ECB exhibited differences in attitudes. The ECB was more relaxed about a final deadline for the abolition of national debit systems, reflecting its sensitivity to the high costs to the banking system. It also preferred to accelerate change by prioritizing the Euro Area states over the rest of the EU and the European Economic Area. In the case of the development of an electronic payment and settlement system (TARGET and TARGET2), timetables and roadmaps were easier to negotiate. The ECB had more direct influence because the key actors were the constituent central banks of the Eurosystem. TARGET2 was phased in as a shared central bank platform between November 2007 and May 2008 (the Bank of England and the Swedish central bank chose not to migrate).

More problematic were TARGET2S and SEPA. In order to complete these projects it was necessary to use temporal devices to mobilize the banking sector and users, especially in the corporate sector. TARGET2S was highly controversial because it raised issues of whether it was appropriate for the ECB to enter into securities clearing and settlement by offering its TARGET system as the platform. Already two private-sector competitors, Clearstream and Euroclear, had invested heavily and feared effects on their business models. The ECB was motivated by the desire to internalize the use of central bank money in securities settlement and the belief that TARGET2S would offer a level of security and cost reduction in settlements that would constitute a major competitive gain for European securities markets. The ECB's problem was to gain agreement on a timetable of 2013 from the key market players. Without their active participation the advantages of TARGET2S would be reduced. The problem of getting market commitment to a timetable for the TARGET2S proposal was that the ECB was using this commitment to expand its own tasks rather than simply act as a catalyst in mobilizing change within markets.

In contrast, the mobilization of market actors was easier in two private-sector, market-driven projects, Short-Term European Paper (STEP) and SEPA. Easiest was STEP, which was initiated and led by the Financial Markets Association to promote convergence of standards in the short-term European paper markets. This development was closely linked to the single monetary policy and hence involved a central supportive role for the ECB in its stages of development. SEPA was more ambitious and complex. It was developed by European banks to make the whole range of electronic payments in euro by credit transfers, direct debits and credit cards as straightforward across Europe as domestic ones. The negotiation of SEPA focuses on the European Payments Council, which brings together banks and banking associations to propose common instruments, standards and business rules, especially on charges. Though it involves the 31 states of the European Economic Area (the EU-27 plus Iceland, Liechtenstein, Norway and Switzerland), the centre remains the Euro Area states.

The Commission, backed by the ECB, took the lead in presenting an ambitious timetable and roadmap for launching SEPA payment instruments for transfers (on 1 January 2008), debits and finally credit cards, completing full transition to SEPA by the end of 2010. This timetable was seen as essential to mobilize commitment to the expensive investments involved. It was recognized that the complexity of issues surrounding credit cards in particular required a process in stages, beginning with transfers. However, the high organizational and technical costs to the banking sector, threats to profit margins and problems of managing the perceived threats to established market players like Visa led to an extension of the timetable. The Commission, which had acted to produce the legislative basis for SEPA by 2006, was more resistant to this deferral. By 2007 the timetable was credit transfers from January 2008, direct debits from November 2009 and credit cards by the end of 2010. Standardization of cards proved a difficult issue for the European Payments Council, with the ECB wanting cross-nationally active banks to agree on a common European card. The ECB wanted a clear final deadline for full conversion to SEPA of five to seven years after its start in 2008 and a termination date for national transfer instruments.

Policing the boundaries of institutional autonomy: the SGP

The SGP provides a carefully choreographed temporal sequencing in disciplining domestic fiscal policies. Designed by legal and economic experts, it develops the excessive deficit procedure in Article 104 of the Maastricht Treaty by speeding up the stages in the decision-making sequence: from initiation by the Commission, through issuing an 'early warning' (requiring Council approval), specified deadlines for corrective measures, to sanctions. EU member states are committed to an annual reporting process on their convergence (for euro outsiders) and stability (for insiders) programmes and to timely imposition of SGP procedures. However, the Council retains effective control over this temporal sequencing, as it demonstrated by rejecting the Commission's recommendations on France and Germany in November 2003. This episode highlighted for the second time the delicate issues of political timing facing the Commission. In 2001 it had suffered the political embarrassment of Irish rejection of Commission criticism of the inconsistency of its budget policy with the BEPGs. The BEPG process was discredited.

After 1999 the main problems of non-compliance focused on relations of large states with the Commission, notably France, Germany and Italy. They displayed greater political sensitivity to erosion of their time-setting autonomy. Overall, however, the SGP was associated with an improvement in the aggregate fiscal performance of the EU. Moreover, despite the high profile of the 2003 SGP crisis, its 2005 reform was not fundamental. Reform was constrained by four factors: an enduring consensus amongst states about the need for time-rules; a blocking coalition of small states against more radical reforms; the Treaty basis of the excessive deficit procedure (EDP); and the enduring support in German public opinion for its core values.

The 2005 reform involved two main changes to time-rules. First, it was recognized that the earlier rules were a case of 'too tough, too late'. The focus on the 'corrective' arm of the Pact failed to offer incentives to build up 'safety margins' through budget surpluses in upswings. In consequence, the risks of non-compliance with the 3 per cent deficit rule were increased during the downswing, especially if as in 2001–05 it proved protracted. Hence rule changes focused on strengthening the 'preventive' arm of the Pact and thereby supporting anti-cyclical behaviour. The Lisbon Reform Treaty sought to strengthen the Commission by giving it the right to directly address an opinion to a member state with lax budget policies. However, despite ECB pressure, and with past experiences in mind, the Commission remained reluctant to use this instrument against France and Italy in early 2008.

Secondly, the emphasis shifted from the one-size-fits-all 'close to balance or in surplus' objective to country-specific medium-term budgetary objectives. States were to follow an adjustment path over the cycle that aimed at an improvement in the structural balance by 0.5 per cent gross domestic product (GDP) per annum. In addition, a number of procedural deadlines were extended under the corrective arm, in line with a greater scope for exceptional circumstances. Consequently, the Council had greater discretion to extend deadlines for correcting excessive deficits. This discretion made allowance for short-term costly structural reforms, for instance to pensions or employment policy, that would aid fiscal consolidation over the long term.

Synchronizing clocks of macroeconomic co-ordination

The time-rules of European macroeconomic co-ordination mechanisms evolved in an ambivalent manner. Though they had some success in better synchronizing different clocks, they proved ineffective in meeting the challenge of mobilizing domestic reforms and securing commitment and compliance. The challenge of synchronizing clocks was formidable. In first designing macroeconomic co-ordination, the annual BEPG process was seen as the pivot of a series of different processes, each with distinctive rules and fora: the SGP, employment policy (the Luxembourg process), structural reform policies (the Cardiff process), and the Macro-Economic Dialogue. Complexity increased when the Cologne European Council in 1999 tied the latter three into the European Employment Pact (as its 'three pillars') and the Lisbon strategy was added in 2000.

In the absence of precise prioritized objectives, clear roadmaps and firm deadlines, macroeconomic co-ordination mechanisms were weak in mobilizing member state governments. This weakness was most apparent in the Lisbon strategy. The Lisbon strategy reflected the ambitions of centre-Left governments to place growth at the centre of EU policy. However, in place of initial discussions about committing to a 3 per cent annual growth objective, the Lisbon European Council in 2000 agreed to a target date of 2010 for transforming the EU into 'the most dynamic and competitive knowledge-based economy in the world, capable of sustainable economic growth with more and better jobs and greater social cohesion'. This vague objective was to be achieved through the open method of co-operation, notably reliance on benchmarking best practice. The lack of a precise roadmap and of a clear objective tied to a timetable reflected the unwillingness of member state governments to be taken hostage to firm commitments. It resulted in the depressing conclusions of the 2004–05 mid-term review that the Lisbon strategy had failed to deliver sufficient structural reforms. The relaunched Lisbon strategy of 2005 de-emphasized the 2010 target date, focused more precisely on growth and employment, and redesigned the governance framework.

In redesigning the governance framework the 2005 review produced a closer synchronization of the various clocks of European macroeconomic co-ordination: the Cardiff process (reforms to product and capital markets), the Employment Guidelines and the BEPGs. Following the model of the BEPG reform in 2003, they were to be synchronized in a new three-year package, known as the Integrated Guidelines for Growth and Jobs. The Integrated Guidelines formed the basis for three-year national reform programmes, which offered a roadmap of domestic structural reforms to product, services, labour and capital markets, to be co-ordinated by new high-level national Lisbon co-ordinators, as well as for a three-year EU-level programme.

CONCLUSION: TIME AS ORDERING DEVICE, TIME AS CONTESTED CONCEPT

The evolving circles of 'internal' time in European economic governance have a complex relationship to the EU and Euro Area member states. The incentive to embrace the distinctive time-discourse, rules and strategies of monetary policy derives from the primacy of rescuing states from the unprecedented financial volatilities and crises that characterized the post-Bretton Woods era. Long time-horizons and clear time-rules offered insurance for governments against the scale, speed, complexity and opacity of globalizing financial markets. At a time when states were caught up in radical time–space compression, 'taking time seriously' provided stability, a semblance of rational order and a basis for restoring an image of governing competence. Monetary union – with its long time-horizons and bias to firm time-rules – has, in consequence, assumed a vanguard role in European economic governance. In dealing with the challenge of a synchronization of different time-rules, the EU bias has been to synchronize around a linear conception of time; in dealing with the challenges of mobilization and commitment, the bias has been to see time-rules as not sufficiently clear and firm. Monetary policy has provided the benchmark standards of rational political time.

These ordering and stabilizing functions of time have coexisted with contest about time. Contest derives in part from the functional specificities of different circles of European governance: whether they are seen as indivisible public goods like price stability and financial infrastructure or whether costs and gains are unevenly distributed across space and time, as with economic reforms. The proximity to monetary policy and the anchoring of dates in Treaty have been decisive for the role of time in mobilizing market and political actors. In contrast, direct, specific and redistributive effects alert governments to difficult issues of time management in controlling for political risks from incompatibilities of EU commitments (e.g. to fiscal retrenchment or benefit and labour-market reforms) with domestic electoral calendars.

The fragility of European economic governance illustrates the simultaneous and paradoxical efforts of member state governments to insure against short-term destabilizing financial market turbulence – by embracing the linear temporal discourse of monetary economics – and to insure against risks from the domestic electoral calendar – by evading commitments and compliance requirements. Strategic arguments for using European economic governance to 'squeeze the national present' by binding hands coexist with strategic arguments for breaking free. This ambivalence about time runs through European economic governance and offsets the radiating effects from monetary policy.

In consequence of these compression effects on European states, European economic governance raises serious issues about the quality of modern democracy (Goetz 2009). From one perspective, its distinctive time-discourse, rules and strategies have stabilized European states by making for more sustainable policies over time. They have facilitated a clearer, more rational debate about political choices and offered new, linear benchmarks by which to assess political credibility and reliability. Underlying parameters and assumptions of economic debate have been altered. From another perspective, European economic governance can be seen as hollowing out domestic democratic competition by suppressing the articulation of political preferences and centralizing executive powers so as to deliver on commitments. By narrowing the range of debate, its time-discourse and rules open up opportunities for populist Euro-sceptic mobilization and the threat of less cohesive party systems and governments (Collignon 2003). It is, however, by no means clear that, in abrogating commitments under European economic governance, states would be able to regain more control over political time. In more directly exposing themselves to the full force of global financial markets, they would have to bind their own hands even more firmly (Eichengreen 2007). In such a context democracy is even less likely to flourish.

Biographical note: Kenneth Dyson is Research Professor at the Cardiff School of European Studies, Cardiff University, UK.

REFERENCES

Adam, B. (2004) *Time*, Oxford: Blackwell.
Alesina, A. (1987) 'Macroeconomic policy in a two-party system as a respeated game', *Quarterly Journal of Economics* 102: 651–78.
Bulmer, S. (2009) 'Politics in time meets the politics of time: historical institutionalism and the EU timescape', *Journal of European Public Policy* 16(2): 307–24.
Collignon, S. (2003) *The European Republic*, London: The Federal Trust.
Dyson, K. (2000) *The Politics of the Euro Zone*, Oxford: Oxford University Press.

Dyson, K. (2008) 'The first decade: credibility, identity and institutional "fuzziness"', in K. Dyson (ed.), *The Euro at Ten: Europeanization, Power, and Convergence*. Oxford: Oxford Universtiy Press, pp. 1–34.

Dyson, K. (ed.) (2006) *Enlarging the Euro Area: External Empowerment and Domestic Transformation in East Central Europe*, Oxford: Oxford University Press.

Dyson, K. and Featherstone, K. (1999) *The Road to Maastricht: Negotiating Economic and Monetary Union*, Oxford: Oxford University Press.

Dyson, K. and Quaglia, L. (2008) 'Committee governance in economic and monetary union: policy experts and their images of europe', *Communities of Experts in the European Union: Final Report*, EU INTUNE, Department of Politics, University of Exeter.

Eder, K. (2004) 'The two faces of Europeanization: synchronizing a Europe moving at varying speeds', *Time and Society* 13(1): 89–107.

Eichengreen, B. (2007) *The Euro: Love It or Leave It?*, 19 November; www.voxeu.org/index.php?q=node/729

Ekengren, M. (1997) 'The temporality of European governance', in K. Jorgensen (ed.), *Reflective Approaches to European Governance*, Basingstoke: Macmillan, pp. 68–86.

Ekengren, M. (2002) *The Time of European Governance*, Manchester: Manchester University Press.

European Central Bank (2004) *The Monetary Policy of the ECB*, Frankfurt am Main: ECB.

Giavazzi, F. and Pagano, M. (1988) 'The advantage of tying one's hands: EMS discipline and central bank credibility', *European Economic Review* 32: 1055–82.

Goetz, K.H. (2009) 'How does the EU tick? Five propositions on political time', *Journal of European Public Policy* 16(2): 202–20.

Goetz, K.H. and Meyer-Sahling, J.-H. (2009) 'Political time in the EU: dimensions, perspectives, theories', *Journal of European Public Policy* 16(2): 180–201.

Harvey, D. (1990) *The Condition of Postmodernity: An Enquiry into the Origins of Cultural Change*, Cambridge, MA: Blackwell.

Heipertz, M. and Verdun, A. (2005) 'The Stability and Growth Pact – theorising a case in European integration', *Journal of Common Market Studies* 43(5): 985–1008.

Hirschman, A. (1970) *Exit, Voice and Loyalty*, Cambridge, MA: Harvard University Press.

Kindleberger, C. (2005) *Manias, Panics and Crashes*, Basingstoke: Palgrave.

Kydland, F. and Prescott, E. (1977) 'Rules rather than discretion: the inconsistency of optimal plans', *Journal of Political Economy* 85: 473–93.

Lucas, R. (1976) 'Econometric policy evaluation: a critique', *Carnegie-Rochester Conference Series on Public Policy* 1: 19–46.

Meyer-Sahling, J.-H. and Goetz, K.H. (2009) 'The EU timescape: from notion to research agenda', *Journal of European Public Policy* 16(2): 325–36.

Moran, M. (1991) *The Politics of the Financial Services Revolution*, London: Macmillan.

Moravcsik, A. (1998) *The Choice for Europe*, Ithaca, NY: Cornell University Press.

Nowotny, H. (1994) *Time: The Modern and Postmodern Experience*, Cambridge: Polity Press.

Parsons, N. and Pochet, P. (2008) 'Wages and collective bargaining', in K. Dyson (ed.), *The Euro At Ten: Europeanization, Convergence and Power*, Oxford: Oxford University Press.

Putnam, R. (1988) 'Diplomacy and domestic politics: the logic of two level games', *International Organisation* 3: 427–60.

Riescher, G. (1994) *Zeit und Politik: Zur institutionellen Bedeutung von Zeitstrukturen in parlamentarischen und praesidentiellen Regierungssystemen*, Baden-Baden: Nomos.

Rogoff, K (1987) 'Equilibrium political business cycles', NBER Working Paper 2428.

Savage, J. (2005) *Making the EMU: The Politics of Budgetary Surveillance and the Enforcement of Maastricht*, Oxford: Oxford University Press.

Schedler, A. and Santiso, J. (1998) 'Democracy and time: an invitation', *International Political Science Review* 19(1): 5–18.

Schmitter, P. and Santiso, J. (1998) 'Three temporal dimensions to the consolidation of democracy', *International Political Science Review* 19(1): 69–92.

Stark, J. (2007) 'Wir machen Geldpolitik und betreiben keine Vogelkunde', *Börsen-Zeitung* 29 December.

Umbach, G. (forthcoming) *Intent and Reality of a New Mode of Governance*, Baden-Baden: Nomos.

Politics in Time meets the politics of time: historical institutionalism and the EU timescape

Simon Bulmer

ABSTRACT This article considers what light historical institutionalism (HI) may be able to shed on the European Union's (EU's) timescape. Drawing on Paul Pierson's work *Politics in Time* it reviews what HI has to say about the dual dynamics of path dependent incremental development and radical change (termed punctuated equilibrium or critical junctures) as well as relating to timing, sequencing and long-term processes. It then suggests three areas of EU studies for exploring these contrasting dynamics, namely the integration process as a whole, EU policy dynamics and Europeanization. Applications of HI in EU studies have tended to be empirical and have often neglected to engage with the temporal theorizing embraced by Pierson. The special issue's appeal for a new research agenda on the EU timescape offers the opportunity, it is argued, to rectify the insufficiency of theoretical reflection.

INTRODUCTION[1]

What light can historical institutionalism (HI) shed on the European Union's (EU's) timescape? In addressing this question I focus on the broad research agenda of EU politics and seek to complement the editors' research agenda, while extending coverage beyond the specific applications in other contributions to this volume. I accept Goetz and Meyer-Sahling's (2009) understanding of a timescape as the manner in which time is institutionalized in a political system along the polity, politics and policy dimensions. The notion of timescape therefore encompasses the broader temporal landscape of the EU. Thus, I depart from a focus on time-rules and concentrate on the macro-level of analysis: on the post-war reconstruction of the state in Europe. I am therefore concerned with the evolution of the European Coal and Steel Community through to today's EU; with the evolving relationship between this supranational level and the member states; with the shifting of authority between these levels; with the transfer of policy responsibilities between them; and with the transfer of some aspects of political contestation to a level beyond the member states.

The title of the article acknowledges the contribution made by Paul Pierson, whose book *Politics in Time* is one of the most influential statements of HI (Pierson 2004).[2] As Pierson has put it elsewhere:

> [HI] scholarship is *historical* because it recognises that political development must be understood as a process that unfolds over time. It is *institutionalist* because it stresses that many of the contemporary implications of these temporal processes are embedded in institutions, whether these be formal rules, policy structures, or social norms.
> (Pierson 1998: 29, italics in original; see also Steinmo 2008)

Pierson developed his HI analysis as a corrective to ahistorical tendencies in the predominant rational choice perspective in American political science more generally. But he was also critical in his work on the EU of the time horizons explored in liberal intergovernmentalist theorizing on the (Pierson 1996, 1998). The concern here, however, is not with critiquing other theoretical approaches to the EU but, rather, to join the editors' plea for devoting greater analysis to political time in the EU. The article does so by advocating HI as a way of capturing some of the longer-term dynamics which are important to understanding the EU's timescape.

The article first spells out the temporal concerns of HI and their significance to the understanding of EU politics. As will be seen, not all HI research – whether generally or on the EU – is primarily concerned with 'the temporal'. Furthermore, an emergent polarization within political science between rationalist and constructivist analysis has tended to put a squeeze on HI amongst the different variants of institutionalism.[3] In emphasizing HI's temporal dimension I then turn to three key areas of the political analysis of the EU – namely integration, policy evolution and Europeanization – and suggest how HI has provided, or might provide, distinctive insights. My broad proposition is that an understanding of time is as important to understanding the evolution of the EU as it is to more specific rules, such as those relating to the legislative cycle (see Kovats 2009). I also therefore discuss how this paper's research agenda fits with that identified by the editors.

HISTORICAL INSTITUTIONALISM AND TIME

From its initial explicit formulation by Thelen and Steinmo (1992), HI has been centrally concerned with how institutional or policy choices create a path dependency in future development. Patterns of institutional or policy evolution are generally regarded as slow-moving and incremental. However, they may be subject to episodes of sudden transformative change, typically referred to in earlier new institutionalist analysis as 'punctuated equilibrium' (Krasner 1984: 240–43). At first blush HI therefore offers considerable potential for insights into time, timing and tempo both generally as well as in the EU context specifically.

A second aspect of HI, emphasized in particular in Hall and Taylor's account of the three 'new institutionalisms', is that HI occupies a middle ground between the rationalist and sociological variants: between calculus- and culture-based explanations of political action (Hall and Taylor 1996: 940).[4] Also intrinsic to this middle ground is the position advanced by Thelen and Steinmo relating to the impact of institutions upon political actors, namely that they affect not only 'the strategies but also the goals that actors pursue' (1992: 8). From this perspective HI may assist the understanding of politics at the interface between what March and Olsen term the logic of consequentialism and the logic of appropriateness (see the discussion in March and Olsen 1989, 1998). One consequence of this mooted bridge-building role for HI is that some of its empirical applications have been less concerned with issues of time than with matters of analytical strategy and 'brand differentiation'. Nevertheless, in his own HI analyses, notably on British, and later comparative, economic policy, Peter Hall placed an emphasis on the temporal (Hall 1992, 1986). In another important contribution to HI Peter Hall explored the role of ideas as a source of change in policy practice (e.g. Hall 1989).

The attention devoted to this second aspect of HI doubtless lies behind Paul Pierson noting that 'those associated with historical institutionalism have generally been more explicit in discussing the "institutionalist" dimensions of their framework than the "historical" ones' (2004: 8). In focusing specifically within this special issue upon the politics of time, institutional and policy *change* is pushed to the forefront of an HI research agenda. Guy Peters has noted about HI that 'The entire analytical framework appears premised upon the enduring effects of institutional and policy choices made at the initiation of a structure', thus apparently making it better suited to explain persistence than change (Peters 1999: 68). However, to portray HI crudely as having a deterministic effect on institutional or policy change is to neglect the work its exponents have conducted on punctuated equilibrium (Krasner 1984) or critical junctures (Collier and Collier 1991) or similar work by policy change analysts on critical institutional events (Baumgartner and Jones 1993). These analyses bring in the second dynamic of radical change to challenge the default position of path dependence. The difficulty lies in *predicting* or *accounting for* this type of change rather than in identifying it, *ex post*, in empirical accounts of institutional or policy evolution. Hence Paul Pierson's early caution in *Politics in Time* that 'Many of the key concepts needed to underpin analyses of temporal processes, such as path dependence, critical junctures, sequencing events, duration, timing and unintended consequences, have received only very fragmented and limited discussion' (2004: 6). Given its temporal focus, historical institutionalists tend to argue that politics must be seen as a movie rather than a series of individual snapshots.

In *Politics in Time* Pierson elaborates on a number of concepts which make the study of the temporal/historical dimension of politics important, namely path dependence, timing, sequence and the nature of long-term processes. Path dependence is not just expressing the point that history matters; it highlights how political processes entail trajectories that are difficult to reverse because they are underpinned by mechanisms of positive feedback and increasing returns, as reflected in sunk costs and vested interests (Pierson 2004: ch. 1). Path dependence does not signify stasis and its impact is likely to vary across policy areas. Whilst path dependence is the aspect of HI that is most typically associated with its application in the EU, this bias is frankly rather unconvincing. Although there are strong elements of continuity in the EU's evolution, one of the most striking aspects about its trajectory since the mid-1980s has been the number of major constitutional reforms, policy innovations and so on. Path dependence has important purchase on the EU's evolution but there have also been major changes as well, such as the introduction of a single currency, so the exploration of critical junctures or punctuated equilibrium must be brought into focus as well.[5]

Timing, sequencing and conjunctures have been the concern of a number of political scientists concerned with macro-social development (e.g. Lipset and Rokkan 1967; Tilly 1975; Skowronek 1982). Different sequencing of events can produce significant cross-national differentiation in the development of states and political systems, as studies such as these attest. Understanding the long-term development of the EU in comparative-historical terms, rather than through integration theory, has been a quite limited research domain (see, e.g. Bartolini 2005; Milward 1992).[6] Tilly has expressed the issue of timing thus: '*when* things happen within a sequence affects *how* they happen' (quoted in Pierson 2004: 54). Thus challenges posed for European integration were quite different in the post-war period compared to that following the end of the Cold War. At the same time, how the EU responded to the latter challenge was also shaped in no small measure by the experience afforded by 40 years of the integration process set down in the *acquis communautaire*. On a smaller scale of illustration, namely the single market, policy solutions adopted at the height of the initiative (that is, 1985–92) combined a strong component of supranational delegation accompanied by the less intrusive market mechanisms of mutual recognition. However, sectoral 'leftovers', such as the single markets in electricity and telecommunications, then had to be dealt with in a post-Maastricht climate of attention to subsidiarity. The range of legislative solutions was narrowed accordingly (Bulmer *et al.* 2007: 133). Pierson's work has much to say about how to investigate the temporal sequences of social processes (2004: ch. 2). His work seeks to complement the game-theoretical approaches which are prominent in rational choice (and which are relevant to highly iterative processes between a few actors, such as in the EU's inter-institutional relations).

A final contribution made by Pierson is to place emphasis on long-term processes at a time when the time horizons of rational choice analysis may privilege attention to the shorter term (Pierson 2004: ch. 3). 'Slow-moving processes may be cumulative, involve threshold effects, or require the unfolding of extended causal chains' (Pierson 2004: 82). Equally, *outcomes* may also be slow-moving. These processes risk being neglected in studies with a short time-frame. The latter are akin to natural scientists focusing only on tornadoes (short time-horizons for both cause and outcome) and neglecting longer-term climate developments, notably global warming, which is unfolding slowly in causal terms and with long-term consequences (Pierson 2004: 81). European integration is a response to a series of long-term processes such as: the search for a peaceful system of international relations in Europe; promoting market integration; building a zone of democratic values and rights; the changing role of the state; population movements; new security challenges and so on. Hence it is important that research on the EU timescape encompasses these longer-term developments. The 'governance turn' in EU studies (Kohler-Koch and Rittberger 2006) has gone hand-in-hand with a withdrawal from theorizing the longer-term forces which underlie integration. Even where the driving forces *are* explored, notably in Moravcsik's work (1998), the treaty or other negotiated bargain represents the outcome. This perspective neglects that the consequences of the bargain take years to unfold. Integration in itself is a long-term process.

Pierson, of course, is not the only exponent of HI. Other authors such as Peter Hall, James Mahoney, Theda Skocpol, Sven Steinmo and Kathleen Thelen have made important contributions (for a sample and overview of such work, see Mahoney and Rueschemeyer 2003). In a notable development Orion Lewis and Sven Steinmo have argued that historical institutionalists should 'take evolutionary theory more seriously', drawing on biological sciences to help understand institutional evolution. Such an approach may also shed light on the EU's organic development over the long term. The purpose of focusing on Pierson's work here is principally as a device to identify areas of empirical research on the EU where HI may offer valuable insights into the EU timescape.

One final observation is in order at this stage. HI's distinctive claim to be concerned with the longer-term processes through its understanding of politics as a movie rather than as snapshots has been challenged in work by Adrienne Héritier (2007; also see Farrell and Héritier 2005). Her analysis of five 'rule changes', for instance relating to the European Parliament's (EP's) legislative role, is based on a set of consecutive snapshots. Each snapshot explores *ex ante* hypotheses based on rational choice institutionalism. In examining the iterative contestation of rule change she demonstrates how the shorter time-horizons of rational choice do not preclude capturing longer-term processes of institutional development.[7] This is important work in its own right but it also challenges assumptions that HI's focus on the 'movie' places it in a privileged position for exploring longer-term processes of institutional and policy change.

HISTORICAL INSTITUTIONALISM, TIME AND INTEGRATION

HI has untapped potential to shed new light on the integration process. That is not to say that it offers a 'silver bullet' in accounting for the fitful timescape of the integration process, namely whether the EU's temporality is able to 'keep pace' with the political, social, economic and technological challenges it faces (Meyer-Sahling and Goetz 2009: 327). But it may be able to assist with disaggregating the different dynamics that bear upon the integration process in a way that existing macro-theories of integration have themselves struggled with. First of all, let us briefly consider the temporal dynamics of European integration and how these have aligned with the two main macro-theories of integration.

The teleological characteristics of neo-functionalist integration proved to be its weakness. Its explanation of the dynamics of integration went awry in the 1960s once French President Charles de Gaulle obstructed the functional and political spillover associated with putting the common agricultural policy (CAP) into effect at the same time as creating a supranational budget and moving to qualified majority on a range of policy areas. Spillover, a central component of neo-functionalism and with implicit assumptions for an integrative timescape, was challenged as the political integration process was stopped in its tracks. Haas, as is often noted, declared integration theory to be 'obsolescent' in the mid-1970s (Haas 1975). However, he was not declaring integration theory or neo-functionalism to be dead. Some neo-functionalists shifted attention to the European Communities as a political system (Lindberg and Scheingold 1970; for commentary, see Rosamond 2000: 85–93). In any event, neo-functionalism left an important legacy for HI analysts and others (e.g. see the papers in Börzel 2005).

The liberal intergovernmentalist account of the temporal dimension of integration is represented in the work of Andrew Moravcsik (1993, 1998). In his account, represented most clearly by his book, *The Choice for Europe*, the timescape of integration is driven by major events, namely the decisions of government heads, intergovernmental conferences (IGCs) and other treaty-negotiating arenas. The key episodes he examines are undoubtedly important to the direction of integration. However, we have arguably already identified the major distinction between the two major macro-integration theories in respect of the timescape, portrayed graphically by Philippe Schmitter (2004: 47–8). Neo-functionalism is based on an epistemology of attention to incremental political processes. By contrast, liberal intergovernmentalism is based on a research strategy of gathering evidence on dramatic political events. HI offers the opportunity to focus on the two different dynamics of change as well as on the short- and long-term nature of political processes relating to integration. This is an important consideration for researching the EU timescape.

In his critique of liberal intergovernmentalism Paul Pierson explained why it is insufficient just to focus upon major events at which the member governments are the key actors (Pierson 1998: 34–50). He explained why gaps emerge between the preferences of the governments and actual political practice. He questioned whether the delegation of authority to supranational institutions through such decisions could possibly ensure conformity to the intentions of those who were party to the original agreement (Pierson 1998: 34–50). His full argument cannot be rehearsed here but it clearly contained an important temporal dimension, illustrated by the restricted time-horizons of negotiators failing to capture the longer-term consequences of their decisions and by shifts over time in member state preferences. In addition, and drawing on neo-functionalism, he noted the problem of controlling the incremental dynamics that develop in the supranational institutions. EU decision rules – especially where unanimity applies – render it difficult for member governments to regain control, while the sunk costs and vested interests surrounding the incremental practices may make the reassertion of control impossible politically.

If the integration process is thought of in terms of a timescape it is possible to identify several related endogenous dynamics that contribute to the state of the EU at a particular time-point. First, there are the politically negotiated reforms to the constitutional and institutional order of the EU. These reforms should not just be understood as IGCs. Also important are the successive enlargements of the EU (Meyer-Sahling and Goetz 2009). These change the shape of interests and concerns that are refracted through existing policies, while at the same time giving rise to new concerns that later may become matters for IGCs. The origins of the European Regional Development Fund in the aftermath of the 1973 enlargement (reflecting British and Irish concerns) and the successive refocusing of the structural funds after southern and eastern enlargements illustrate the way in which enlargement impacts upon the shape of the EU's policy profile. Thus each of the IGCs and rounds of enlargement brings about significant change to the trajectory of the EU as a whole, while impacting on individual policy regimes as well. There has been considerable theoretically informed work on the socialization and incentive effects of enlargement upon the accession/new member states themselves (see, e.g., Schimmelfennig and Sedelmeier 2004). However, there has been little effort to theorize the impact upon the timescape of the EU's existing policy profile of the successive rounds of enlargement.

Second, as highlighted by Pierson's critique of liberal intergovernmentalism, there are the political dynamics that develop between these major reforms, as the institutions – both supranational and intergovernmental – put those agreements into operation. The interaction of these dynamics has been taken up in the study of treaty reform (Falkner 2002a). The first and second dynamics are what Christiansen and Jørgensen (1999) have referred to as the 'summits' and 'valleys' of the integration process. Quite apart from the 'valleys' being missed by those whose research is biased towards dramatic political events, the relatively short intervals between the 'summits' has encouraged 'event-following' in EU studies. I suggest that the dual dynamics of change present in HI should facilitate an ability to research the summit and the succeeding valley in order to explore the longer-term processes unleashed and the EU timescape more broadly.[8] The tempo of integration may be quicker in connection with the 'summits' but, to understand the long-term process that is European integration, it is necessary to include attention to the 'valleys' as well.

A related incremental dynamic concerns what might be termed the proceduralization of constitutional politics in the EU. Christiansen has argued (2002) that the process of treaty reform has become proceduralized to some degree and may consequently constrain the pattern of negotiations.[9] Falkner (2002b: 7) refers to the development of an *acquis conférenciel*. A question which arises from this proceduralization of constitutional politics is whether it has impacted on the speed of reform. Certainly the domestic ratification process has become more hazardous and potentially slower because of the need, following recent enlargements, to secure approval in 27 member states. The process of enlargement has also become proceduralized over time. However, as Graham Avery's contribution to this volume reveals, the historic challenge of eastern enlargement required a large measure of change to past practice (Avery 2009). Incremental adaptation of past enlargement procedures was not feasible, and there were adjustments to the timetable, notably in what he calls the 'battle of dates'.

Third, there is the judicial dynamic arising from the jurisprudence of the European Court of Justice (ECJ). The state of the EU's constitutional order is not simply the product of treaty reforms, enlargements and the developments which take place between them. An important additional contribution derives from ECJ jurisprudence (see, for instance, Stein 1981; Weiler 1991). The timescape of ECJ jurisprudence is quite different from that of the day-to-day policy process because its interventions are frequently concerned with the interpretation of the treaties or the legislation arising from the policy process. There is necessarily a time-lag in relation to the original political decision on the treaty or legislation. To illustrate the different timescape of ECJ jurisprudence it should be recalled that some of the most fundamental decisions on the supranational character of European law were handed down in the mid-1960s, at precisely the same time as the resurgence of national governments following the 1965 empty chair crisis.

A beginning has been made in using HI to explore the different dynamics of integration, focusing particularly on treaty reform (see Christiansen *et al.* 2002). Greve and Jørgensen (2002) have sought to introduce the legal context into analysis of the dynamics of treaty reform. These studies have shown a way forward but they have also emphasized the institutional rather than the temporal aspects of HI, exploring the theoretical propositions made by Pierson.[10] Hence my conclusion from this review is that HI offers the potential to capture key macro-level processes in the timescape of European integration. There might be particular merit in making a connection between HI and evolutionary theory in understanding the EU's development.

HISTORICAL INSTITUTIONALISM, TIME AND POLICY EVOLUTION

The application of HI analysis to the political system of the EU has chiefly been undertaken in connection with policy analysis. However, as has already been noted, the emphasis has been on HI's institutional contribution rather than its historical or temporal contribution.[11] The twin dynamics of path dependence and radical change have relevance to understanding EU policy dynamics, since policy pathways may be subject to occasional 'punctuations' (Pollitt 2008: 42). Goetz (2009) has suggested in his second proposition that EU political time is linear, suggesting a contrast with the more cyclical nature of time at the national level. For example, the EP's electoral cycle is not associated with a government–opposition dynamic and legislation does not fall at the end of a parliamentary term, unlike in most national systems. Linearity is further underlined by presidency work programmes which may provide continuity during the 'changing of the guard' in the Parliament and the Commission. Linearity offers support to understanding EU policy development as incremental. However, it should be noted that where 'punctuations' occur in policy, they may be considered non-linear in nature.

What the literature on EU policy dynamics lacks at present is a wider literature that systematically explores such issues as those raised by Chris Pollitt:

- What mechanisms keep policies on particular pathways?
- Under what circumstances do significant changes take place?
- Is path dependency widespread or limited to particular circumstances?
- How should 'within path' changes be distinguished from punctuations?
- And, finally, what is the velocity of policy down a pathway (Pollitt 2008: 43)?

Addressing questions such as these may assist with comparison of the dynamics across policy sectors. For example, do policy areas where authority is delegated to non-majoritarian agencies demonstrate greater path dependence than others?

Amongst the temporal factors which impact on a policy's timescape are: electoral cycles at national level and in the EP; the Commission's term of office; the presidency's term of office (including recent developments towards 'trio presidencies'); and, as Tholoniat has identified (2009), the Commission's planning cycle. The EU's financial perspectives provide an important budgetary timescape. Through interaction effects the jurisprudence of the European courts may impact in a major way on existing policy such that existing incremental developments are subjected to a critical juncture, resulting in a major new direction unfolding. As illustrations of such rulings of the European Court it is possible to identify the 1979 *Cassis de Dijon* ruling's impact upon the internal market; the 1987 *Philip Morris* judgment's impact on regulating concentrations (mergers and acquisitions); and the 1986 *Nouvelles Frontières* ruling on air transport liberalization (Armstrong and Bulmer 1998: 149–51, 95–6, 177–8 respectively). Each of these decisions recalibrated the policy debate and made a substantial contribution to the development of a new policy trajectory that departed from the incremental path dependence theretofore.

Another form of interaction effect can arise when a round of constitutional reform may recalibrate inter-institutional relations, for example by introducing qualified majority voting into a policy area, adding dynamism to stalled legislative proposals. Similarly, changes in EU-level competences can also impact upon policy development, for instance by providing the Commission with clear authority to initiate legislation rather than using soft-law methods.[12] This kind of impact can also work in the reverse direction. Recent reforms to the common agricultural policy CAP have reduced the extent of its interventionism and led to a reorientation towards rural policy. This development, when taken in conjunction with the devolution of powers in the UK since 1999, has opened up space for the practice of distinct rural policies in

England, Wales and Scotland (Burch *et al.* 2005: 470). Thus, to the extent that policy is repatriated to the member state, it may contribute to a critical juncture in the practice of policy at the latter level. As was noted earlier in the article, enlargements also impact on policy dynamics by changing the pattern of interests in the Council.

Policy evolution itself may be characterized by temporal measures. A policy review may be written into legislation or be agreed politically as a way of returning to issues unresolved in negotiations. As illustration of the former, the 1989 Merger Control Regulation included specific provision for a review (originally scheduled for 1993) because member governments had reached an uneasy compromise on the threshold at which mergers and acquisitions would be subject to supranational regulation. More recently, Tony Blair secured a political agreement at the European Council in December 2005 that there should be a midterm review of the budget in 2008–09, seeking thereby to put further pressure for its reorientation away from the CAP (Howarth 2006: 93). Another form of temporal measure is the setting of headline objectives, such as the 2010 Lisbon Strategy target regarding European competitiveness or the Commission's 'roadmap' on enlargement, outlined by Avery (2009). Such devices of 'governing by timetable' are designed to prevent policy stasis and 'lock in'.

In order to explore the role of temporality in policy evolution more thoroughly, and to develop better defined analytical tools, comparison is essential. A comparison between the CAP and the budget, for instance, can be revealing in exploring policy dynamics (Pollack 2005: 21–2). The development of the CAP from the 1960s entailed many sunk costs which reinforced path dependence. However, it was the associated force of agricultural vested interests – the sector generally and certain member states in particular – which explained the maintenance for so long of a policy trajectory that, in the words of Rieger, followed 'non-economic objectives [which gave] the CAP a rationale of its own' (Rieger 2000: 180). It typically necessitated stimuli from outside of agriculture and interaction effects with other EU policies to force major-order policy change upon reluctant agriculture ministers and the policy community: the threat of exhausting the EU's budget in the 1980s; pressures from world trade negotiations from the late 1980s; and in the late 1990s the challenge of extending the CAP regime to new, more agrarian, member states with the 2001 enlargement (Donaghey 2003; Feindt 2008).

By contrast, the EU budget is subject to revision at seven-year intervals as part of bargains between the member governments over the so-called 'financial perspectives'. The resultant sequence of reviews enables some flexibility, although the need for unanimity on the medium-term settlements still imposes constraints on fundamental change. Thus, in the case of the EU budget the timing and tempo of change are very much predetermined, with more significant change being agreed at the seven-year review point and a pattern of incremental change from year to year. Nevertheless, the existence of review points provides clear prospects for critical junctures in policy evolution (for empirical illustration, see Laffan 2000).

The illustrations above reveal how the timescape of EU policies could become a more explicit focus for research. Path dependence, critical junctures, timing, sequencing and conjunctures are all concepts which can shed light on the comparative timescapes of different EU policies. The empirical papers in this special issue illustrate the importance of time. My conclusion here is that this research agenda will be enhanced further if attention is paid to long-term trends of policy evolution and to the comparative dynamics across policy areas.

HISTORICAL INSTITUTIONALISM, TIME AND EUROPEANIZATION

The final area of the EU timescape which is considered here relates to Europeanization. Although institutionalism has been intrinsic to many studies of Europeanization, the application of HI has been negligible (for an exception, see Bulmer and Burch 2001). However, as Klaus Goetz (2009: 191) has argued, 'the impact of EU time on political time in the member states' is an important component of the EU timescape. Goetz's concern is with the impact of EU political time upon the political timescape in the member states, developing a theme previously explored by Ekengren (2002). I would like to consider here how the timescape of EU integration has impacted upon institutional change within the member states.[13] I focus specifically on how member states 'deal with "Europe"', although there are wider impacts upon the state that could also be covered, such as the domestic political economy or the democratic process. Specifically, the focus is upon subnational government.

Two observations are in order at the outset. First, any EU member state has to develop domestic institutional arrangements to deal with the duties of engagement that accompany membership. These duties are downstream (*reception*, for example by transposing European legislation) and upstream (*projection*, namely engagement in the EU policy-making process). The second observation is that the timing of accession matters. No fewer than 27 member states have had to adjust to EU membership. We know from evidence relating to the 15 members prior to enlargement in 2001 that each state dealt with the EU in a distinctive way even though they were participating in the same supranational organization (e.g. see Kassim 2003, 2005; Wessels *et al.* 2003). Each state responded to accession in accordance with an embedded institutional pattern; we could term this the 'national varieties of state institutions' thesis. However, the response of individual member states has also been conditioned by the timing of their accession.

For the original six member states, the downstream impact of membership was not a major issue in the 1950s, since the priority was on the upstream flow from central government to the supranational level as part of the construction of the European Communities. Europeanization (and its study) really only gained momentum as a result of the development of the single market and further reform in the 1992 Maastricht Treaty. With each successive enlargement the adjustment pressures placed on acceding states have increased because of the growth of EU rules, policies, procedures and legislation (the *acquis communautaire*). The pressures were especially pronounced for ten of the recent member states because accession followed quite recent democratic transitions in the aftermath of the end of the Cold War and the break-up of the Soviet Union (Goetz 2005). The later that a member state joins the EU, the greater in principle will be the pressure for major domestic reform upon accession. Whether major reform takes place is a matter for empirical study. There is, notably, an interaction effect with the embeddedness of domestic institutions: a condition influenced by the timescape at that level.

Rather than reflecting on how the timing of accession impacts at the member state level, I consider it in relation to the engagement with subnational authorities (SNAs) in EU policy-making. The EU's main impact on territoriality came with the development of the structural funds from the mid-1970s onwards. For the founding member states and those joining in 1973 there had been no major impact on the territoriality of the state. Consequently, incremental domestic adjustment took place using informal arrangements. However, with the growth of the structural funds in the late 1980s the impact of the EU was significant. Given the territorial nature of German government, the Maastricht Treaty became an opportunity for the *Länder* to 'strike back' (Jeffery 1994). The *Länder* (with support from Belgian SNAs) projected demands into the Maastricht negotiations for greater subnational sensitivity and secured the creation of the Committee of the Regions, the right of subnational ministers to sit in the Council and the introduction of the subsidiarity principle. At the same time the domestic ratification of the Maastricht Treaty gave the *Länder* governments leverage so that they could achieve a domestic constitutional reform (Article 23, Basic Law), enabling them to have formalized domestic participation rights where European policy impacted on their powers (see Bulmer *et al.* 2000: 33–40).

The Spanish experience has been characterized by a growing empowerment of the authorities beyond Madrid, but under different circumstances. When Spain acceded in 1986 it was a new democracy and its own internal territorial distribution of authority was not strongly embedded. Over the period since membership the historic nationalities, especially in Catalonia and the Basque country, have sought to strengthen their authority, including over European policy. The key opportunities in respect of the latter have not come at the time of new developments at EU level but as a result of domestic opportunities arising from government formation in Madrid. These opportunities have derived from the fact that the different Catalan and Basque political parties have on occasion occupied a crucial role in ensuring a majority to the governing party in the Spanish parliament. The asymmetrical decentralization within Spain has resulted in the historic nationalities (Basque country, Catalonia and Galicia) securing not only an important role for themselves but also for the other autonomous communities (Morata 2007).

These illustrations reveal the interaction of two timescapes. The EU's impact on SNAs gradually increased, especially with the development of the structural funds. At the member state level the territorial distribution of powers may itself be relatively stable or scarcely embedded at all, as in the case of the new Spanish democracy in the mid-1980s.[14] For Germany the territorial challenge confronted the *Länder* well after accession and it was necessary to convince the federal government to take up their cause, as well as finding allies such as in Belgium to do likewise. The Maastricht Treaty negotiations offered the opportunity for strengthening participation rights for SNAs, reinforced by the veto power held by the *Länder* in the Bundesrat. In the case of Spain, however, the domestic timescape for territorial reform was insufficiently advanced to take such action. The autonomous communities had not established their domestic constitutional authority. Reform to the communities' role in EU policy-making came later (in late 2004) as a result of domestic electoral timing and domestic dynamics rather than responding to a specific reform at that time from the EU level (Morata 2007). The interaction of the two timescapes is fertile ground for further research, and could encompass other states where the territorial ramifications of EU membership have been pronounced: for instance Belgium, Austria and the United Kingdom. The UK case is interesting because a domestic change in an embedded, centralized system – the election of the Blair government in 1997 – prompted reforms that brought British territorial governance into much greater alignment with the multi-levelled and partnership modes on the European mainland (see Bache 2008).

There is abundant scope to develop the research agenda further on the interaction of the EU and domestic timescapes. Martin Burch and I have explored the historical trajectory of UK central government's adjustment to European integration (Bulmer and Burch 2009, forthcoming). We found that the system of 'dealing with Europe' was initiated in 1961 at the time of the first application for membership of the European Communities. Subsequent critical junctures occurred in 1973 with accession, as the system was recalibrated for new tasks; following the 1992 Maastricht Treaty, when it became more fragmented as a result of the EU's three-pillar system; and under the Blair government because of greater investment in strategic thinking about European policy as well as domestic reforms associated with devolution. However, a much more differentiated timescape was identified when attention moved to how individual ministries 'deal with Europe' (Bulmer and Burch 2009, forthcoming: ch. 8; see also Jordan 2002 on the timescape for the UK Department of the Environment).

My conclusion here, therefore, is that analysis of the impact of the EU timescape at domestic level can form a rewarding research agenda. The impact on domestic political parties and party systems in particular deserves further examination (see Mair 2007). Europeanization entails handing off some control of the domestic timescape to the EU level but the consequence is that the EU timescape becomes a driver of change at the domestic level (Ekengren 2002: ch. 5). The timing and scale of these changes, I suggest, are fundamental to understanding EU–member state relations.

CONCLUSION

The editors of this volume have made a strong case for greater attention being paid to political time in the EU. In this article I have argued that the broader picture of the EU timescape should not be neglected. The evolution of the EU's constitution, long-term policy trends and realignments of authority between the EU, the member states and subnational authorities, I argue, should be integral to this research agenda. HI offers a number of key concepts to capture the timescape, namely path dependence, punctuations, sequencing events, duration, timing and unintended consequences. Pierson's *Politics in Time* sets out an agenda to underpin the application of these concepts and thereby to shift attention to the temporal aspect of HI analysis. HI analysis has no monopoly over this research agenda, as the work of Adrienne Héritier has illustrated (2007). However, I have suggested here a tentative research prospectus for taking forward analysis of some of the key issues of the EU timescape. HI is not without its critics. It can better explain developments *ex post* than offer predictive hypotheses. Nevertheless, it can capture macro-level political development: a scale of research which seems to be slipping from view in the analysis of the EU.

Biographical note: Simon Bulmer is Professor at the Department of Politics, University of Sheffield, UK. He is Director of the Graduate School in Politics and of the Centre for International Policy Research.

NOTES

1. I am grateful for comments received on the paper, including those from my colleague, Ian Bache.
2. For a review of a range of the contributions, see also Mahoney and Rueschemeyer (2003).
3. In the context of EU studies, see, for instance, the limited attention paid to HI in Cini and Bourne (2006), where a chapter is devoted to each of rational choice and sociological variants. Pollack includes historical institutionalism in three paragraphs within a chapter on rational choice approaches (2006: 48–9), presumably a reflection of the prominence he gives to Paul Pierson's role in HI (see also Pollack 1996).
4. Hall and Taylor's proposition that HI might act as a bridge between two important approaches in political science has been contested by Hay and Wincott, who consider that calculus- and culture-based explanations have incompatible 'social ontologies' (Hay and Wincott 1998: 951). Indeed, they argue that HI has its own distinctive ontology.
5. An important task in such analysis is devising generic criteria to enable identification of a critical juncture: a task not undertaken here. Monetary union followed on from policy co-operation on currency matters dating from the late 1960s. However, the physical introduction of the euro and the transfer of interest rate decisions to the European Central Bank represented a fundamental break with previous patterns of policy co-operation.

6 For a preliminary institutionalist prospectus for such a study, see Bulmer (2008).
7 For instance, her exploration of the EP's role in the legislative process starts with the Treaty of Rome and culminates in the revisions proposed in the Constitutional Treaty of 2004 (Héritier 2007: 69–121).
8 See Armstrong and Bulmer (1998) for exploration of the single market/Single European Act and developments in a set of case studies for the decade following the 1985 agreement on the single market White Paper.
9 The 'Convention Method' that started the process leading to the Lisbon Treaty represented a new departure in the process, of course.
10 Other individual contributions to understanding the timescape of integration from an institutionalist standpoint can be found in Sandholtz and Stone Sweet (1998) and Stone Sweet *et al.* (2001). However, the empirical subject matter is very varied and the institutionalist perspectives differ across the authors.
11 See, for instance, Susanne Schmidt's testing of historical institutionalist against rational choice institutionalist explanations of the practices of agenda-setting (Schmidt 2001). Her findings emphasize that *formal rules* may be an insufficient basis for explanation. However, and this is not to criticize that paper, the time dimension is not explored.
12 As an illustration, the Single European Act's introduction of what was then Article 118a (EEC Treaty) on health and safety offered a way to regulate maternity rights: an issue that had previously only been addressed through soft-law norms (see Armstrong and Bulmer 1998: ch. 9).
13 This discussion draws on Bulmer and Burch (2009, forthcoming: ch. 9).
14 For a detailed examination of institutional adjustment in Germany and Spain, but predating the most recent developments in the latter, see Börzel (2002)

REFERENCES

Armstrong, K. and Bulmer, S. (1998) *The Governance of the Single European Market*, Manchester: Manchester University Press.
Avery, G. (2009) 'Uses of time in the EU's enlargement process', *Journal of European Public Policy* 16(2): 256–69.
Bache, I. (2008) *Europeanization and Multilevel Governance: Cohesion Policy in the European Union and Britain*, Lanham, MD: Rowman & Littlefield.
Bartolini, S. (2005) *Restructuring Europe: Centre Formation, System Building, and Political Structuring between the Nation State and the European Union*, Oxford: Oxford University Press.
Baumgartner, F. and Jones, B. (1993) *Agendas and Instability in American Politics*, Chicago, IL: University of Chicago Press.
Börzel, T. (2002) *States and Regions in the European Union: Institutional Adaptation in Germany and Spain*, Cambridge: Cambridge University Press.
Börzel, T. (2005) 'Special Issue: The Disparity of European Integration: Revisiting Neofunctionalism in Honour of Ernst Haas', *Journal of European Public Policy* 12(2): 215–396.
Bulmer, S. (2008) 'Building a multi-level polity in Europe', in U. Sverdrup and J. Trondal (eds), *The Organizational Dimension of Politics*, Bergen: Fagbokforlaget, pp. 170–85.
Bulmer, S. and Burch, M. (2001) 'The "Europeanisation" of central government: the UK and Germany in historical institutionalist perspective', in G. Schneider and M. Aspinwall (eds), *The Rules of Integration*, Manchester: Manchester University Press, pp. 73–96.
Bulmer, S. and Burch, M. (2009, forthcoming) *The Europeanisation of Whitehall: UK Central Government and the European Union*, Manchester: Manchester University Press.

Bulmer, S., Jeffery, C. and Paterson, W. (2000) *Germany's European Diplomacy: Shaping the Regional Milieu*, Manchester: Manchester University Press.

Bulmer, S., Dolowitz, D., Humphreys, P. and Padgett, S. (2007) *Policy Transfer in European Union Governance: Regulating the Utilities*, London: Routledge.

Burch, M., Gomez, R., Hogwood, P. and Scott, A. (2005) 'Devolution, change and European Union policy-making in the UK', *Regional Studies* 39(4): 465–76.

Christiansen, T. (2002) 'The role of supranational actors in EU treaty reform', *Journal of European Public Policy* 9(1): 33–53.

Christiansen, T. and Jørgensen, K.E. (1999) 'The Amsterdam process: a structurationist perspective on EU treaty reform', *European Integration Online Papers* 3(1), at: http://eiop.or.at/eiop/texte/1999-001a.htm; accessed 15 September 2008.

Christiansen, T., Falkner, G. and Jørgensen, K.E. (2002) 'Theorizing EU treaty reform: beyond diplomacy and bargaining', *Journal of European Public Policy* 9(1): 12–32.

Cini, M. and Bourne, A. (eds) (2006) *Palgrave Advances in European Union Studies*, Basingstoke: Palgrave Macmillan.

Collier, R.B. and Collier, D. (1991) *Shaping the Political Arena: Critical Junctures, the Labour Movement, and Regime Dynamics in Latin America*, Cambridge: Cambridge University Press.

Donaghey, R. (2003) 'Agenda setting in the EU agricultural policy process', Ph.D. thesis, Manchester: University of Manchester, Department of Government.

Ekengren, M. (2002) *The Time of European Governance*, Manchester: Manchester University Press.

Falkner, G. (2002a) 'Special Issue: EU Treaty Reform as a Three-level Process: Historical Institutionalist Perspectives', *Journal of European Public Policy* 9(1): 1–146.

Falkner, G. (2002b) 'Introduction: EU treaty reform as a three-level process', *Journal of European Public Policy* 9(1): 1–11.

Farrell, H. and Héritier, A. (2005) 'A rationalist-institutionalist explanation of endogenous regional integration', *Journal of European Public Policy* 12(2): 273–90.

Feindt, P. (2008). 'Interpreting policy change – the role of paradigm shifts, side effects and crises in agricultural policies'. Paper for the 58th Political Studies Association Annual Conference, Cardiff, 1–3 April; available at: http://www.psa.ac.uk/2008/pps/Feindt.pdf; accessed 15 September 2008.

Goetz, K. (2005) 'The new member states and the EU: responding to Europe', in S. Bulmer and C. Lequesne (eds), *The Member States of the European Union*, Oxford: Oxford University Press, pp. 254–80.

Goetz, K.H. (2009) 'How does the EU tick? Five propositions on political time', *Journal of European Public Policy* 16(2): 202–20.

Goetz, K.H. and Meyer-Sahling, J.-H. (2009) 'Political time in the EU: dimensions, perspectives, theories', *Journal of European Public Policy* 16(2): 180–201.

Greve, M. and Jørgensen, K.E. (2002) 'Treaty reform as constitutional politics a longitudinal view', *Journal of European Public Policy* 9(1): 54–75.

Haas, E. (1975) *The Obsolescence of Regional Integration Theory*, Berkeley, CA: University of California Institute of International Studies, Research Paper No. 25.

Hall, P. (1986) *Governing the Economy: The Politics of State Intervention in Britain and France*, Cambridge: Polity Press.

Hall, P. (1989) *The Power of Economic Ideas*, Princeton, NJ: Princeton University Press.

Hall, P. (1992) 'The movement from Keynesianism to monetarism: institutional analysis and British economic policy in the 1970s', in K. Thelen, S. Steinmo and F. Longstreth (eds), *Structuring Politics: Historical Institutionalism in Comparative Analysis*, Cambridge: Cambridge University Press, pp. 90–113.

Hall, P. and Taylor, R. (1996) 'Political science and the three new institutionalisms', *Political Studies* 44(5): 936–57.

Hay, C. and Wincott, D. (1998) 'Structure, agency and historical institutionalism', *Political Studies* 46(5): 951–7.
Héritier, A. (2007) *Explaining Institutional Change in Europe*, Oxford: Oxford University Press.
Howarth, D. (2006) 'Internal economic and social policy developments', *Journal of Common Market Studies* 44(Annual Review): 81–99.
Jeffery, C. (1994) 'The Länder strike back: structures and procedures of European integration policy-making in the German federal system', Leicester: Leicester University, Discussion Papers in Federalism No. FS 93/2.
Jordan, A. (2002) *The Europeanization of British Environmental Policy: A Departmental Perspective*, Basingstoke: Palgrave Macmillan.
Kassim, H. (2003) 'Meeting the demands of EU membership: the Europeanization of national administrative systems', in K. Featherstone and C. Radaelli (eds), *The Politics of Europeanisation*, Oxford: Oxford University Press, pp. 83–111.
Kassim, H. (2005) 'The Europeanization of member state institutions', in S. Bulmer and C. Lequesne (eds), *The Member States of the European Union*, Oxford: Oxford University Press, pp. 285–316.
Kohler-Koch, B. and Rittberger, B. (2006) 'Review article: The "governance turn" in EU studies', *Journal of Common Market Studies* 44(Annual Review): 27–49.
Kovats, L. (2009) 'Do elections set the pace? A quantitative assessment of the timing of European legislation', *Journal of European Public Policy* 16(2): 239–55.
Krasner, S. (1984) 'Approaches to the state: alternative conceptions and historical dynamics', *Comparative Politics* 16(2): 223–46.
Krasner, S. (1988) 'Sovereignty: an institutional perspective', *Comparative Political Studies* 21(1): 66–94.
Laffan, B. (2000) 'The big budgetary bargains: from negotiation to authority', *Journal of European Public Policy* 7(5): 725–43.
Lewis, O. and Steinmo, S. (n.d.) Taking evolution seriously. Manuscript at http://spot.colorado.edu/~steinmo/TakingEvolution.pdf; accessed 4 September 2008.
Lindberg, L. and Scheingold, S. (1970) *Europe's Would-be Polity*, Englewood Cliffs, NJ: Prentice-Hall.
Lipset, S.M. and Rokkan, S. (eds) (1967) 'Cleavage structures, party systems and voter alignments: an introduction', *Party Systems and Voter Alignments*, New York: Free Press.
Mahoney, J. and Rueschemeyer, D. (eds) (2003) *Comparative Historical Analysis in the Social Sciences*, Cambridge: Cambridge University Press.
Mair, P. (2007) 'Political parties and party systems', in P. Graziano and M. Vink (eds), *Europeanization: New Research Agenda*, Basingstoke: Palgrave Macmillan, pp. 154–66.
March, J. and Olsen, J. (1989) *Rediscovering Institutions*, New York: Free Press.
March, J. and Olsen, J. (1998) 'The institutional dynamics of international political orders', *International Organization* 52(3): 729–58.
Meyer-Sahling, J.-H. and Goetz, K.H. (2009) 'The EU timescape: from notion to research agenda', *Journal of European Public Policy* 16(2): 221–38.
Milward, A. (1992) *The European Rescue of the Nation State*, London: Routledge.
Morata, F. (2007). 'The European Union and the Spanish state of the autonomies'. Paper given at CONNEX Research Group conference, 7–9 June, available at: http://www.mzes.uni-mannheim.de/projekte/typo3/site/fileadmin/BookSeries/Volume_Three/chapter14.pdf; accessed 18 September 2008.
Moravcsik, A. (1993) 'Preferences and power in the European Community: a liberal intergovernmentalist approach', *Journal of Common Market Studies* 31(4): 473–524.
Moravcsik, A. (1998) *The Choice for Europe: Social Purpose and State Power from Messina to Maastricht*, Ithaca, NY: Cornell University Press.
Peters, B.G. (1999) *Institutional Theory in Political Science: The 'New Institutionalism'*, London: Cassell.

Pierson, P. (1996) 'The path to European integration: a historical institutionalist analysis', *Comparative Political Studies* 29(2): 123–63.

Pierson, P. (1998) 'The path to European integration: a historical-institutionalist analysis', in W. Sandholtz and A.Stone Sweet (eds), *European Integration and Supranational Governance*, Oxford: Oxford University Press, pp. 27–58.

Pierson, P. (2004) *Politics in Time: History, Institutions and Social Analysis*, Princeton, NJ: Princeton University Press.

Pollack, M. (1996) 'The new institutionalism and EC governance: the promise and limits of institutional analysis', *Governance: An International Journal of Policy and Administration* 9(4): 429–58.

Pollack, M. (2005) 'Theorizing EU policy-making', in H. Wallace, W. Wallace and M. Pollack (eds), *Policy-Making in the European Union*, 5th edn, Oxford: Oxford University Press, pp. 13–48.

Pollack, M. (2006) 'Rational choice and EU politics', in K.E. Jørgensen, M. Pollack and B. Rosamond (eds), *Handbook of European Union Politics*, London: Sage Publications, pp. 31–55.

Pollitt, C. (2008) *Time, Policy, Management: Governing with the Past*, Oxford: Oxford University Press.

Rieger, E. (2000) 'The common agricultural policy', in H. Wallace and W. Wallace (eds), *Policy-Making in the European Union*, 4th edn, Oxford: Oxford University Press, pp. 179–210.

Rosamond, B. (2000) *Theories of European Integration*, Basingstoke: Macmillan Press.

Sandholtz, W. and Sweet, A.Stone (eds) (1998) *European Integration and Supranational Governance*, Oxford: Oxford University Press.

Schimmelfennig, F. and Sedelmeier, U. (2004) 'Governance by conditionality: EU rule transfer to the candidate countries of Central and Eastern Europe', *Journal of European Public Policy* 11(4): 661–79.

Schmidt, S. (2001) 'A constrained Commission: the informal practices of agenda-setting in the Council', in G. Schneider and M. Aspinwall (eds), *The Rules of Integration*, Manchester: Manchester University Press, pp. 125–46.

Schmitter, P. (2004) 'Neo-neofunctionalism', in A. Wiener and T. Diez (eds), *European Integration Theory*, Oxford: Oxford University Press, pp. 45–74.

Skowronek, S. (1982) *Building a New American State: The Expansion of National Administrative Capacities 1877–1920*, Cambridge: Cambridge University Press.

Stein, E. (1981) 'Lawyers, judges and the making of a transnational constitution', *American Journal of International Law* 75(1): 1–27.

Steinmo, S (2008) 'Historical institutionalism', in D. della Porta and M. Keating (eds), *Approaches and Methodologies in the Social Sciences: A Pluralist Perspective*, Cambridge: Cambridge University Press, pp. 118–38.

Sweet, A.Stone, Sandholtz, W. and Fligstein, N. (eds) (2001) *The Institutionalization of Europe*, Oxford: Oxford University Press.

Thelen, K. and Steinmo, S. (1992) 'Historical institutionalism in comparative politics', in K. Thelen, S. Steinmo and F. Longstreth (eds), *Structuring Politics: Historical Institutionalism in Comparative Analysis*, Cambridge: Cambridge University Press, pp. 1–32.

Tholoniat, L. (2009) 'The temporal constitution of the European Commission: a timely Investigation', *Journal of European Public Policy* 16(2): 221–38.

Tilly, C. (ed.) (1975) *The Formation of National States in Western Europe*, Princeton, NJ: Princeton University Press.

Weiler, J. (1991) 'The transformation of Europe', *The Yale Law Journal* 100(8): 2403–83.

Wessels, W., Maurer, A. and Mittag, J. (eds) (2003) *Fifteen into One? The European Union and Its Member States*, Manchester: Manchester University Press.

The EU timescape: from notion to research agenda

Jan-Hinrik Meyer-Sahling and Klaus H. Goetz

ABSTRACT This article outlines how the notion of an EU timescape may be developed into a fruitful research agenda. It sets out central tasks involved, including clarification of the concept of an EU timescape; of the key empirical questions to be asked; and of the status of political time in variable-oriented research. The article illustrates the potential value-added of a time-centred approach to the study of the EU by highlighting temporal issues in EU enlargement, differentiated integration and democratization. It concludes with thoughts on the comparison of democratic timescapes.

THE EU TIMESCAPE: MORE THAN AN ATTENTION-DIRECTING NOTION?

What does it mean to study the EU timescape? The articles collected in this volume offer selective insights into the manner in which political time in the European Union (EU) is institutionalized along the dimensions of polity, politics and public policy. They provide evidence of how political time matters in EU politics, and how scholars may use it as a dependent and independent variable in analyses of diverse aspects of the EU political system. But is there more to the study of political time than the potential to make a series of more or less connected observations about the relevance of time in a range of diverse institutional, decisional and policy settings? If time is seemingly 'everywhere', is there not a danger that its study ends up 'all over the place'? And what, if anything, is to be gained by advancing the notion of an EU timescape? Can it be more than what Johan Olsen (2002), with reference to Europeanization, has called an 'attention-directing device' that encourages scholars of the EU to focus on the importance of time in the EU political system? Does it instead have the potential to serve as what he calls an 'explanatory concept', or, if we are less ambitious, one that may help to guide research and integrate empirical findings?

The following sketches out some of the key tasks that will need to be tackled if we want to advance research on political time in the EU as an empirical research agenda centred around the EU timescape as a potentially integrative concept.

This outline of what needs to be done is interspersed with arguments about why we think such time-centred analysis is a worthwhile undertaking. There are at least four tasks to be tackled: first, clarification of terms and concepts, including 'political time', 'timescape' and 'EU timescape'; second, clarification of the empirical phenomena to be described and explained; third, clarification of the analytical status of time in causal arguments; and, finally, illustration of the potential value-added of time-centred research.

CONCEPT, SUBSTANCE AND CAUSATION

Terms and concept

None of the three time-related terms that have been frequently employed in this volume – political time, timescape, and EU timescape – have so far been tightly defined and none is readily operationalizable. Of the three, the term most familiar to political scientists will be 'political time'. It has been the central focus of Skowronek's (1993, 2008) work on the American presidency and, within that context, essentially refers to the specific historical-temporal location of a presidency, and the specific challenges, opportunities and constraints with which American presidents have been confronted as a result. By contrast, our usage of the term has not been about locations in historical-political time and the impact of historical time on politics. Rather, we have employed political time as a convenient shorthand for a very diverse range of rules, norms, conventions and understandings that relate to time as a resource and constraint for political institutions and actors; in political decision-making; and in the structuring of public policies.

We have borrowed the notion of a timescape from the sociologist Barbara Adam (1998, 2004, 2008), who defines a timescape as 'a cluster of temporal features, each implicated in all the others, but not necessarily of equal importance in each instance' (Adam 2004: 143). Its key elements include time-frames, temporality, timing, tempo, duration, sequence and temporal modalities (past, present, future) (Adam 2008).

To employ this concept of a timescape with specific reference to a political institution or political system – the EU timescape – is attractive for two main reasons. First, as Adam (2008; 1; emphasis in the original) notes, 'the "scape" part of the concept acknowledges that we cannot embrace time without simultaneously encompassing space and matter ... a *timescape's* perspective acknowledges this spatiality, materiality and contexuality but foregrounds the temporal side of the interdependency.' In the context of the EU, this means, in particular, that a time-centred analysis of the EU political system cannot get us very far without paying attention to the substantive issues at the heart of the EU political processes and the partial re-spatialization of politics that European integration entails (Bartolini 2005).

Second, the timescape concept invites a focus on the linkages and interdependencies between different dimensions of the temporal constitution of a political system. As will be shown in more detail at the end of this article, this point is especially relevant with regard to the combination of temporal features that exist across the polity, politics and policy dimensions of different political timescapes. Adam (2008: 2) argues that when several of these dimensions 'are brought together we begin to see patterns of rhythmicity, periodicity and cyclicality'. This implies that it is, in principle, both capable of guiding research – as an attention-directing notion – and may help to integrate diverse empirical findings in the sense that it encourages the search for both regularities and interconnections of the varied temporal features of the EU system.

Whilst the EU timescape may serve as an integrative concept, the degree of stability and orderliness in the institutionalization of the temporal features of the EU political system is a matter for empirical observation. Given the material fluidity of the EU system – in terms of institutions, decision-making modes and policies – and its shifting boundaries (both external and internal), the EU timescape is likely to be dynamic rather than static or what Zerubavel (1981) calls 'rigidified'. Political conflict over deepening and widening does, therefore, inevitably also involve arguments over time. Moreover, there is evidence of distinct *Eigenzeiten* in different policy domains (Dyson 2009), and we must also allow for a degree of randomness and contradiction across temporal arrangements.

Substance

The components of a timescape enumerated by Adam open up a very wide agenda for empirical research. If research on the EU timescape is to benefit from, and contribute to, political science scholarship on political time, it seems advisable to focus, in the first instance, on the three dimensions introduced earlier (Goetz and Meyer-Sahling 2009): terms, time budgets, time horizons and their effects; questions concerning timing, tempo, sequence and duration of decision-making processes and their effects; and the temporal properties of EU policies and their effects. In respect of effects, we suggest that a focus on the implications of time for the distribution of power, system performance and legitimacy will help to ensure that research on the EU timescape can contribute to key debates in the analysis of the EU political system.

Causation

Making causal arguments, preferably based on general theoretical assumptions, is, of course, the Holy Grail of scientific analysis. Much of contemporary research – whether qualitative or quantitative – operates more or less explicitly with research designs based on independent and dependent variables. In this tradition, it is relatively easy to determine the analytical status of political time or the timescape as an independent or a dependent variable – it can obviously be both depending on the question that is asked – and the usual standards and methods for making casual inferences can be employed. In this sense, there is nothing special about political time.

There are, however, at least two issues to which time-centred analysis needs to be especially sensitive. First, there is a propensity in political science accounts of time to include different aspects of time both on the 'independent' and the 'dependent' variable. For example, arguments about political business cycles link observations about lengths of terms and election timing – independent variable – to temporal properties of policies (e.g. timing, intertemporal trade-offs) – as the dependent variable. In a similar vein, historical institutionalist accounts of institutional and policy development ascribe key explanatory power to temporal categories – such as actors' time horizons and decisional sequences – in trying to account for developments 'over time' (Bulmer 2009). Given the many guises that political time can take, there is, in principle, nothing wrong with time being part of both the explanans and the explanandum, though the dangers for confusion and circularity are real.

Second, as noted above, the close association between political time, political substance, and political space means that it is not easy and, in many instances, not desirable to try to isolate a time-centred cause or effect. For example, analysing the importance of sequences for the success or failure of policy reforms can only yield insights if sequence and substance are considered together (Beyer 2008; Ganghof 2008). Similarly, the impact of politicians' time budgets and time horizons on substantive policy decisions cannot be assessed without information on substantive policy options and actors' preferences.

VALUE-ADDED: ASKING QUESTIONS ABOUT EU TIME

What does research that 'foregrounds' time have to add to the analysis of the EU? We have already noted how temporal analysis links in with considerations about power, performance and legitimacy. In the following, we offer some illustrative examples of how time-centred analysis ties in with key debates about the EU, including enlargement, differentiated integration and democratization. The questions in Table 1 relate to polity, politics and policy dimensions and, for illustrative purposes, distinguish between political time as a dependent and an independent variable.

Enlargement

EU decision-making is often – rightly or wrongly – perceived as slow and cumbersome, and enlargement has been seen by many as a further threat to the timeliness and expeditiousness with which decisions are made. With the exception of work on legislation (see Kovats 2009, with further references), we still have little systematic data on whether successive enlargements have been accompanied by a slowing down of the Commission, the Council, the European Parliament (EP), or the European Court of Justice. Is König's (2007) finding of 'an ever-slowing' EU legislative process generalizable to other processes – for example, under the open method of co-ordination – making for progressive gridlock or have successive enlargements also entailed successful time-saving innovations?

Table 1 Debates in EU integration and examples of their temporal dimension

Issue	Time as a dependent variable	Time as an independent variable
Enlargement	Does enlargement slow down EU policy-making?	How have actors' time budgets and time horizons affected enlargement decisions?
Differentiated integration	How can we explain temporal aspects of differentiated integration?	Do cycles help to explain differentiated integration?
Democratization	Can the EU 'keep pace' with its economic, social and technological environments?	Do inter-institutional differences in terms, time budgets and time horizons help or hinder deliberative decision-making?

Source: Authors' compilation.

Helen Wallace's (2007) detailed review of scholarship on the impact of the 2004 enlargement on the EU institutions leads her to argue 'that the "business as usual" picture is more convincing than the "gridlock picture" as regards practice in and output from the EU institutions since May 2004' (Wallace 2007: 5–6; emphasis in the original). As data reported by Best and Settembri (2007) for the Council indicate, important legislation does, as is to be expected, take longer than 'ordinary' or 'minor' legislation, 'but there is no significant difference between the EU15 and EU25: Ordinary acts are actually decided, significantly faster . . . after enlargement' (Best and Settembri 2007: 6). This raises not only the question as to why more member states do not need more time to take decisions, but also many more issues that arise with regard to how successive enlargements – in combination with other factors – have affected timing, tempo, sequence and duration in EU policy-making. Moreover, enlargement has had consequences for other dimensions of political timescapes. Enlargement is likely to have affected the choice of terms, for instance, the 18 months' troika Presidencies of the Council, and the choice of time-related features of EU policy, such as the phasing out of the traditional common agricultural policy with its reliance on guaranteed prices over the next decade.

Treating time as an independent variable, we may ask how the respective terms, time budgets and time horizons of national and EU participants in the EU accession process have materially affected enlargement decisions, such as the willingness to ask for and concede derogations. To give an example, the investiture of the Prodi government in 1999 and especially the appointment of a Commissioner for Enlargement created a strong incentive within the Commission to complete the eastern enlargement of the EU within the time budget of five years (see Avery 2009; Lass-Lennecke and Werner 2009). Similarly, the end of the EP term and the elections scheduled for June 2004 created a specific time horizon for EU institutions and for candidate states which narrowed down the alternatives for the choice of an enlargement date. In other words, it is likely to be difficult to explain enlargement of the EU without recourse to temporal categories, especially the terms, time budgets and time horizons of the relevant actors.

Differentiation[1]

Political and academic debate surrounding the phenomenon of differentiated integration is replete with time-centred images and metaphors. In Stubb's (1996) categorization, time is one of the three main variables of differentiated integration, the others being 'space' and 'matter'. The notions frequently employed in discussions of temporal differentiation include, for example, multi-speed Europe, vanguards or laggards. Following Stubb, major examples of such temporal differentiation include transition periods, temporary derogations, or the temporal structuring of European monetary union (EMU) and of the adoption of the single currency.

Next to analysing such patterns of temporal differentiation, appreciating the potential of, and limitations to, differentiated integration as a political tool also invites us to consider temporal aspects of differentiation. For example, what can we say about the *speed* with which such arrangements have been introduced or abolished? Answering this question may help us to judge whether differentiation is a short-term expediency or part of longer-term institutional design. And what do we know about the *duration* of differentiated institutional decision-making and, in particular, policy arrangements? For example, if one compares different enlargement rounds, has there been a lengthening or a shortening of transitional arrangements and temporary derogations? If this were to be the case, it might indicate that full integration is becoming ever more difficult to achieve.

If we turn to time as an independent variable, it is interesting to note how not only historical-institutionalism, but also neo-functionalism and 'neo-neofunctionalism' (Schmitter 2004) emphasize temporal factors as central to their causal accounts of integration, although the implications for *differentiated* integration require some teasing out. Thus, Schmitter (2004), building on work first published more than 30 years previously (Schmitter 1970), seeks to elucidate the temporal logic that underlies functional spillovers in economic-social integration and the spillover of the latter into political integration. In so doing, he puts emphasis on the fundamental importance of cycles, including 'initiation cycles', 'priming cycles' and 'transforming cycles'. Whilst initiation cycles constitute the start of the integration process, priming cycles are about changes that 'define the context of a crisis that is compelling actors to change their strategies' (Schmitter 2004: 61). During a 'transformative cycle', a qualitative transformation takes place: the member states 'will have exhausted the potentialities inherent in functionally integrating their economies and dedicate more and more of their efforts to functionally integrating their polities' (Schmitter 2004: 65–6).

With reference to differentiated integration, it is especially relevant to note that the idea of a cyclical development is closely linked to notions of asynchronic change in the key variables that drive actors to change their strategies. Thus, Schmitter hypothesizes that during priming cycles asynchrony 'in rates of change at the national level sets up – due to their differing marginal impacts – asynchrony in rates of regional change. This, in turn, enhances the probability that less convergent, and possibly divergent, actor strategies will be promoted and this makes the adoption of a joint policy vector more and more difficult' (2004: 64).

Several implications flow from these suggestions. First, if it makes sense to think of European integration as a process with cyclical elements, it might also be instructive to explore evidence for differentiated integration as a cyclical phenomenon. Second, in thinking about such stages, it might be useful to refer to the idea of 'interstitial institutional change', as developed by Farrell and Héritier (2007). The decisive point here is to understand the dynamics of informal differentiation, on the one hand, and formal differentiation, on the other. Third, the notion of asynchronic development in national conditions that shape integration – both within and across states – might help to understand the emergence of demands for differentiation and the durability or transience of the latter.

Democratization

Is the EU able to 'keep pace' with its economic, social and technological environment? Does it have an appropriate timescape to meet the challenges it faces? Several authors have highlighted the tension between growing acceleration in economic, social and technological developments, on the one hand, and traditional democratic timescapes, on the other. Scheuerman (2004; see also Scheuerman 2001), in his stimulating book *Liberal Democracy and the Social Acceleration of Time*, argues that social

> acceleration poses fundamental challenges to the temporal fundaments of the separation of powers ... High-speed society tends to favor high-speed political institutions, and traditional liberal democratic assumptions about temporality unwittingly aggrandize executive power and weaken broad-based popular legislatures.
>
> (Scheuerman 2004: 26)

In a similar vein, Rosa (2003, 2005) has suggested that we witness an increasing 'desynchronization' between politics and its social, economic, cultural and technological environments. On the one hand, he argues, 'the time needed for democratic political decision-making is not just hard to accelerate, since processes of deliberation and aggregation in a pluralist democratic society inevitably take time' (2003: 23). In fact, for a variety of reasons, including, *inter alia*, growing calls for regulation and more time needed for consensus-building, the demand for time resources increases. On the other hand, the speed with which societies change accelerates, leading to a politics that becomes increasingly 'situationalist' and the shifting of decisions to other, faster decision-making arenas (like the economy or the legal system – juridification) (Rosa 2003: 23f.).

Examining EU time from this perspective begs the question of which parts of the EU institutional order might be strengthened as a result of pressures for speedy decisions. More generally, it invites research on how quickly the EU – as compared to national institutions – succeeds in detecting and problematizing new challenges, on the one hand, and manages to generate acceptable policy responses, on the other. Existing data on the legislative process can only provide a partial response to this question. First, they do not cover the often extended period of consultation and preparation prior to the formal submission of draft legislation by the Commission. For example, how long does it take to produce a Green Paper and how much time on average elapses between a Green Paper and a White Paper and the tabling of a legislative proposal by the Commission? Second, there is, of course, a big part of policy-centred activity in the EU that is not oriented towards the production of legislation (or in which legislation plays only a minor part).

Turning to time as an independent variable, perhaps the overarching question in the context of democratization concerns the consequences of distinct configuration of terms, time budgets and time horizons of the different EU policy-makers (Goetz 2009). Does the fact that EU policy-makers across the different institutions do not work to the same clock systematically encourage the opening up of 'windows of opportunity' for deliberation? Or, on the contrary, are the resultant pressures for intra-institutional and inter-institutional co-ordination and synchronization so strong as to encourage 'governing by timetable', in which substantive deliberation is sacrificed on the altar of time-efficient policy-making?

THE EU TIMESCAPE IN CONTEXT

This special issue has sought to make a case for studying the manner in which political time is institutionalized in the EU. Studying the EU timescape involves, in particular, an analysis of terms, time budgets, time horizons; of the temporal features of decision-taking; and of the time structures embedded in policies. These issues matter because they affect the distribution of power in, and the performance and legitimacy of, the EU. The specific configurations of the functions of political time in the EU; the precise nature of the time rules that institutions and actor follow; the terms, time budgets and time horizons within which they act; the degrees of temporal autonomy they enjoy; their capacity to set the clock for others; their ability to engage in the discretionary use of time; the temporal properties of EU policies – all are important elements of the EU political timescape, with implications for democracy, transparency and the quality of governance.

For the comparativist, the main question that arises is: what is specific (though not necessarily unique) about the EU timescape? And in seeking to answer this question, what should the EU be compared with – national political systems and, if so, which, or other international organizations? Both questions – about singularity and comparators – are, of course, hardy perennials in EU scholarship.

In the main, the comparative literature that we have referred to in the introduction (Goetz and Meyer-Sahling 2009) concerns national political systems, a fact which at least in part reflects our own background in comparative politics rather than international relations. Certainly, the democratic timescapes of parliamentary versus presidential systems and unitary versus federal systems can be expected to differ significantly, notably in the degree to which terms, time budgets and time horizons are synchronized across institutions and levels of government. We would expect a greater degree of synchronicity in parliamentary and unitary systems, whereas presidential systems of government and federal systems have a higher degree of asynchronicity built into their constitution.

The lack of synchronization of the political terms at the EU level, in particular, the Presidency of the Council and the EP (see Goetz 2009), might suggest that the inter-institutional timescape of the EU political system is closer to a federal parliamentary system as found, for example, in Germany, or a federal presidential system, as in the US. The introduction of a President of the European Council to be appointed for two and a half years, as envisaged by the Lisbon Treaty, would increase the temporal alignment of EU institutions and support arguments that point towards the parliamentarization of the EU; but, for the moment, 'most similar cases' are unlikely to be found in parliamentary systems.

Yet the scope of political timescapes should not be limited to the alignment of terms, time budgets and time horizons across institutions. Rather, we would expect that political systems systematically group together specific temporal features at the polity, politics and policy dimensions. The literature on political business cycles suggests that the dimensions of polity, politics and policy are temporally closely interrelated, as time budgets – polity – influence the use of temporal rules in decision-making – politics – which in turn favours particular temporal patterns of policy.

In the case of the EU, there is no dominant political cycle and there is no dominant political time-setter (Goetz 2009). Instead, political terms are at best partly synchronized and the rights to use time in the legislative process are shared among the three core institutions of the EU. The discussion of EU policy in the introductory article also points in the direction of higher levels of continuity, consistency and gradualism as characteristic features of EU policy time.

This combination of temporal features contrasts above all with parliamentary systems of a Westminster-type, which combine a synchronization of institutional cycles with the allocation of temporal powers in the legislative process (by and large) exclusively to the government (Döring 2004). Moreover, debates on the politics of tax policy, economic policy, and administrative reform – to mention but a few examples – have traditionally identified a greater propensity for stop-and-go policies, policy U-turns, radical reforms and a higher pace of reform in Westminster systems such as in the UK and New Zealand (Steinmo 1993; Hall 1986; Hood 1994).

In short, a case can be made for the cross-dimensional patterning of temporal features and thus the presence of different timescapes of political systems much in accordance with discussions surrounding different patterns of democracy (Lijphart 1999). But it is, in any case, not without risks to try to undertake comparative analysis at such a systemic level. Especially in the case of the EU, the political system has not reached a point of stability and maturity comparable to that of national political systems. Political time in the EU is, therefore, not only likely to be more changeable than in consolidated national democracies; the EU timescape can also be expected to show greater tensions, contradictions and disjunctures.

Biographical notes: Jan-Hinrik Meyer-Sahling is Lecturer in European Politics at the University of Nottingham, UK. Klaus H. Goetz is Professor of German and European Politics and Government at the University of Potsdam, Germany, and Visiting Fellow at the European Institute, London School of Economics, UK.

NOTE

1 This section draws on Goetz (forthcoming).

REFERENCES

Adam, B. (1998) *Timescapes of Modernity*, London: Routledge.
Adam, B. (2004) *Time*, Cambridge: Polity Press.
Adam, B. (2008) *Of Timescapes, Futurescapes and Timeprints*, Paper presented at Lüneburg University, 17 June 2008.
Avery, G. (2009) 'Uses of time in the EU's enlargement process', *Journal of European Public Policy* 16(2): 256–69.
Bartolini, S. (2005) *Restructuring Europe*, Oxford: Oxford University Press.
Best, E. and Settembri, P. (2007) *Surviving Enlargement: How has the Council Managed?* Paper presented to the EUSA Tenth Biennial International Conference, Montreal, May 2007.
Beyer, J. (2008) 'Wann, wenn nicht jetzt? Konzeptionelle Grundlagen für die Anlayse der Sequenzierung politischer Reformen', in Bertelsmann-Stiftun (ed.), *'Schritt für Schritt' – Sequenzierung als Erfolgsfaktor politischer Reformprozesse?*, Gütersloh: Bertelsmann Stiftung, pp. 10–56.

Bulmer, S. (2009) '*Politics in Time* meets the politics of time: historical institutionalism and the EU timescape', *Journal of European Public Policy* 16(2): 307–24.

Döring, H. (2004) 'Controversy, time constraint, and restrictive rules', in H. Döring and M. Hallerberg (eds), *Patterns of Parliamentary Behaviour: Passage of Legislation across Western Europe*, Aldershot: Ashgate Publishing Ltd, pp. 141–68.

Dyson, K. (2009) 'The evolving timescapes of european economic governance: contesting and using time', *Journal of European Public Policy* 16(2): 286–306.

Farrell, H. and Héritier, A. (eds) (2007) *Contested Competences in Europe: Incomplete Contracts and Interstitial Institutional Change* 30(2), special issue of *West European Politics*.

Ganghof, S. (2008) 'Politikwissenschaftliche und politökonomische Perspektiven auf Reformsequenzierung – Typen, Mechanismen und ländervergleichende Fallbeispiele', in Bertelsmann-Stiftung (ed.), *'Schritt für Schritt' – Sequenzierung als Erfolgsfaktor politischer Reformprozesse?*, Gütersloh: Bertelsmann Stiftung, pp. 57–12.

Goetz, K.H. (2009) 'How does the EU tick? Five propositions on political time', *Journal of European Public Policy* 16(2): 202–20.

Goetz, K.H. (forthcoming) 'Time and differentiated integration', in K. Dyson and A. Sepos (eds), *Whose Europe? The Politics of Differentiated Integration*, Basingstoke: Palgrave.

Goetz, K.H. and Meyer-Sahling, J.-H. (2009) 'Political time in the EU: dimensions, perspectives, theories', *Journal of European Public Policy* 16(2): 180–201.

Hall, P.A. (1986) *Governing the Economy: The Politics of State Intervention in France and Britain*, Oxford and New York: Oxford University Press.

Hood, C. (1994) *Explaining Economic Policy Reversals*, Buckingham: Open University Press.

König, T. (2007) 'Divergence or convergence? From ever-growing to ever-slowing European legislative decision making', *European Journal of Political Research* 46: 417–44.

Kovats, L. (2009) 'Do elections set the pace? A quantitative assessment of the timing of European legislation', *Journal of European Public Policy* 16(2): 239–55.

Lass-Lennecke, K. and Werner, A. (2009) 'Policies, institutions and time: how the European Commission managed the temporal challenge of eastern enlargement', *Journal of European Public Policy* 16(2): 270–85.

Lijphart, A. (1999) *Patterns of Democracy: Government Forms and Performance in Thirty-Six Countries*, New Haven, CT: Yale University Press.

Olsen, J. (2002) 'The many faces of Europeanization', *Journal of Common Market Studies* 40(5): 921–52.

Rosa, H. (2003) 'Social acceleration: ethical and political consequences of a desynchronized high-speed society', *Constellations* 10(1): 3–33.

Rosa, H. (2005) *Beschleunigung: Die Veränderung von Zeitstrukturen in der Moderne*, Frankfurt a. M: Suhrkamp.

Scheuerman, W.E. (2001) 'Liberal democracy and the empire of speed', *Polity* XXXIV(1): 41–67.

Scheuerman, W.E. (2004) *Liberal Democracy and the Social Acceleration of Time*, Baltimore, MD: Johns Hopkins University Press.

Schmitter, P.C. (1970) 'A revised theory of regional integration', *International Organization* 24(4): 836–68.

Schmitter, P.C. (2004) 'Neo-neofunctionalism', in A. Wiener and T. Diez (eds), *European Integration Theory*, Oxford: Oxford University Press, pp. 45–73.

Skowronek, S. (1993) *The Politics Presidents Make: Leadership from John Adams to George Bush*, Cambridge, MA: Belknap/Harvard University Press.

Skowronek, S. (2008) *Presidential Leadership in Political Time: Reprise and Reappraisal*, Lawrence, KS: University Press of Kansas.

Steinmo, S. (1993) *Taxation and Democracy: Swedish, British and American Approaches to Financing the Modern State*, New Haven, CT: Yale University Press.
Stubb, A. (1996) 'A categorization of differentiated integration', *Journal of Common Market* 34(2): 283–95.
Wallace, H. (2007) *Adapting to Enlargement of the European Union: Institutional Practice since May 2004*, Brussels: TEPSA.
Zerubavel, E. (1981) *Hidden Rhythms: Schedules and Calendars in Social Life*, Chicago and London: University of Chicago Press.

Index

Page numbers in *Italics* represent tables.
Page numbers in **Bold** represent figures.

accession criteria 95, 100
accession negotiations 83–6, 87, 88
Accession Treaty 85
acquis 79, 80, 83, 87, 93, 94, 95, 96
acquis conférenciel 134
action plans 47
Action programmes 83
Acts of Accession 94
Adam, B. 28, 147, 148
agenda powers 68, 69, 73
American presidency 147
Amsterdam Treaty 56
Annual Management Plan 51, 53
Annual Policy Strategy (APS) 49, 51
asynchronic change 16
Austria 84, 115, 140
automaticity 116
Avery, G. 17, 77–90, 95, 96

Balint, T. *et al* 103
Baltic states 118
battle of dates 78, 83–5
Bauer, M.W. 103
Becker, R.: and Saalfeld, T. 62
Belgium 62, 140
Bellier, I. 98
Best, E.: and Settembri, P. 150
Britain 115, 118, *see also* United Kingdom (UK)
Broad Economic Policy Guidelines (BEPGs) 114
budget (EU) 2, 46, 137
budgetary chapter 81, 82
Bulgaria 118
Bulmer, S. 17, 128–45
Bundesbank 113
Bundestag 62
bureaucratization 54

central banking 110, 116–19
Central and East European countries 79, 83, 85, 87, 92
centralization 36
chapter desks 98–9, **99**
chief executives: terms of office 12
coalition governments 65
cohabitation 13
Commission 9, 17, 94, 95; as agenda-setter 43; as a broker 45–6; as building-block 43, 45; and collegiality principle 46–7; and communication 47; consolidation phase 56; and European Council 66; initiatives 68–71, *70*, **71**; and multi and supranational regime 46; and policy horizons 47; and procedural changes 100–2; and regulation 47, 56; and structural changes 97–100; and temporal constitution 2–59; temporal parameters *44*, *45*; and time 43–7; and time management 97–102
Commission President: term of office 25
Commissioners 28
Commission's Legislative and Work Programme (CLWP) 49, 51
committee governance 116
Committee of Permanent Representatives (COREPER) 7, 29
common agricultural policy (CAP) 133, 136–7
Common Market Organization for wine 10
consensual-type democracies 13
constitution-making 6, 12
constructivist perspective 15
Copenhagen criteria 77, 78–9, 80, 87, 94, 95
Council membership: turnover 33

INDEX

Council of Ministers 29, 36
Council presidencies 8, 9, 12, 23, 28–9
country desks 98, 99, **99**, 100
Cox, G.W.: and McCubbins, M.D. 60
Croatia 86
cycles 24–5
cyclical time 27, 28, 38
Cyprus 98
Czech Republic 118

decision-making 8–10
democracy 3, 60, 62, 78, 79, 80, 108, 125
democratic time 4
democratization 8, 12, 152–3
Denmark 115, 118
DG Enlargement 17, 98, 99, 100, 101
differentiation 84, 151–2
Directorate-Generals (DGs) 53, 97, 98, 101
Donahue, K.: and Warin, T. 37
Draft Common Positions (DCPs) 99, **99**
Dyson, K. 17, 107–27

early agreements 1, 13, 15, 31
Eastern enlargement 17, 91–106, 135
economic criteria 101
Economic and Financial Affairs Council (ECOFIN) 112
Economic and Financial Committee (EFC) 111
economic and monetary union (EMU) 28, 110, 111, 114, 117, 151, *see also* monetary union
Economic Policy Committee (EPC) 111
economic theory of legislation 60, 61, 64, 66, 67
Eigenzeit 16, 17, 24, 32, 34, 37, 38, 148
Ekengren, M. 15, 35, 36, 108
elected magistrate: term of office 4–5
elections 60–76, 64
electoral cycle 6, 11, 25, 28, 46, 107, 108
electoral terms 7
enlargement 77–90, 134, 149–51
enlargement policy 28, 31–2, 92, 102
Estonia 84
Euro Area 108, 115, 119, 120, 124
Euro Group 112
European Central Bank (ECB) 7, 110, 113, 115, 118, 120, 121, 122; members 1
European Constitution 31
European Court of Auditors 28
European Court of Justice (ECJ) 135

European economic governance 107–27; and internal/proper time 113–16; and time functions 111–13
European integration 15, 16, 35–8, 129, 131, 132, 133, 134
European Parliament (EP) 12; and elections 61; electoral cycle 135–6; electoral term 26; and enlargement 85; legislative role 132; members 1; and voting patterns 64
European Payments Council 121
European Regional Development Fund 134
Europeanization 34, 35, 36, 43, 129, 138–40, 146
Euroscepticism 32
Eurostat 116
evolutionary theory 132

Farrell, H.: and Héritier, A. 152
financial markets 118, 119; infrastructure 120–2
France 13, 114–15, 116, 122, 123
functional adaptation 103

game theory 83
Germany 9, 62, 84, 116, 122, 139, 140, 154
Goetz, K.H. 16, 23–41, 94, 138; and Meyer-Sahling, J.-H. 1–22, 18, 87, 146–57
Goodin, C. 31
governance turn 132
government *pro tempore* 3–4
gradualism 12
Greece 115

Hall, P. 130; and Taylor, R. 129–30
Hayes-Renshaw, F.: and Wallace, H. 24
Héritier, A. 132; and Farrell, H. 152
Hirschman, A. 119
historical institutionalism 2, 17, 119, 128–45, 149, 151; and Europeanization 138–40; and integration 132–5; and policy evolution 135–8; and time 129–32
human rights 78, 79, 80
Hungary 8, 80, 84, 85, 118

impact assessments (IAs) 51–2, 53, 54, 55
inflation 107, 117
initiation cycles 151
institutional change 15, 92, 93

INDEX

institutionalization 33
institutions (EU) 2, 31, 55, 94, 96
integration *150*
integration theory 2, 15, 131
International Monetary Fund (IMF) 108
interstitial institutional change 152
Italy 62, 66, 116, 122, 123

Jacobs, A.M. 11
Jerneck, M. 35

Kardasheva, R. 9
Kinnock reforms 49, 97, 103
König, T. 149
Kovats, L. 17, 60–76
Krasner, S. 129

Lagona, F.: and Padovano, F. 66–7
Lass-Lennecke, K.: and Werner, A. 17, 91–106
legislation 17, 60–76, 150; adoptions 71–3, *72*, **73**; cycles 61–2, 64–8
legislative process: initiation of 65–6
legislative system: and time 63–4
legislative time 8–9
legitimacy 13–14
Lewis, O.: and Steinmo, S. 132
liberal intergovernmentalism 113, 133
linearity 136
Linz, J. 3–4
Lisbon Strategy 28, 32, 54, 108, 112, 114, 117, 120, 123–4
Lisbon Treaty 8, 23, 30, 154
Lithuania 115
Loomis, B. 24, 25
Luxembourg 62
Luxembourg group 80

Maastricht Treaty 7, 25, 37, 111, 114, 117, 122, 138, 140
McCubbins, M.D.: and Cox, G.W. 60
macroeconomic co-ordination 123–4
Mair, P. 36
non-majoritarian institutions 7, 11, 29
majoritarian systems 13
March, J.G.: and Olsen, J.P. 103, 130
market economy 78
matrix system 98, 99
Mayhew, A. 95
medium-term perspective 78–80, 95
meetings: frequency of 10

Members of the European Parliament (MEPs) 5, 26
membership (EU) 77, 138–9; criteria 78, 84
Meyer-Sahling, J.-H.: and Goetz, K.H. 1–22, 18, 87, 146–57
mobilization 26–7, 30, 34, 36
modernization 54
monetary policy 108, 109, 112, 117–18
monetary theory 117–18
monetary union 78, 108, 109, 111, 113, 114, 117, 124, *see also* economic and monetary union (EMU)
Moravcsik, A. 133

national fiscal policy 37
negative binomial regression model (NBRM) 68, 69, 71
neo-functionalism 16, 133, 151
neo-neofunctionalism 16, 151
the Netherlands 62, 115
new institutionalisms 129
New Zealand 155
Nowotny, H. 15
Nugent, N. 93

Olsen, J.P. 146; and March, J.G. 103, 130
ongoingness 31
open method of co-ordination (OMC) 48, 49
openness 31
Organization for Economic Co-operation and Development (OECD) 108, 110

Padovano, F.: and Lagona, F. 66–7
parliamentary systems 6
path dependency 113, 130–1
performance 13
Peters, G. 130
Pierson, P. 128, 129, 130, 131, 132, 133–4
planning 54–6
planning cycle: multi-annual 5
Poland 9, 80, 84, 118
policy 10–12; activism 48; cycles 26; Europeanization of 37; evolution 129; and institutions 91–106; review 137; schedules 31; timing 4
policy reforms: temporality of 12
political business cycles (PBC) 60, 154
political criteria 80, 101
political cycles 27–8
political decision-making 4

INDEX

political time 1–22, 107, 146, 147, 148, 149, 155; five propositions 23–41; institutionalizing 5–12, 14, 23; and legislation 61–4
politics 8–10
politics of when 11–12
polity 6–8
Pollitt, C. 136
Portugal 115
power 12–13
power to delay 9
presidency: rotating 23–4, 28–9
presidential systems 6
priming cycles 151, 152
procedural cartel theory 60, 61, 64
Prodi, R. 83

qualified majority voting (QMV) 63

rapporteurs 9, 15
rationalist perspective 14, 15
rationalization 30
research agenda 3
Rieger, E. 137
Riescher, G. 27, 30
roadmap 78, 80–3, 85, 87, 88, 95–6, 102, 123

Saalfeld, T.: and Becker, R. 62
Santer Commission 97
Santiso, J.: and Schedler, A. 3; and Schmitter, P. 8
Schedler, A.: and Santiso, J. 3
Scheuerman, W.E. 152
Schmitter, P. 151, 152; and Santiso, J. 8
Secretariat General 53
sequencing 131
Settembri, P.: and Best, E. 150
Short-Term European Paper (STEP) 121
Single Euro Payments Area (SEPA) 110, 113, 121, 122
Skowronek, S. 147
Slovakia 118
Slovenia 84
social time 15
soft law paradox 47–9
Spain 82, 139, 140
spillover 113, 120
Stability and Growth Pact (SGP) 37, 110, 114, 115, 116, 122–3
stabilization 30
Steinmo, S.: and Lewis, O. 132; and Thelen, K. 130
Stone Sweet, A. 2

strategic planning and programming (SPP) 49, **50**, 51, 52, 53, 54
subnational authorities (SNAs) 139, 140
Sweden 115, 118
synchronization 27, 30, 108, 153, 154

TARGET2S 110, 121
Taylor, R.: and Hall, P. 129–30
temporal autonomy 33–4
temporal grids 10, 100–2, 103
temporality 77, 80, 86
Thelen, K.: and Steinmo, S. 130
Tholoniat, L. 16–17, 42–59
Tilly, C. 131
time 35–6; consistency 117; horizons 109–10, 117; inconsistency 107, 108, 118; linear 27, 28, 38; theorizing 14–16
time management 92–3
time rules 10, 13; and governance 11
time-space compression 110
timescape 128, 147, 148, 153–5; and research agenda 146–57
timetabling 30–3
timing 131
transboundary policy problems 29
transforming cycles 151
transition periods 96
transitional measures 86, 88
transparency 56
transtemporal policy problems 29
Treaty on European Union 30
Treaty on functioning of European Union 30
treaty reform 134, 135
treaty revisions 26
troïka presidency 13, 55, 150
Turkey 86

United Kingdom (UK) 8, 140, 155, *see also* Britain

Verheugen, G. 82, 83

Wallace, H. 150; and Hayes-Renshaw, F. 24
Warin, T: and Donahue, K. 37
Werner, A.: and Lass-Lennecke, K. 17, 91–106

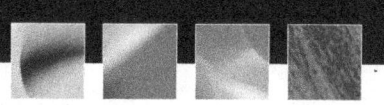

AUTHOR SERVICES

Publish With Us

The Taylor & Francis Group Author Services Department aims to enhance your publishing experience as a journal author and optimize the impact of your article in the global research community. Assistance and support is available, from preparing the submission of your article through to setting up citation alerts post-publication on **informa**world™, our online platform offering cross-searchable access to journal, book and database content.

Our Author Services Department can provide advice on how to:

- direct your submission to the correct journal
- prepare your manuscript according to the journal's requirements
- maximize your article's citations
- submit supplementary data for online publication
- submit your article online via Manuscript Central™
- apply for permission to reproduce images
- prepare your illustrations for print
- track the status of your manuscript through the production process
- return your corrections online
- purchase reprints through Rightslink™
- register for article citation alerts
- take advantage of our i*OpenAccess* option
- access your article online
- benefit from rapid online publication via i*First*

See further information at:
www.informaworld.com/authors

or contact:
Author Services Manager, Taylor & Francis, 4 Park Square, Milton Park, Abingdon, Oxon OX14 4RN, UK, email: authorqueries@tandf.co.uk